I0803124

IMAGES
of America

ERIE STREET CEMETERY

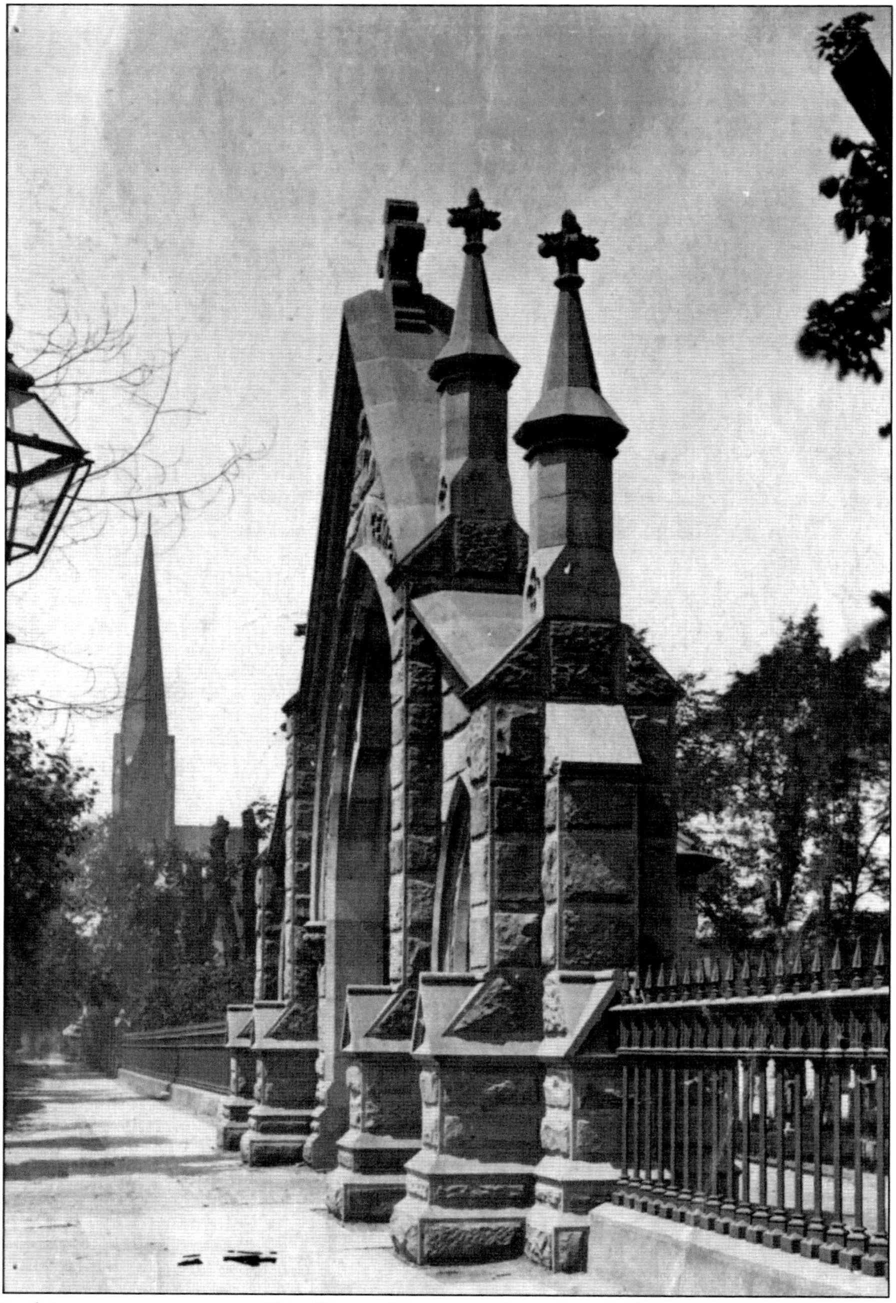

The Gothic entrance gate at Erie Street Cemetery has changed little since it was erected in 1870. During that year, the gate and wrought iron fence were built. According to the 1874 Atlas of Cuyahoga County, the steeple beyond the gate is that of the Evangelical Lutheran Church. (Western Reserve Historical Society.)

On the Cover: In this photograph from the collection of the Western Reserve Historical Society, well-dressed men visit the Erie Street Cemetery in the 1860s. (Western Reserve Historical Society.)

IMAGES
of America

ERIE STREET CEMETERY

John D. Cimperman

ARCADIA
PUBLISHING

ISBN 978-0-7385-8342-6

Published by Arcadia Publishing
Charleston, South Carolina

Printed in the United States of America

Library of Congress Control Number: 2010939282

For all general information, please contact Arcadia Publishing:
Telephone 843-853-2070
Fax 843-853-0044
E-mail sales@arcadiapublishing.com
For customer service and orders:
Toll-Free 1-888-313-2665

Visit us on the Internet at www.arcadiapublishing.com

To all those buried in Erie Street Cemetery and those who are working to preserve this historic site

CONTENTS

ACKNOWLEDGMENTS

This book was written to draw attention to one of Cleveland's most historic locations and to continue the work of the Early Settlers Association in preserving the burial grounds of many of the early pioneers of the city.

Material for this book has been gathered from many sources, and I hope I do not forget to thank all those who provided information, photographs, or their special collections. Throughout the book I will try to identify the individual, organization, and source of all material rather than in this acknowledgment. Unless otherwise noted, all images are courtesy of the author. I am greatly indebted to the following for their courtesies and help: Janice Petrick, who was a great help in the typing of this book; James Cimperman; Joseph Cimperman; John and Betty Franklin; and Jan Valore. I would also like to thank Ann K. Sindelar, reference supervisor, and Vicki Calozza from the library reference division of the Western Reserve Historical Society Library and Archives; William C. Barrow, special collections librarian from Cleveland State University; Michelle A. Day, president of the Woodland Cemetery Foundation; the staff of the Olmsted Falls Branch of the Cuyahoga County Public Library; Martin Hauserman, chief city of Cleveland archivist; and Veronica Pierce, deputy city of Cleveland archivist.

A special thank you to the Honors and Experimental Learning Program of Cuyahoga Community College (Tri-C), which has undertaken as one of their programs the preservation and restoration of Erie Street Cemetery under the direction of Robert Searson, district director; David A. Bernatowicz, assistant professor in the department of history; and Ashlee Brand, assistant professor and English and Honors Program Coordinator of the Metro Campus, who submitted the project description for the Tri-C program partnership with the Early Settlers Association. Also thank you to the following students in the honors program: Sherrai Watkins, Jasmine Core, Matthew Velotta, Machelle Gay, and Somijata Sakar. It is our hope that this book will assist in their efforts.

INTRODUCTION

The early settlers of the Western Reserve arrived in what became Cleveland to build a new life in the wilderness area. The land became available when Connecticut sold its western land to the Connecticut Land Company, which then offered it for sale for settlement. The history of the Western Reserve is an important part of the early history of the United States. It all began in 1662 when King Charles II of England granted Connecticut all lands bounded by the colony from sea to sea. Following the American Revolution, when the new government was formed, the Congress of Confederation in 1787 established the Northwest Territory. It was an achievement for the new government that would provide an avenue for the establishment of government in the Northwest Territory. Connecticut relinquished all of its western lands to the new federal government except for the land it called the "Western Reserve" or "New Connecticut." The Western Reserve is a section of land that became northeastern Ohio. It is bounded by Lake Erie on the north, Pennsylvania on the east, and extends 120 miles westward and southward from the lake to the 41st parallel. On April 28, 1800, Pres. John Adams signed a bill by which New Connecticut (the Western Reserve) came under the jurisdiction of the US government, at the same time establishing the validity of the Connecticut land title.

Erie Street Cemetery, originally called City Cemetery, is today Cleveland's oldest cemetery and is the final resting place for many of those pioneers who braved the early days of settlement. But Erie Street was not Cleveland's first cemetery. The first cemetery was the Ontario Street Cemetery of 1804 that was located at Prospect Avenue and Ontario Street just off what is today Public Square. When the owner of the property took action to gain possession for building purposes, a new location had to be found for a burial ground. Leonard Case, a prominent Clevelander, purchased about 10 acres of land that he felt was "far out of town" so this would not happen again. The title of the land was transferred to the village for $1 with the agreement that the land would be used for burial purposes.

After the closing of the Ontario Street Cemetery, a burial ground in the village of Newburgh, called Axtell Cemetery, was the oldest cemetery in the county. Its first burial was in 1801, and the cemetery continued in existence until 1880. It was located north of Broadway on what is today East Seventy-Eighth Street and was comprised of about eight acres. It was said to have more than 3,000 bodies within its grounds. Axtell Cemetery was sold to the railroad by the city and the bodies were moved to either Harvard Grove, which had its first burial in 1881; Erie Street Cemetery, established in 1826; or Woodland Cemetery, dedicated June 14, 1853.

The first interment in Erie Street Cemetery was Minerva M. White, daughter of Moses and Mary White, in September 1827. The remaining bodies of the pioneers buried in the Ontario Street Cemetery were exhumed and reburied in Erie Street Cemetery. As Leonard Case had said, and the town had agreed, the location was considered far enough from the town center that it would not hinder new construction as the town grew. But as is now known, that was not the case. The city grew, bringing many threats or suggestions for new uses for the land. Even today, being located just across from Progressive Field—the city's major league baseball stadium and the home of the Cleveland Indians—the cemetery currently finds itself in a very prominent location, especially during baseball season.

When Erie Street Cemetery was established, the population of what was to be the "capital" town of the Western Reserve was just over 800 people. It was a time when the village was beginning to grow with the influx of men looking for work on the Ohio Canal. Construction ended when the canal reached its final destination, the Cuyahoga River and Lake Erie, in 1828.

On the eastern portion of the land acquired for Erie Street Cemetery was a building called the "township poorhouse," which housed elderly patients and those with chronic diseases. In 1837, it was named City Hospital and continued on as a hospital until it was torn down in 1857. What was called Cleveland's first general hospital was housed in a small brick building in St. Vincent's Orphanage on the west side of town. In 1853, the Sisters of Charity of St. Augustine opened the doors of St. Joseph's Hospital to the community. It was the forerunner of St. Vincent Charity Hospital.

In 1840, Erie Street Cemetery was plotted and a register of lots and burials began. Early death records are difficult to find because Ohio did not enact a statute until 1856 that required birth, death, and marriage registration—a law that was generally disregarded. A later 1867 law again required registration of birth and death records. Some of these are extant. Two types of "death records" known to be in existence before 1867 are records of cholera deaths, registered during some epidemics, and veterans' deaths, representing only a small proportion of the deaths that occurred. The third law, which went into effect on December 20, 1908, set up the current record-keeping system in Ohio. Cuyahoga County Probate Court kept death records between 1867 and December 19, 1908.

The saga of early life in Cleveland can be told in the Erie Street Cemetery, from the town's founding to its days as a boomtown, then on to the Industrial Revolution. This book will try to unfold some of that story.

One

THE WESTERN RESERVE

Lorenzo Carter was from Rutland County, Vermont, where at age 21 he bought a farm, cleared the land, farmed, hunted, and fished, and in 1789, he married Rebecca Fuller and fathered two sons.

In 1795, Carter and a companion traveled to Ohio by crossing the Ohio River, then explored the Muskingum River Valley, and wintered in Ohio. In the spring of 1796, they reached the mouth of the Cuyahoga River to search for a homesite on the high ground near the lake.

On May 2, 1797, Carter, Ezekiel Hawley, Elijah Gun, and James Kingsbury arrived with their families to the hardships of the Western Reserve. Because of the harsh winter, Kingsbury returned to New Hampshire for provisions. It took him more than two months to get back. His wife lost their baby to starvation, and she almost died before his return. The hardships of those first settlers were almost unbearable.

That is why the inscription on the Carter gravesite in Erie Street Cemetery reads, "They Remained—Others Fled." During the early years of the settlement, there was no form of local government; Carter was the "law" to the Indians and settlers. He and a man named Stephen Gilbert were appointed the first constables of the village.

When Carter reached Cleveland he was 30 years old. He died in 1814 but accomplished a great deal in those 17 years. At his death he was described as a frontiersman, community leader, and tavern keeper. His cabin was used as a tavern where he welcomed travelers with food, drink, and a bed. His cabin was the center of activity in the village. He launched a ferry to carry travelers across the river and traded with the Indians. Carter also built the first schooner for lake trading, making him the father of Cleveland's shipbuilding industry. There was no one like Lorenzo Carter; he stood out as a true Cleveland pioneer. As detailed in this book, he, along with many of those early settlers, distinguished themselves in Cleveland's early history.

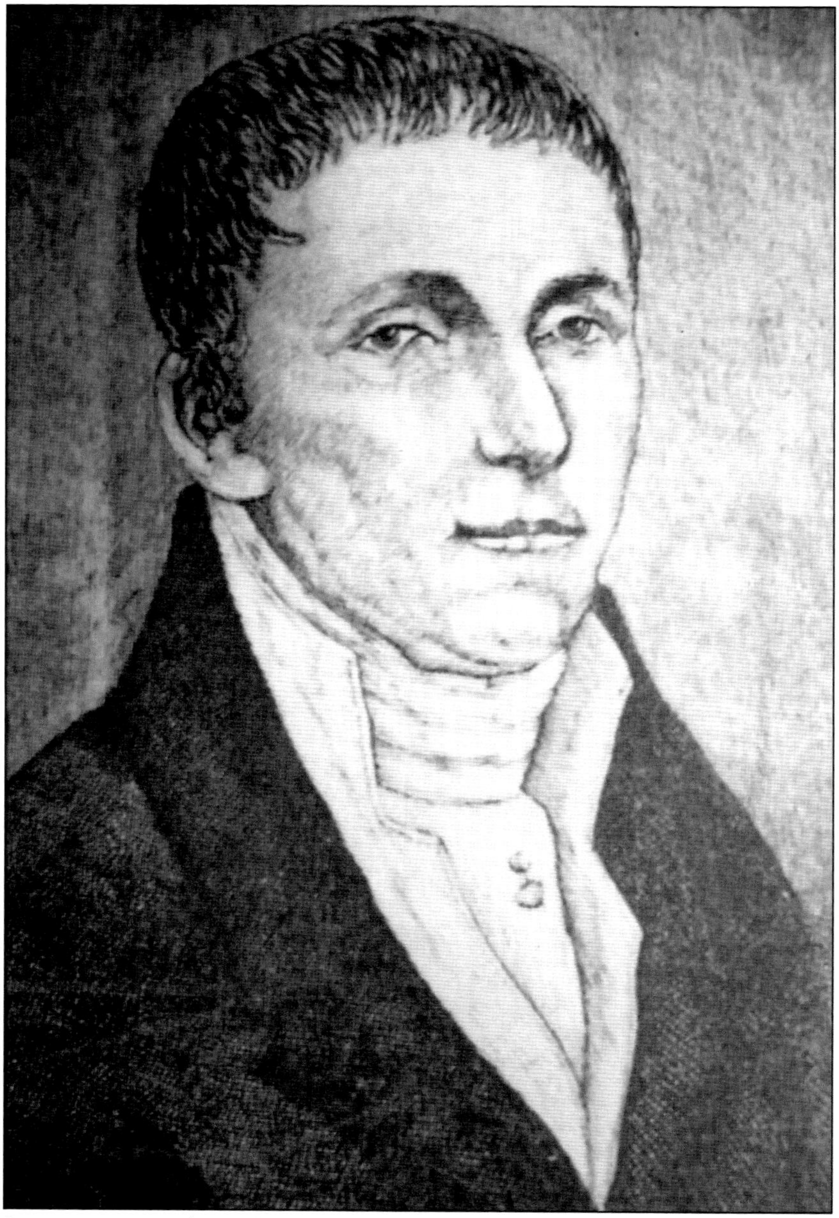

Lorenzo Carter was given the rank of major in the Cleveland militia. He was called the "Pioneer of the Pioneers." His young life began with the loss of his father, Eleazer, who served as a lieutenant in the Continental Army. Eleazer returned home from service and died of smallpox at the age of 37, leaving a widow and six children. The oldest was 11-year-old Lorenzo, who continued to farm for his family. In 1789, he married Rebecca Fuller and began to work his own farm in Castleton, Vermont. He was not happy with his life as a farmer and saw the opportunity that New Connecticut had to offer. In the fall of 1795 or early 1796, Lorenzo went west to investigate the new land. He returned home to Vermont in the fall of 1796. In 1797, he moved his family and the family of his brother-in-law, Ezekiel Hawley, along with Elijah Gun and James Kingsbury and their families, to a new life in the wilderness. (Early Settlers Association.)

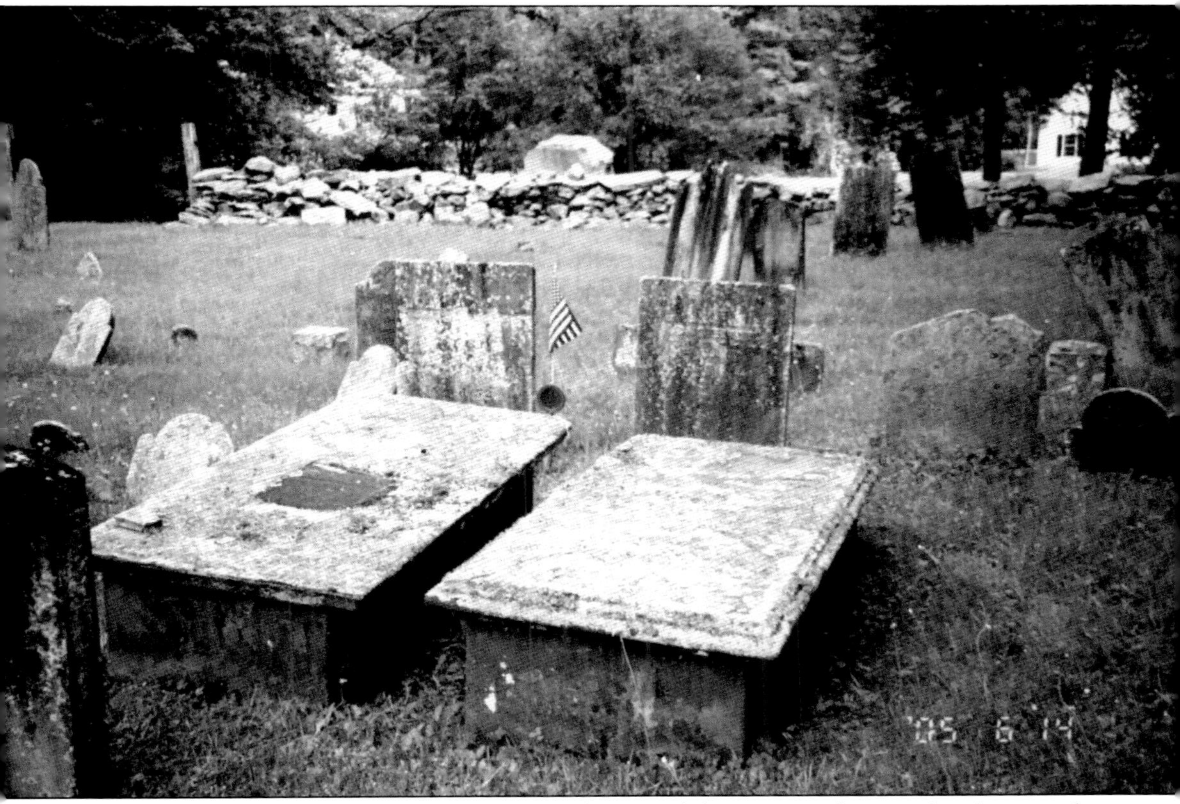

Erie Street Cemetery contains the remains of many of the area's earliest settlers but not the founder of the city. Moses Cleaveland (1754–1806) rests in peace in a cemetery in the town where he was born, Canterbury, Connecticut. He was a lawyer, politician, soldier, and surveyor. He was elected to the Connecticut General Assembly and was commissioned brigadier general of the militia. In 1796, he was asked to lead the survey of the Western Reserve of Connecticut for the Connecticut Land Company. He successfully negotiated the sale of the land with the Mohawk and Seneca Nations. The members of the surveying party named the settlement "Cleaveland" after their leader, and it eventually became known as "Cleveland." This is a photograph of the Moses Cleaveland gravesite in the Canterbury, Connecticut, cemetery. For many years, the Early Settlers Association (ESA) supported the maintenance of this cemetery. There was an effort in 1930 and 1948 to bring his remains to Erie Street Cemetery. Those efforts failed, and his gravesite remains in Canterbury, Connecticut, with other members of his family.

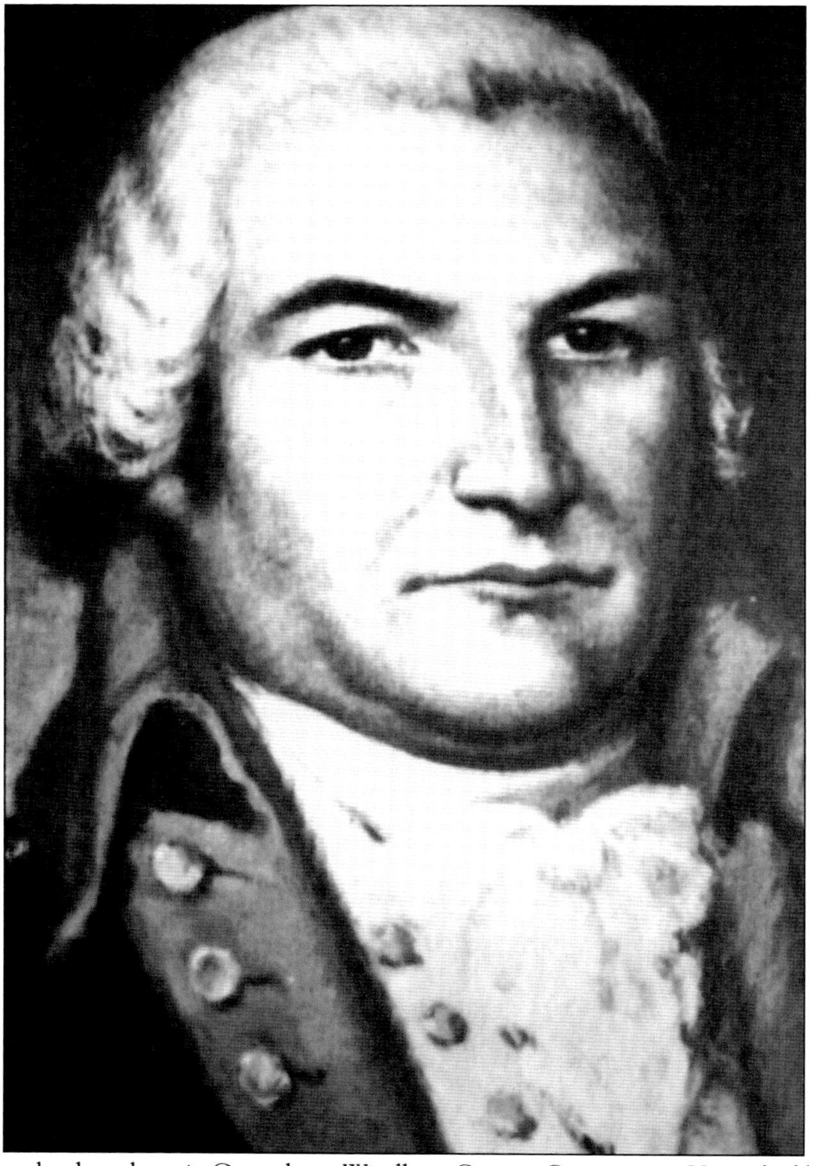

Moses Cleaveland was born in Canterbury, Windham County, Connecticut. He studied law at Yale University, graduating in 1777. With the onset of the Revolutionary War, he was commissioned as an ensign in the 2nd Connecticut Regiment of the Continental Army. In 1779, he was promoted to captain of a company of combat engineers in the newly formed US Army Corps of Engineers. He left the Continental Army in 1781 and went on to practice law. In 1788, he was a member of the Connecticut convention that ratified the US Constitution. He was elected to the Connecticut General Assembly, and in 1796, he was commissioned brigadier general in the Connecticut militia. Cleaveland, who was a shareholder in the Connecticut Land Company, was chosen to lead a survey of the lands of the Western Reserve. The Northwest Territory was established in 1787, and the claims of the colonies had to be settled. Massachusetts, New York, and Virginia had claims for land granted by English kings. All gave up their claims to the new American government except for Connecticut, which retained its Western Reserve. (Early Settlers Association.)

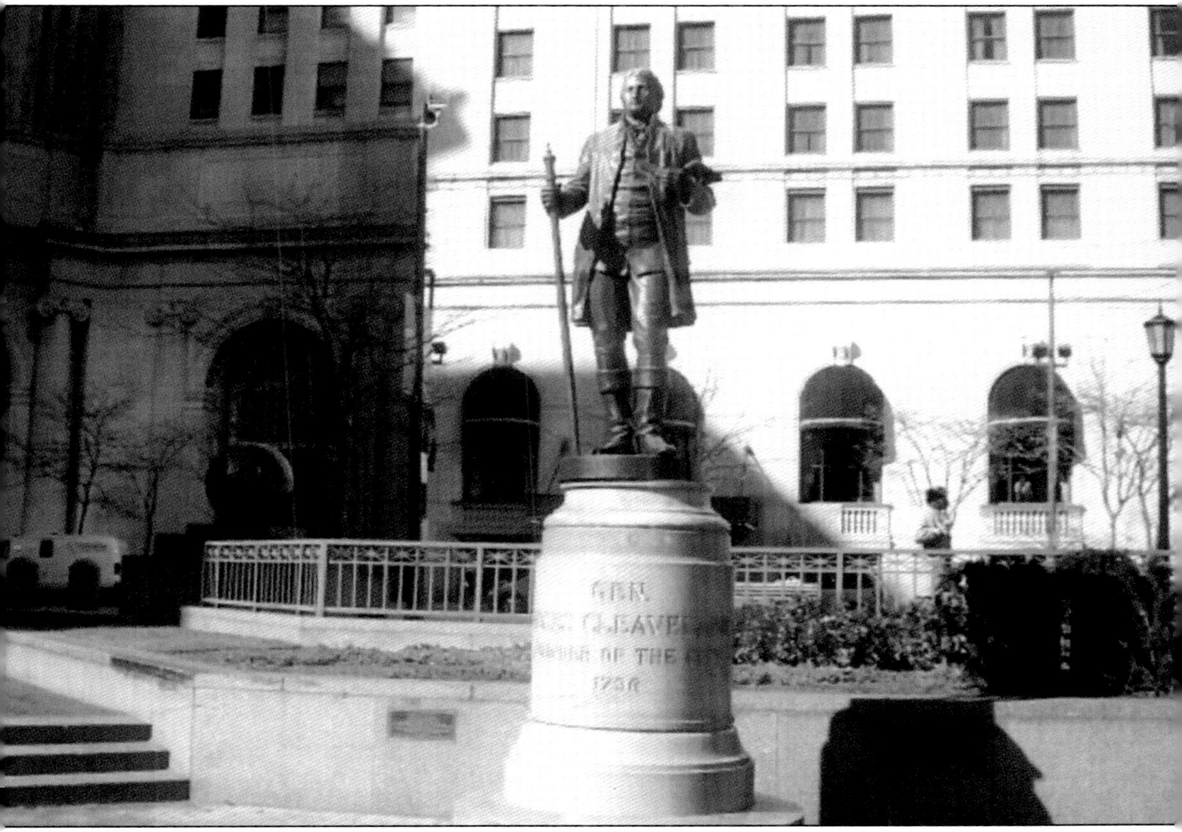

The Early Settlers Association did not succeed in moving Moses Cleaveland's grave from Canterbury, Connecticut, to Cleveland but it did have his likeness erected in granite and placed on Cleveland Public Square. Cleveland celebrated its 92nd birthday by unveiling a statue of Moses Cleaveland. Mayor Brenton D. Babcock accepted the statue for the city. He was mayor from 1887 to 1888. This bronze seven-foot, 10-inch-tall statue on a granite circular pedestal was designed by J.C. Hamilton and given to the city on July 23, 1888, by the Early Settlers Association of the Western Reserve with a grand ceremony. It was reported that more than 500 early settlers and many more Greater Clevelanders attended the unveiling of the statue, located on the southwest quadrant of Cleveland Public Square. The tradition continues today with a celebration and program every July 22 in front of the Moses Cleaveland statue.

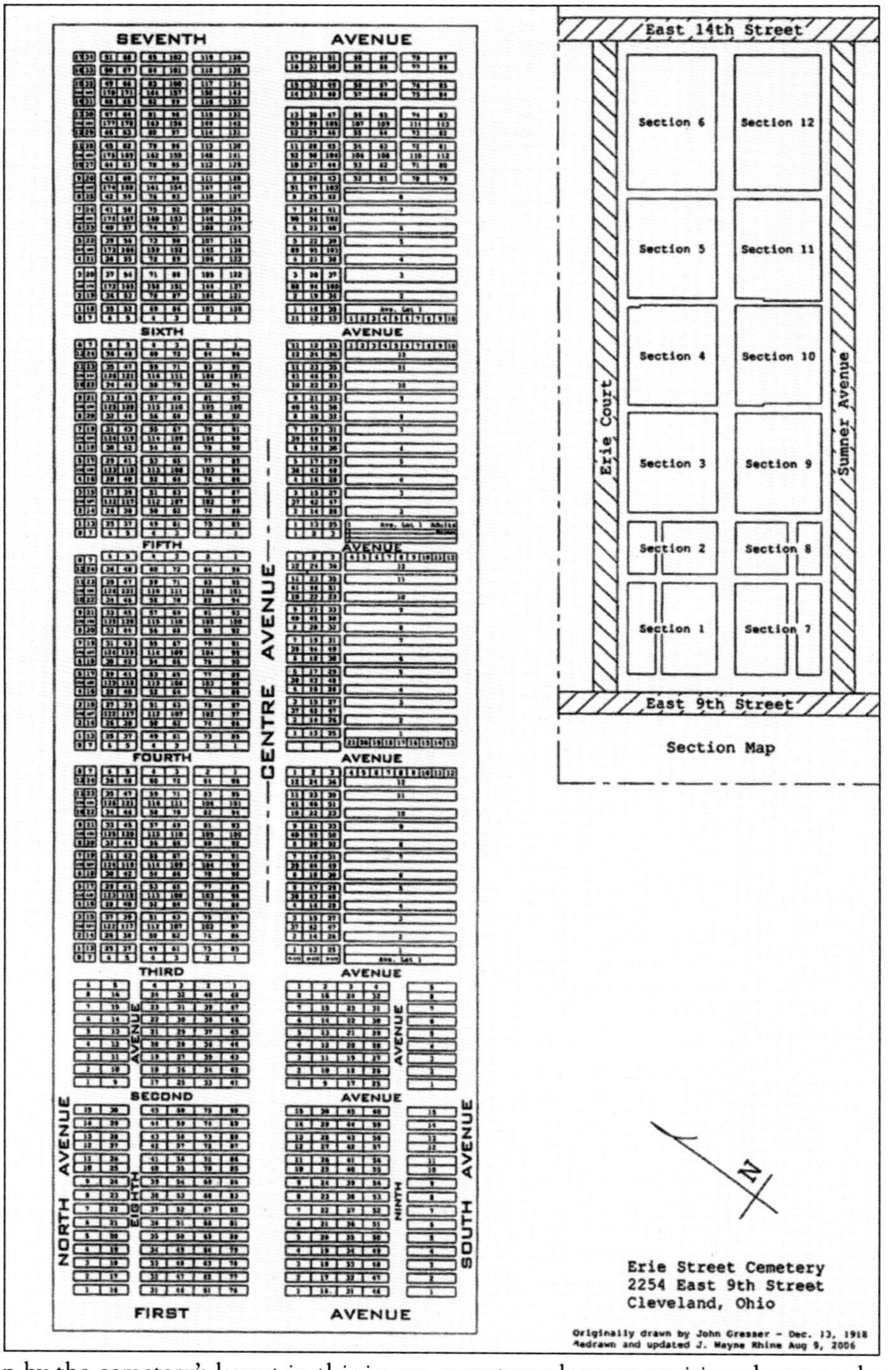

As seen by the cemetery's layout in this image, cemetery planners envisioned avenues breaking up each section. Today, there are no avenues to be seen, but, looking closely, one can find section numbers cut into the curb of what was called Centre Avenue. This map was originally drawn by John Gresser on December 13, 1918, and was redrawn and updated by J. Wayne Rhine on August 9, 2006. (City of Cleveland Archives.)

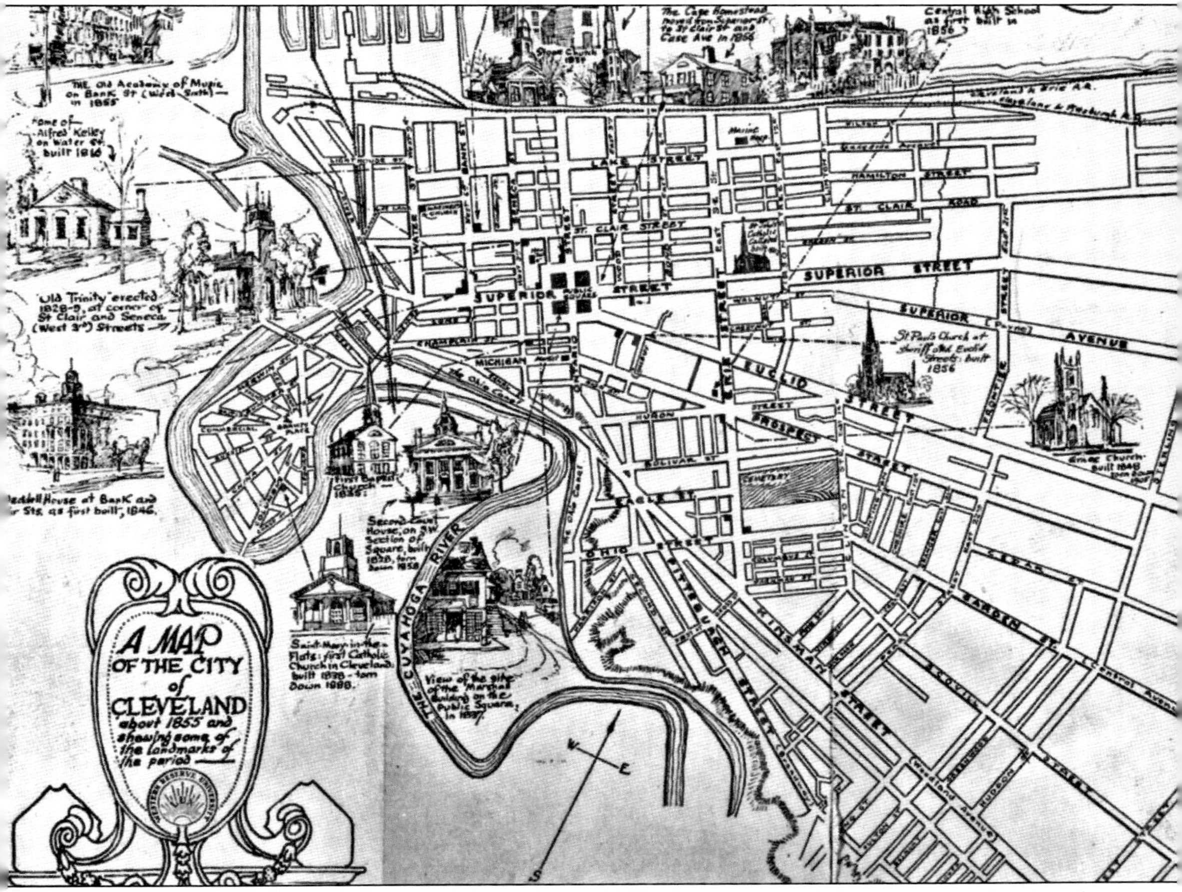

This map of the city of Cleveland, from about 1855, shows some of the important landmarks of the time. The location of Erie Street Cemetery, listed as "cemetery," can be seen at Erie and Eagle Streets. This was 15 years before the Gothic entrance and gatehouse were built. By looking at the map, one can see many churches were being built throughout the city. (City of Cleveland Archives.)

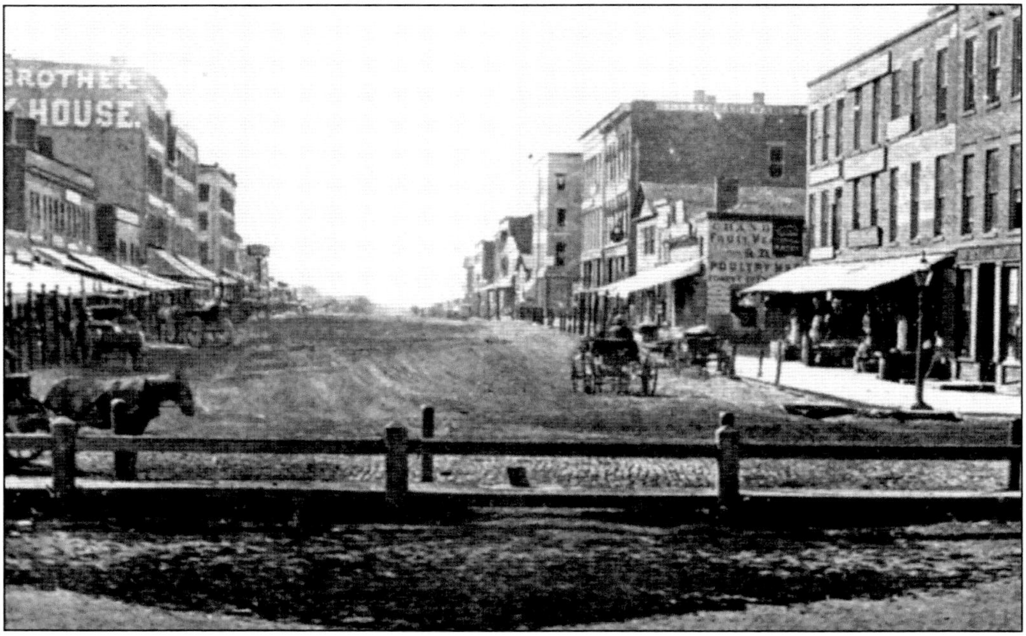

This photograph looks south from Cleveland Public Square along Ontario Street sometime in the early 1860s to where the Central Market would later be built. The square is enclosed by a fence that does not permit access from Ontario and Superior Streets. (Cleveland State University, Cleveland Press Collection.)

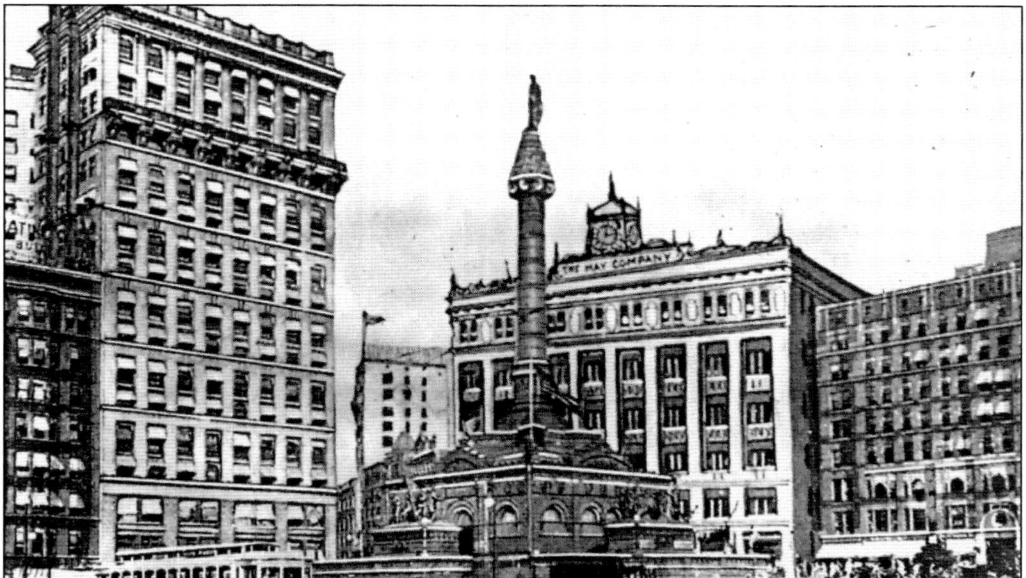

This is a view looking across Cleveland Public Square, past the Soldiers' and Sailors' Monument, to the May Company building where two homes once stood. The Ontario Street Cemetery, Cleveland's first cemetery, was behind the two residences. The Ontario Street Cemetery's ground began at the south end of the May Company building and ran along the east side of Ontario Street before Prospect Avenue (first called Cuyahoga Street) was cut through in 1831.

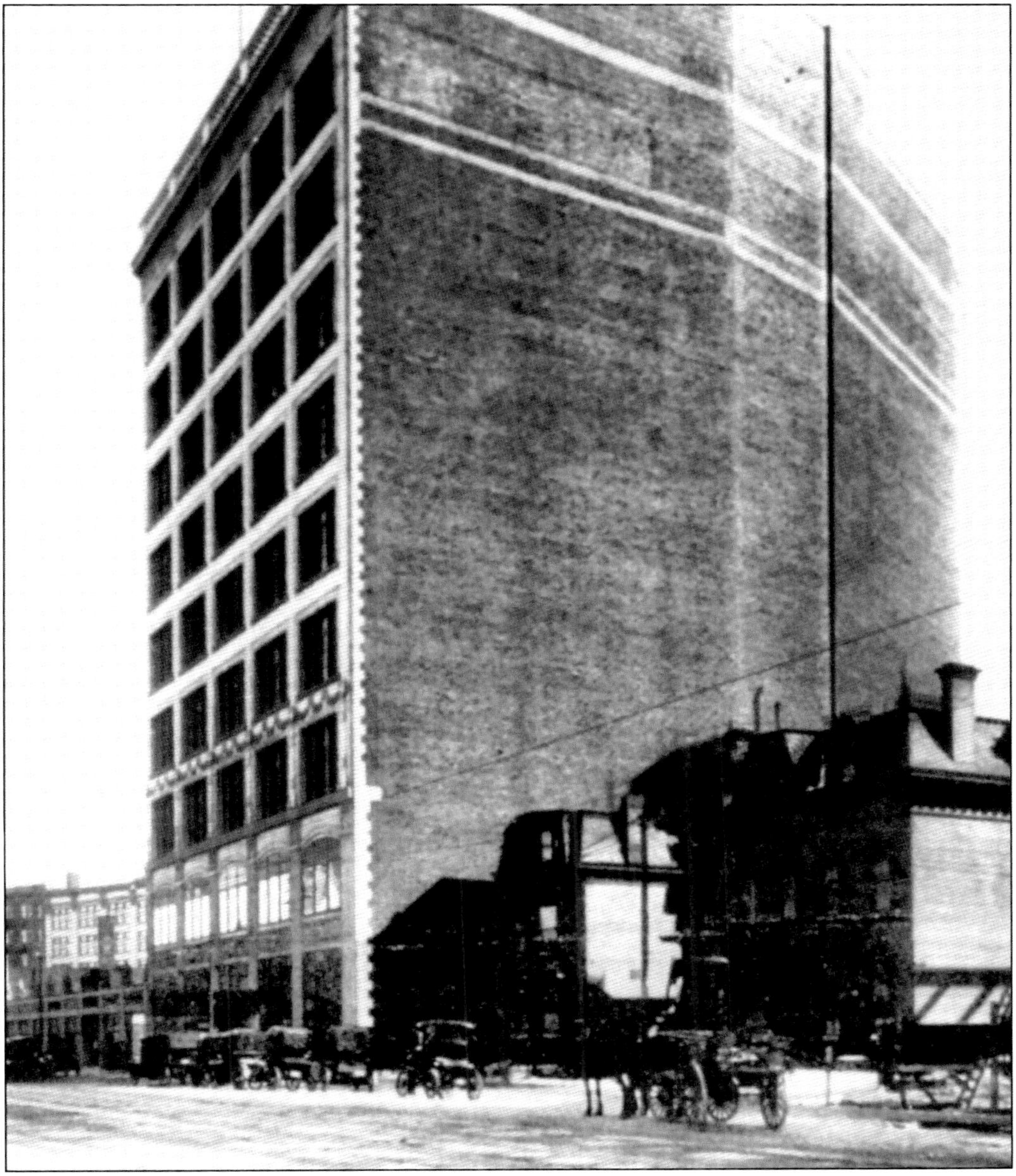

This is a photograph of what was called the Pope Building, now known as the Halle Building, designed in 1907 by Henry Bacon, the architect who designed the Lincoln Memorial in Washington, DC. The building underwent a $30 million restoration by the Forest City Development Corporation in 1984 to develop 400,000 square feet of office space and two levels of retail space. Following the restoration, the building was added to the National Register of Historic Places by the US Department of the Interior. The building is located at 1228 Euclid Avenue in what became Cleveland's Playhouse Square District. Behind this building would have been the Ontario Street Cemetery—a demonstration of how the city was growing. The two homes seen in this photograph are reminiscent of the homes that stood in the developing commercial districts near Public Square. The original structure cost $1 million to build. Additions to the building were constructed in 1947 and 1994. (Cleveland Public Library Collection.)

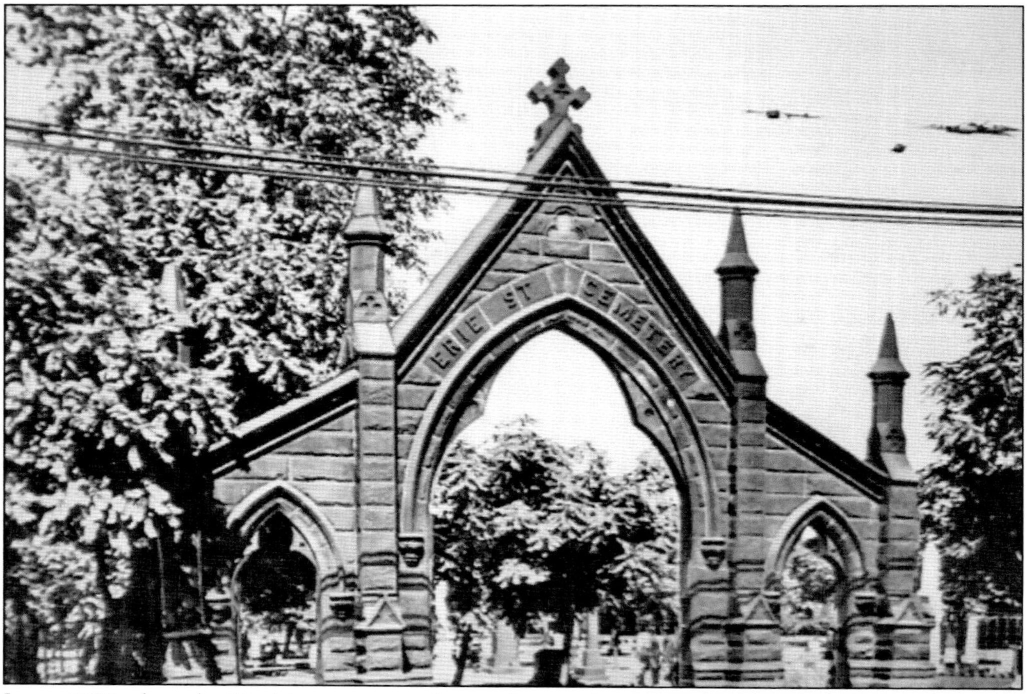

It was 1870 when the Gothic gateway and wrought iron fence were built to enclose the Erie Street Cemetery grounds in order to properly honor those buried there. What might have inspired those early Clevelanders to erect a gate was a ceremony held in 1865 when two heroes of the Civil War were buried at Erie Street Cemetery. Col. William Creighton and Lt. Col. Orrin J. Crane of the famous 7th Ohio Infantry died in the Battle of Ringgold Gap in Georgia. They were buried with full military honors. Of the regiment's 610 Cleveland soldiers who entered the battle, only 14 survived that day. Below is the entrance gate to the cemetery as it appeared on a summer day in 1922. (Cleveland State University, Cleveland Press Collection.)

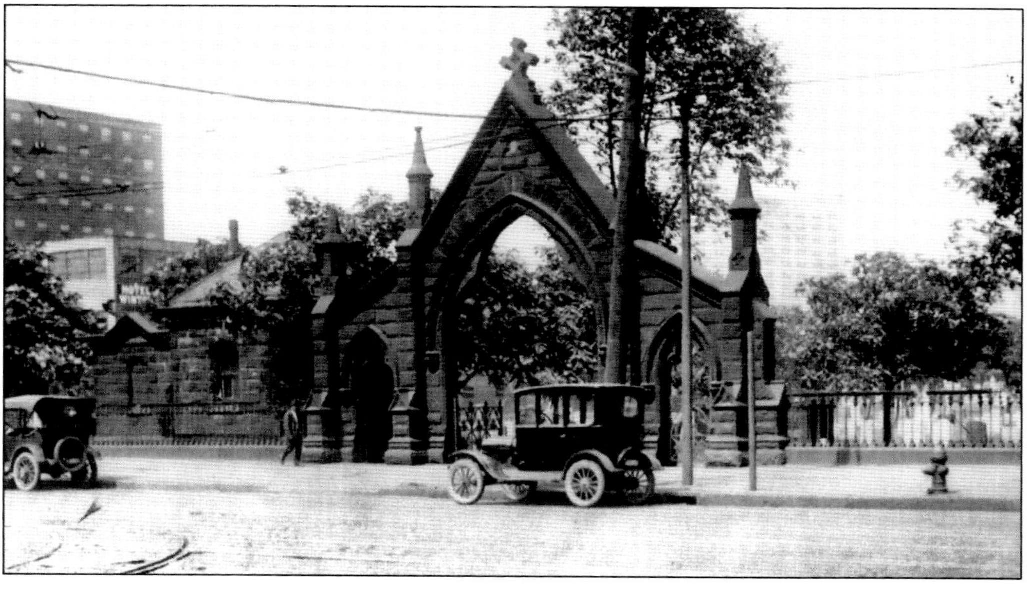

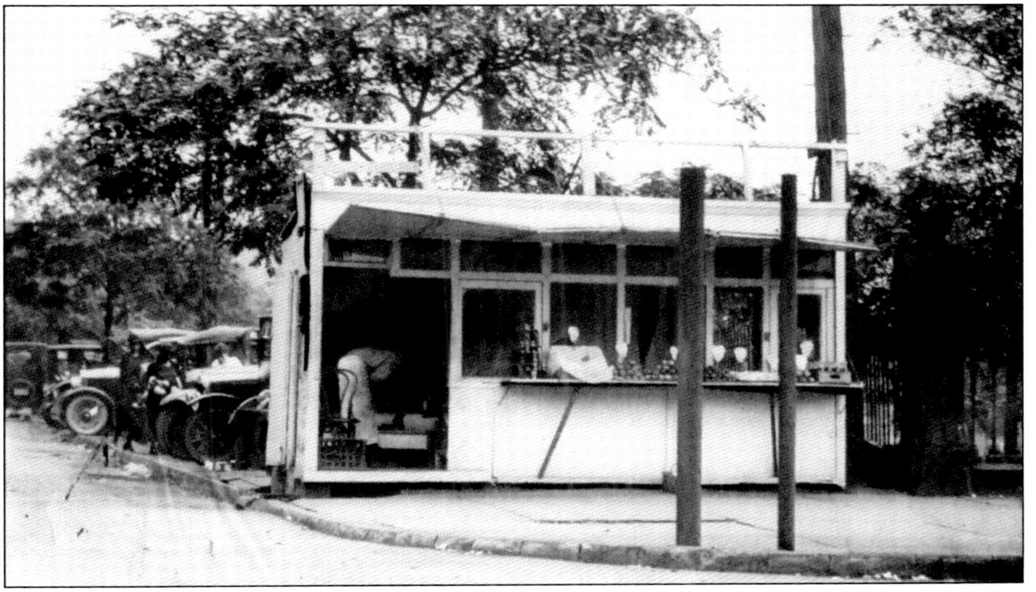

This photograph was taken on July 26, 1926, of a newsstand that stood just north of the Erie Street Cemetery entrance. The newsstand is evidence of how the city had grown by the 1920s. When the cemetery was first planned, it was considered far enough from the city center that it would not impede development. By the 1920s, it became sought-after property. (Cleveland State University, Cleveland Press Collection.)

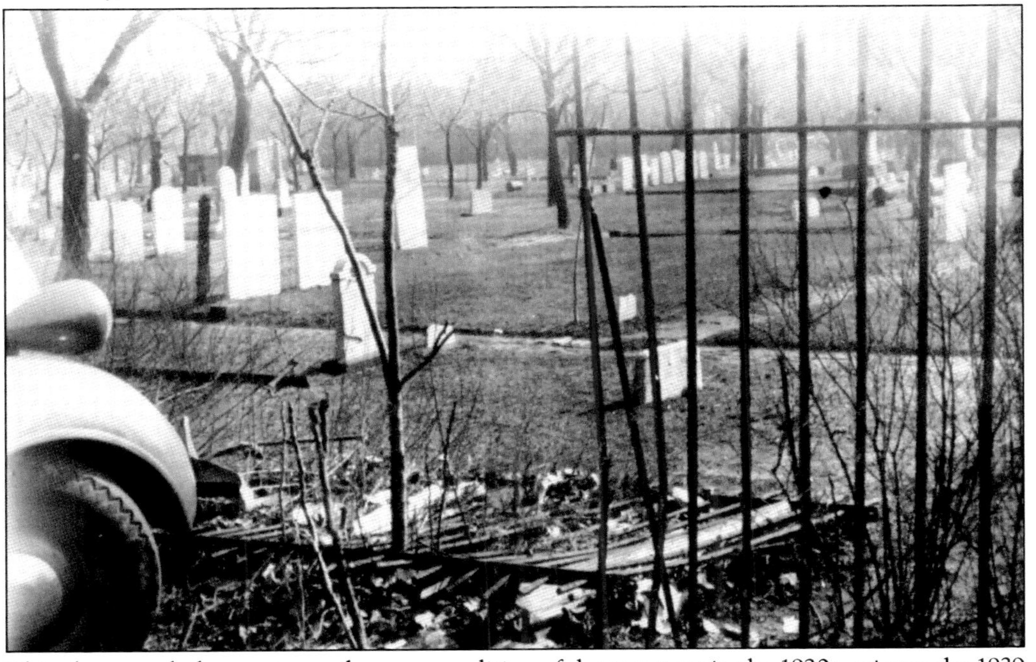

This photograph demonstrates the poor condition of the cemetery in the 1920s, prior to the 1939 and 1940 improvements. As seen in this photograph, the wrought iron fence had deteriorated so badly that it no longer protected the grounds. By 1940, a stone wall replaced the deteriorating wrought iron fence. (Cleveland State University, Cleveland Press Collection.)

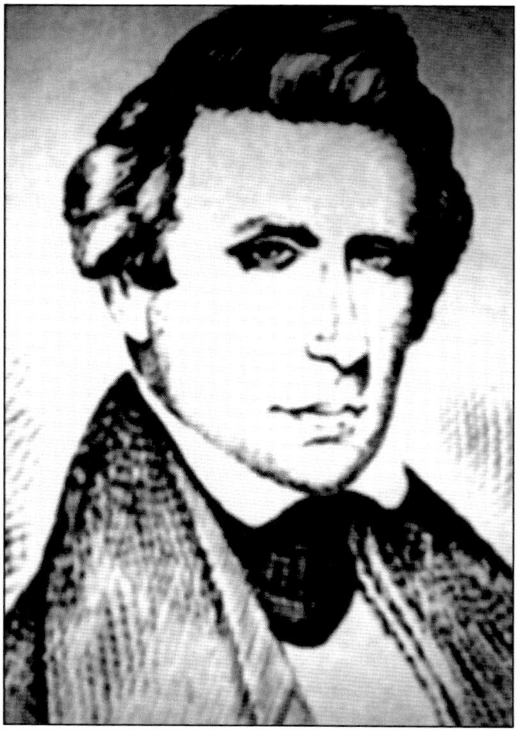

In 1836, Cleveland went from village to a municipality and elected its first mayor, John Wheelock Willey (1797–1841), who served two terms from 1836 to 1837. He came to Cleveland in 1822 from New Hampshire. It was said that he was a brilliant lawyer. Willey also served as a judge and state senator. He was the author of the city's charter. Willey was 28 years old when he reached Cleveland, and he died at the age of 47 while serving as common pleas judge. The salary of the mayor was $500 per year, and a councilman received $1 for each meeting he attended. Willey is buried in Erie Street Cemetery, but his headstone is weathered and very difficult to read. The stone is near the main entrance on the south side across from the Carter gravesite in Section 7. Records show he was reinterred at Lake View Cemetery section 5, lot 13, grave number 4. (Early Settlers Association.)

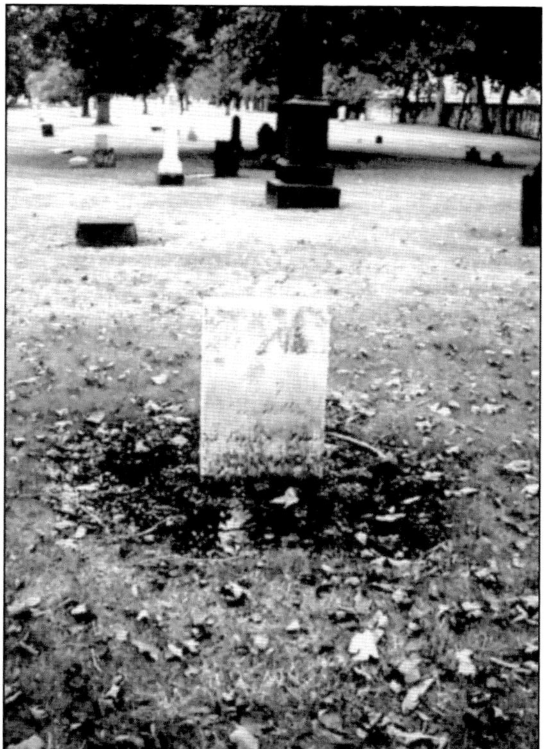

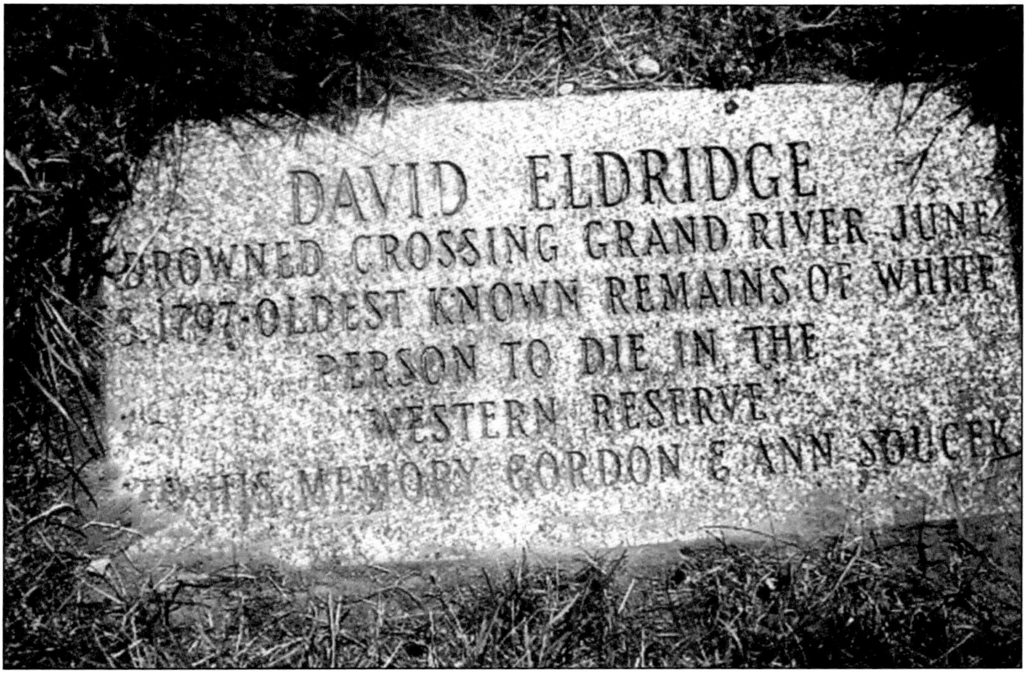

In 1797, the first religious service was reportedly held at a gravesite in Cleveland. It was also the first burial in what became the Ontario Street Cemetery. The service was for David Eldridge, a member of the second surveying party who drowned as he attempted to cross the Grand River. His remains were moved to Erie Street Cemetery when the Ontario Street Cemetery closed. Gordon and Ann Soucek placed the stone in his memory.

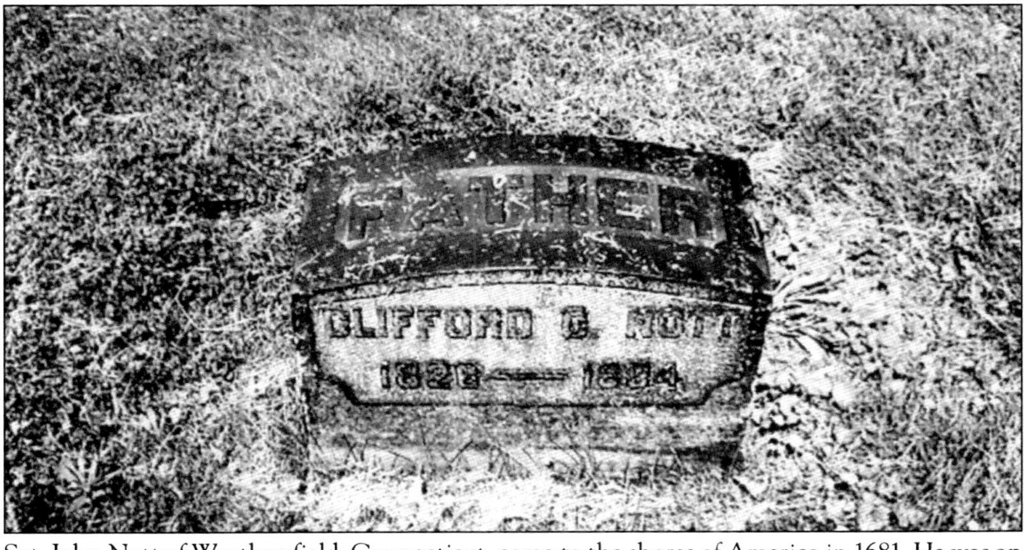

Sgt. John Nott of Weathersfield, Connecticut, came to the shores of America in 1681. He was an American ancestor of a pioneer family of that name who came to the city of Cleveland. William and Laura Belden Nott came to Cleveland where he operated a company that manufactured pump and vessel spars. William, Laura, and several of their children are buried in Erie Street Cemetery. Clifford D. Nott (1828–1884) was another ancestor of the Sgt. John Nott family.

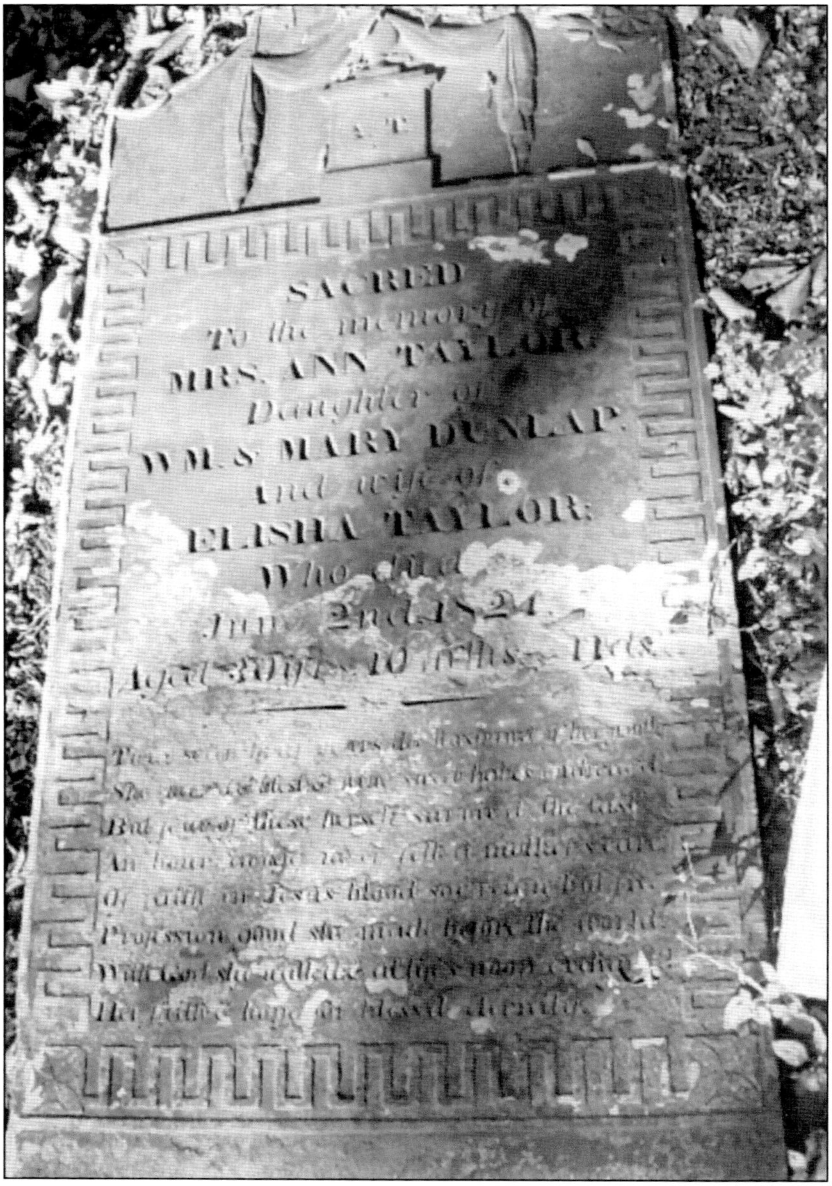

The Taylor family gravestone, which lies flat against the ground, tells an interesting story. Philo Taylor came from New England to Rocky River about 1808 and bought or built a log tavern on the eastern bank. He sold his tavern and moved to Cleveland. In 1816, he helped organize the Commercial Bank of Lake Erie, the pioneer bank of the city. He also owned a general merchandise store and was landlord of a tavern. His wife, Zerviah Davenport Taylor, who was the mother of his 11 children, is buried in Erie Street Cemetery. Elisha Taylor, the son of Philo Taylor, also helped build Cleveland into the metropolis it became. He lived in Cherry Valley, New York, but came to Cleveland around the age of 32 with his young wife, Ann. Elisha became a dry goods merchant dealing primarily with the Indians in furs. He was a deacon and charter member of the Old Stone Church, was the first superintendent of the first Cleveland Sabbath School, and was ardent in his opposition to alcohol.

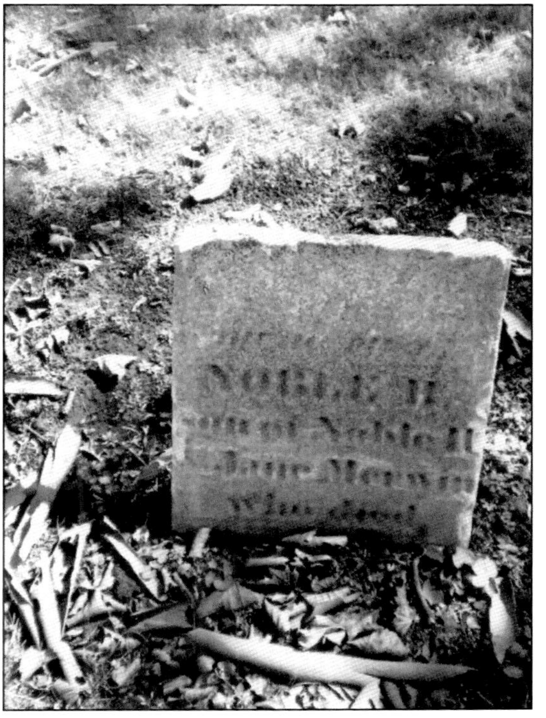

In these photographs are the Noble Merwin gravestone and Lyon monument. The arch symbolizes "the passage to heaven." Noble came to Cleveland from Connecticut in 1811. Minerva Buckingham Merwin joined her husband later the same year. He bought the George Wallace Tavern, which provided him with the money to further his business interests, which included a warehouse. He built small boats that laid the foundation for Cleveland's shipbuilding industry. Minerva conducted the first religious services each Sunday until a missionary was sent to the village. She died in 1823. Noble's second wife, Jane Lyon, was a young widow. They married in 1825, but he died a short time later at the age of 40. Jane's son from her first marriage, Richard, became a very prominent businessman in Cleveland.

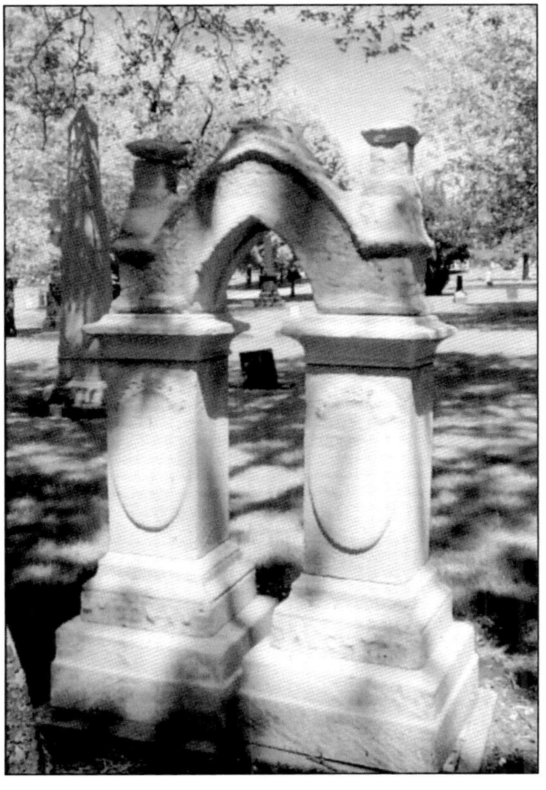

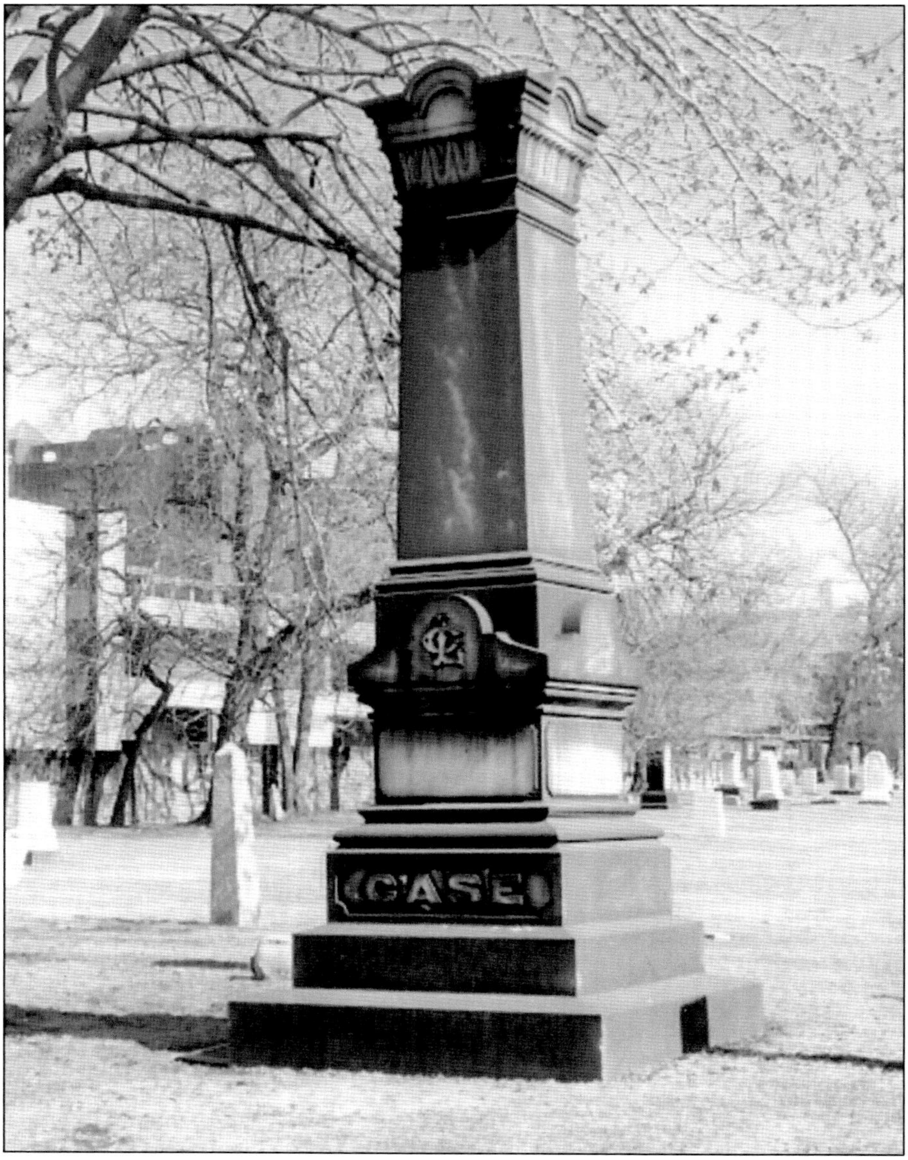

The Case monument is dedicated to the man who donated the land to establish Erie Street Cemetery. Leonard Case Sr. purchased the land and then donated it to the city for burial purposes. To make the donation official, Case was paid $1 for the property. He was born in 1786 in Westmoreland County, Pennsylvania, the son of a pioneer farmer. He came to Cleveland in 1816 from his home in Warren, Ohio, at the request of Judge James Kingsbury to be a cashier at Cleveland's first bank. His career began as what was called a "confidential clerk" to Gen. Simon Perkins, who was a land agent for the Connecticut Land Company in 1807. Case died December 7, 1864. His obituary read, "Although crippled and frail since a boy was said to be a giant of civic, and business actives of Cleveland." He served as president of the village council, was a member of the state legislature, and was the first auditor of Cuyahoga County. He was responsible for an ordinance to plant shade trees on city streets and, along with his son William, fostered the idea of Cleveland as the "Forest City."

It would be hard to ignore the name Case in the study of Cleveland's history, and it is appropriate that the Case monument is one of the most enduring and prominent in Erie Street Cemetery. Leonard Case Sr. (July 29, 1786–December 7, 1864), a businessman and philanthropist, was born in Westmoreland County, Pennsylvania, the son of a poor German couple who moved to Trumbull County, Ohio. Leonard was stricken with what must have been infantile paralysis, a disease not yet detected, that left him with crippled limbs. He studied law, passed the bar in 1814, and came to Cleveland in 1816. In Cleveland, he was hired to be a bank cashier at the newly formed Commercial Bank of Lake Erie. After that bank failed, he stayed in Cleveland practicing law. In 1832, he reorganized the Commercial Bank of Lake Erie and became its president. In the late 1840s, he turned his affairs over to his sons, William and Leonard Case Jr. His body now rests in Lake View Cemetery. (Early Settlers Association.)

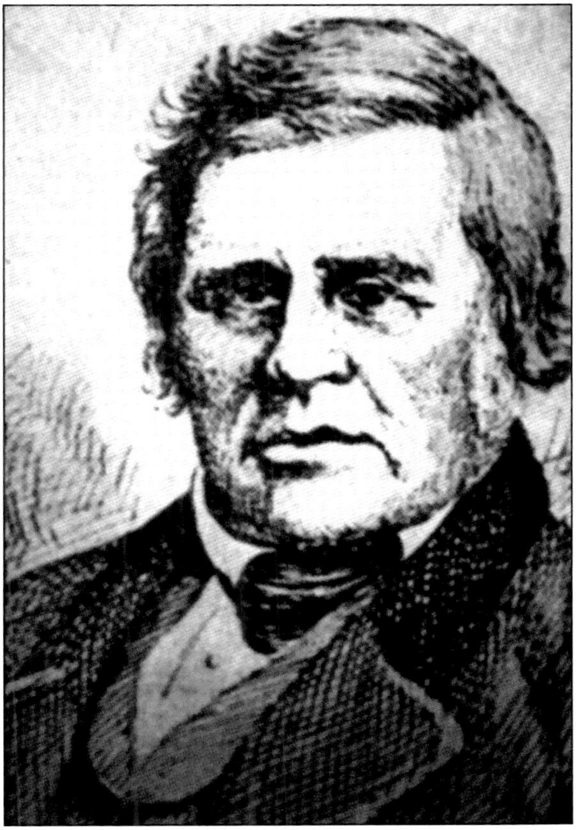

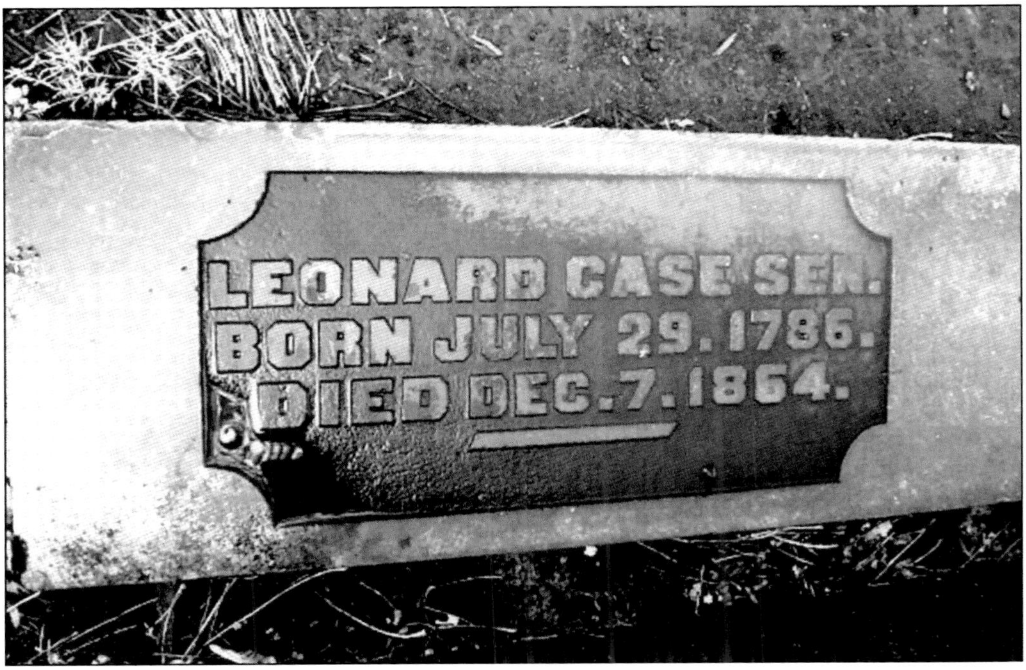

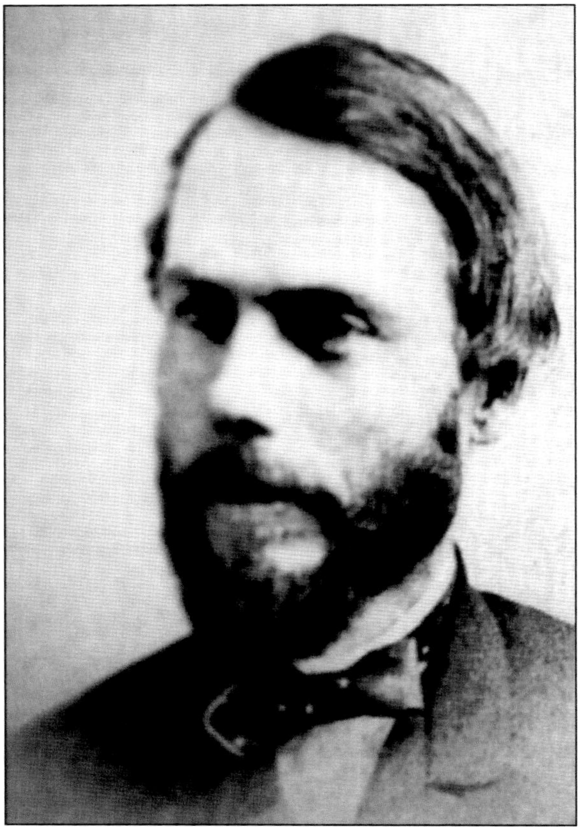

Leonard Case Jr. (June 27, 1820–January 6, 1880) followed his father as a lawyer and philanthropist who endowed the Case School of Applied Science. The school opened in 1881 on Rockwell Avenue then moved to University Circle in 1885. He, along with his brother William, helped form the Cleveland Library Association. Leonard gifted 200 acres for industrial plants and railroad rights-of-way that became the city's first comprehensive industrial district. William Case, as mayor of Cleveland in the 1850s, completed a project his father started and led a tree-planting program in the city that led to the nickname "Forest City." (Early Settlers Association.)

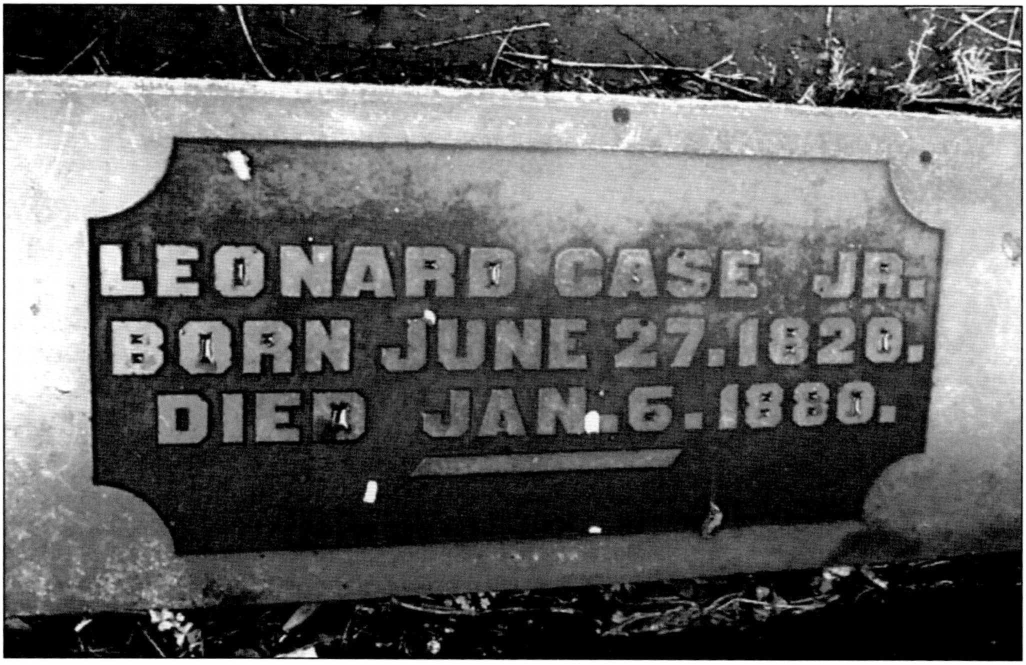

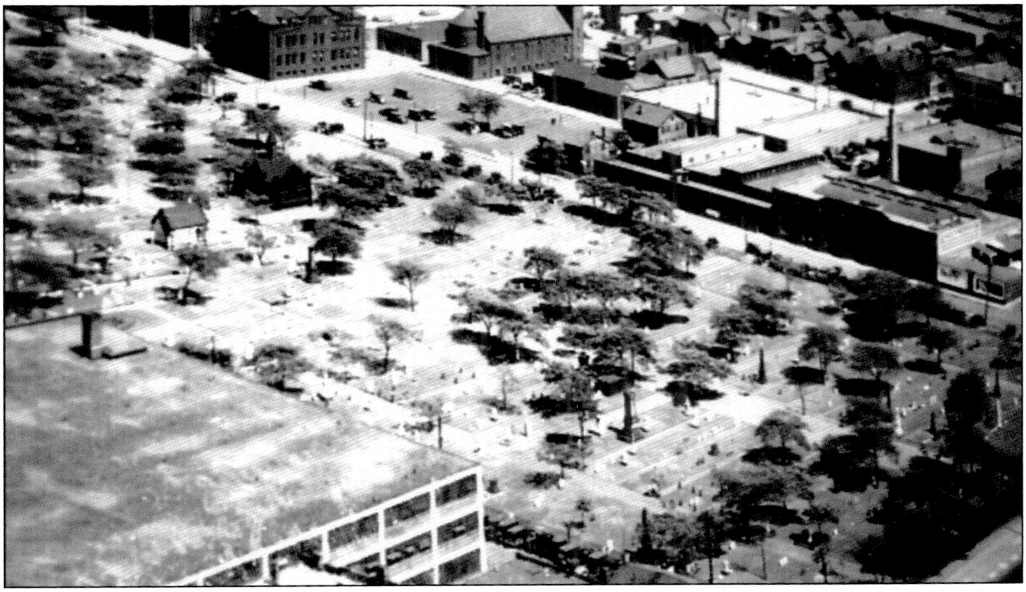

This is an aerial view of Erie Street Cemetery looking southwest, taken in the 1920s. By looking closely, one can see the chapel that once stood near the middle of the cemetery. (Cleveland State University Cleveland Press Collection.)

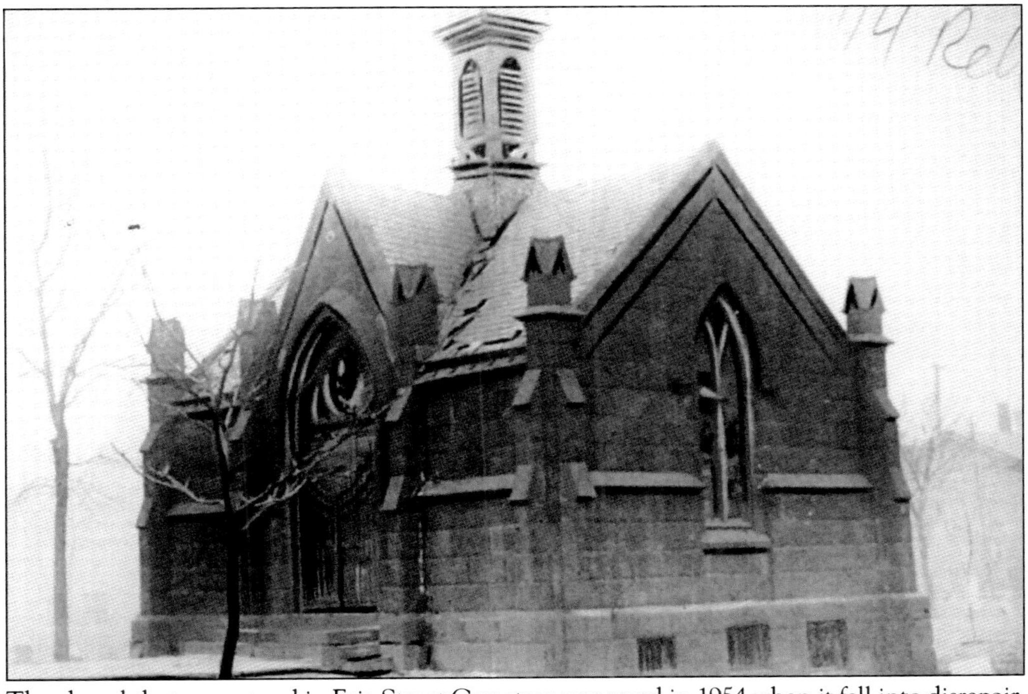

The chapel that once stood in Erie Street Cemetery was razed in 1954 when it fell into disrepair. Supposedly, it had become an eyesore and a source of danger. The Early Settlers Association did not object to the demolition because it was no longer used for its original purpose, as a chapel for the cemetery. In its last years, it was used as a tool shed by cemetery workmen. (Cleveland State University Cleveland Press Collection.)

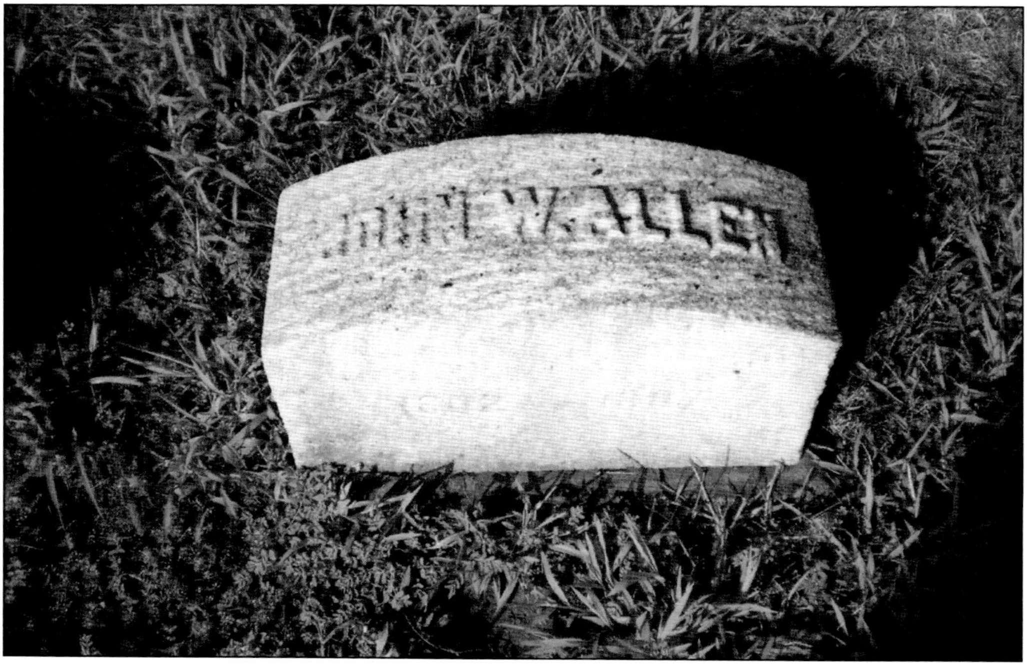

John W. Allen came to Cleveland in 1826, a year after graduating from Harvard. He began his career by petitioning Congress for aid to build a harbor in Cleveland. He was president of the village of Cleveland's board of trustees from 1831 to 1835. During the cholera epidemic of 1832, he established Cleveland's first board of health. He was elected to the Ohio Senate in 1835 and then served two terms in Congress from 1836 to 1841. Allen was a member of the Whig party and then became a Republican. He served as a bank president, was a strong supporter of the railroad industry, and served two terms as postmaster. He was also the editor of one of Cleveland's first newspapers, the *Cleveland Advertiser.* In 1841, Allen was elected the fourth mayor of Cleveland, serving until 1843. The stone to the left is for Harriet Mather, his wife, a relative of Samuel L. Mather.

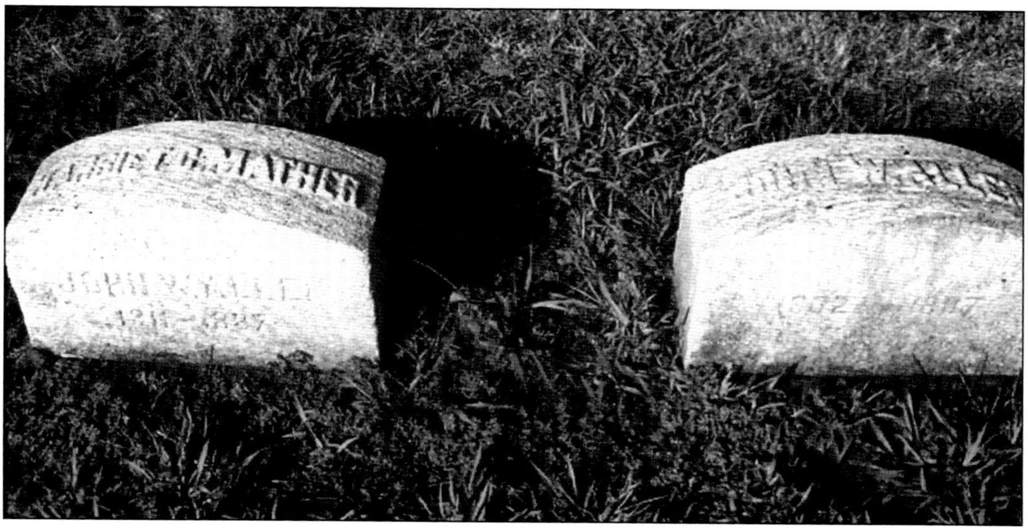

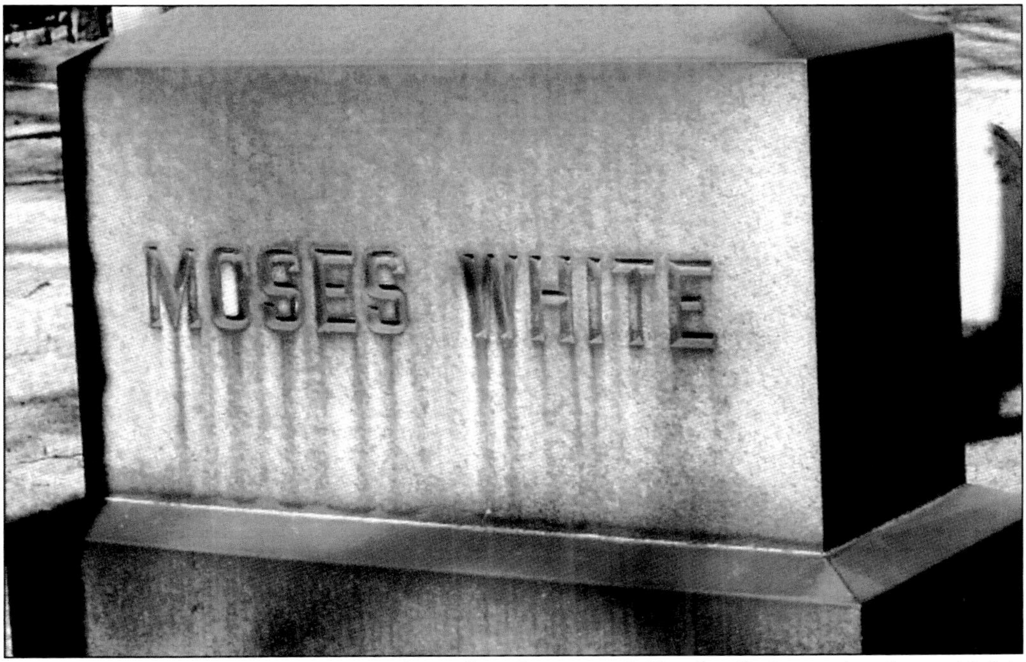

Moses White (1807–1866) was an early settler who opened Cleveland's first tailor shop with his wife, Mary, who was also a tailor. He was discouraged by the absence of organized religion in Cleveland during those early days. He was a man of action and helped organize the first Sunday schools in Cleveland in 1819. This pioneer organization that White, a Baptist layman, developed became the First Presbyterian Church of Cleveland, today known as Old Stone Church on Cleveland Public Square. Seventeen devout Baptists, which included Moses White, organized the First Baptist Society in February 1833. The first interment in Erie Street Cemetery in September 1827 was Minerva M. White, daughter of Moses and Mary White. She was one of eight children, only two of whom survived to maturity.

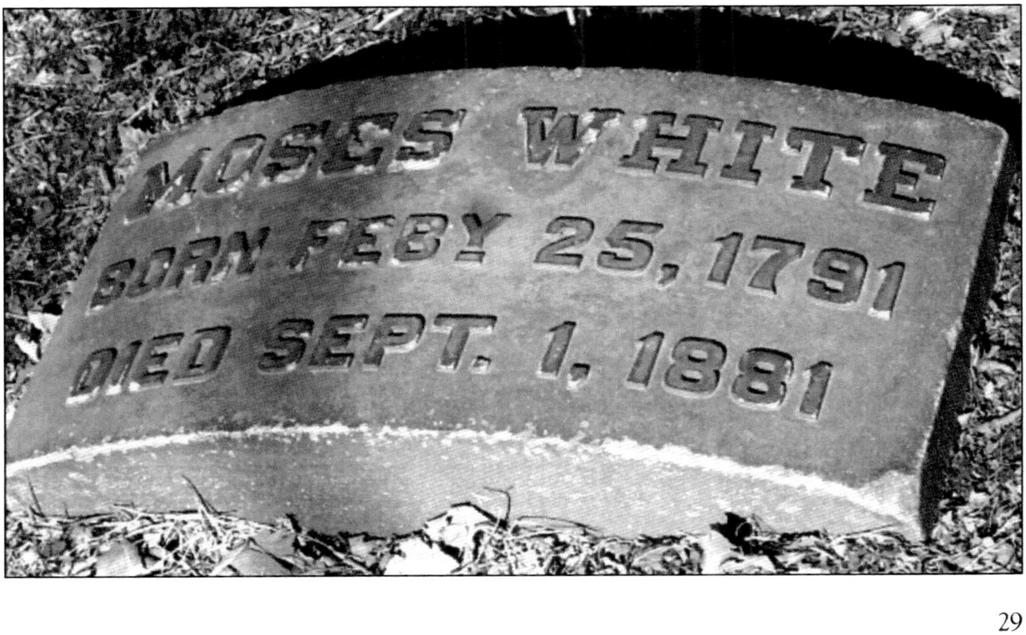

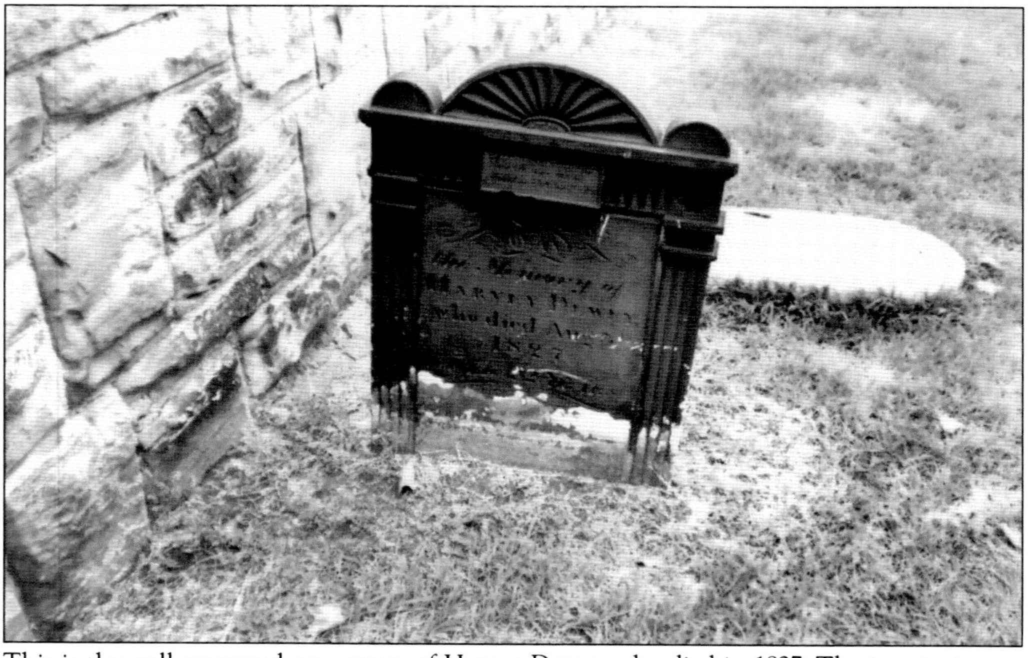

This is the well-preserved gravestone of Harvey Dewey, who died in 1827. The inscription on the top of the stone reads, "Our days on the earth are as a shadow." He was only 22 years old when he died.

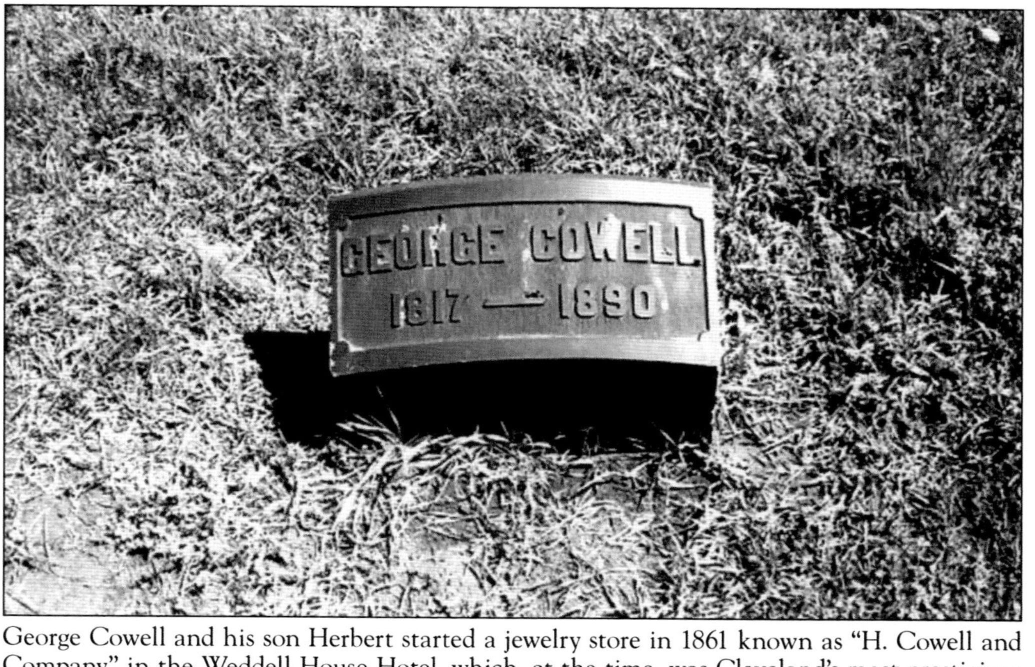

George Cowell and his son Herbert started a jewelry store in 1861 known as "H. Cowell and Company" in the Weddell House Hotel, which, at the time, was Cleveland's most prestigious hotel. When President Lincoln came to Cleveland on the way to his first inauguration, he stayed at the Weddell House Hotel and spoke to a gathering from its balcony.

Peter Weddell (1788–1847) came to Cleveland in 1820 and opened a store that became one of the largest in Ohio. In 1845, he tore down the store that had made him wealthy enough for the construction of the Weddell House Hotel, considered Cleveland's most famous hotel. The hotel was called the Astor House of the Lakes. Unfortunately, Weddell died shortly before it was opened. It was the site of many historic gatherings early in Cleveland's history. Presidents and statesmen spoke from its balcony, including Abraham Lincoln, who stayed at the Weddell House on his way to Washington, DC, for his first inauguration. The east end of the famous hotel was razed in 1905 for the construction of the Rockefeller Building. The west end of the hotel lasted until 1961. Weddell also had a distinguished career as a banker, an incorporator of the Ohio Railroad Co., and a board member of the Cleveland Medical College. He financially supported Western Reserve University in Hudson and helped in the purchase of the land for the Old Stone Church on Public Square. He is buried in Erie Street Cemetery, but his headstone is gone. (Early Settlers Association.)

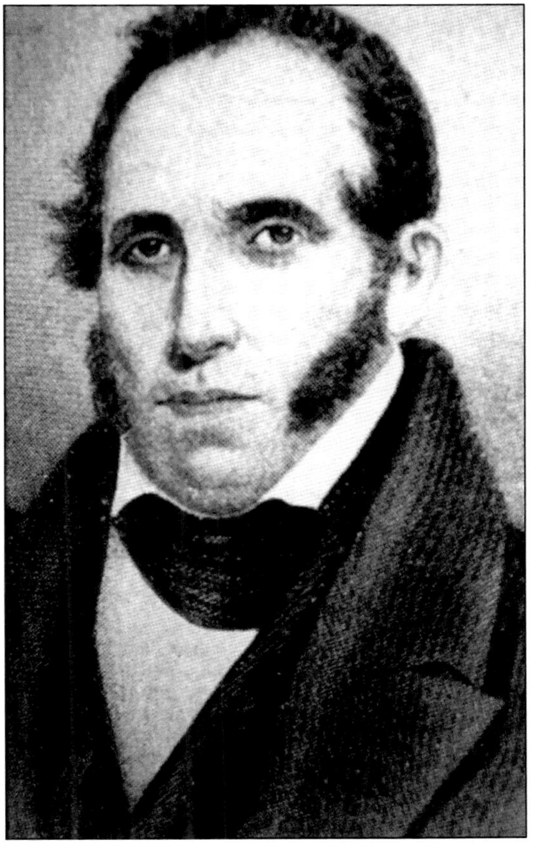

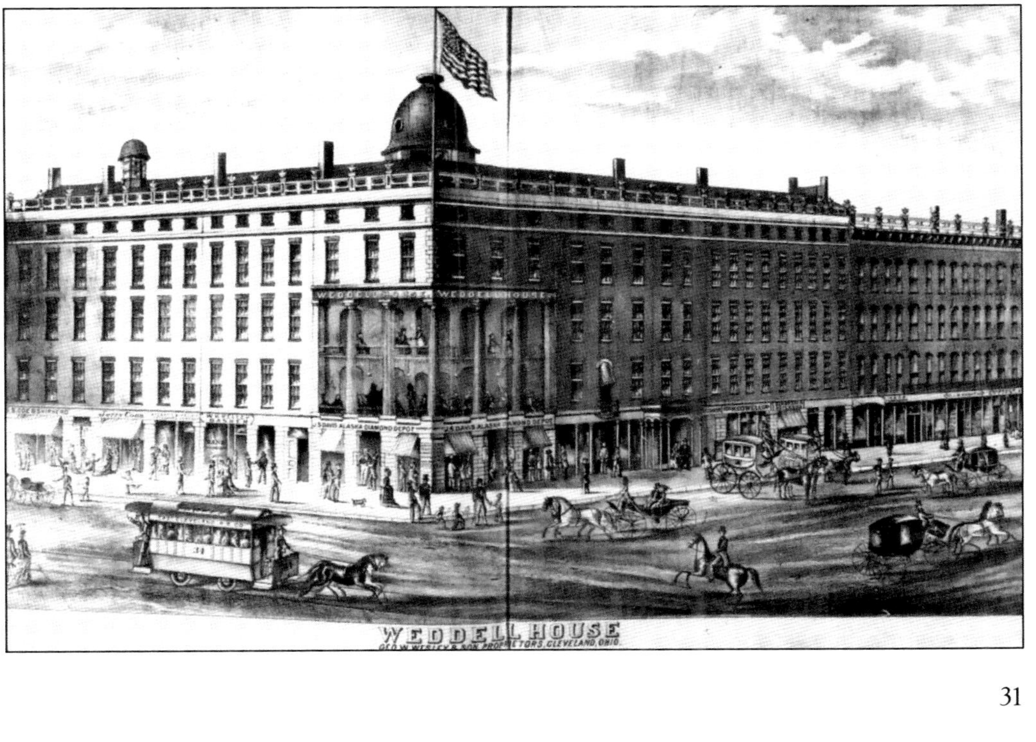

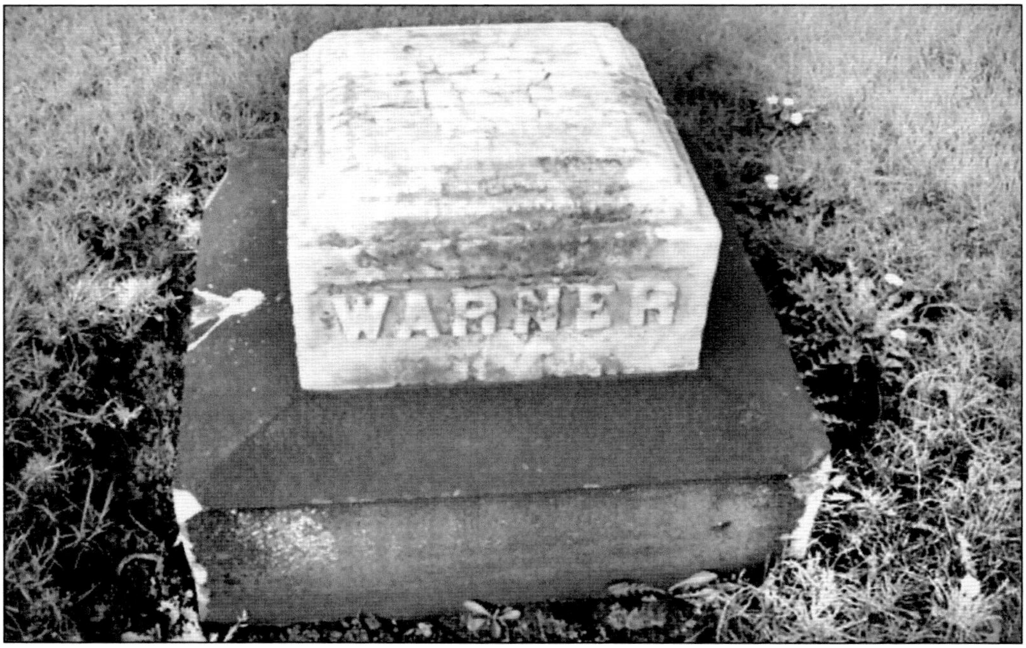

John Fletcher Warner was born in Burlington, Vermont, in 1817. When he was 16 years old, he left Burlington to join his brother who had gone to Cleveland two years earlier. He married Abby Kingsley. His first job in Cleveland was working in a warehouse along the Cuyahoga River. He then advanced to a job as bookkeeper for Ransom, Baldwin & Co., a commission merchants business.

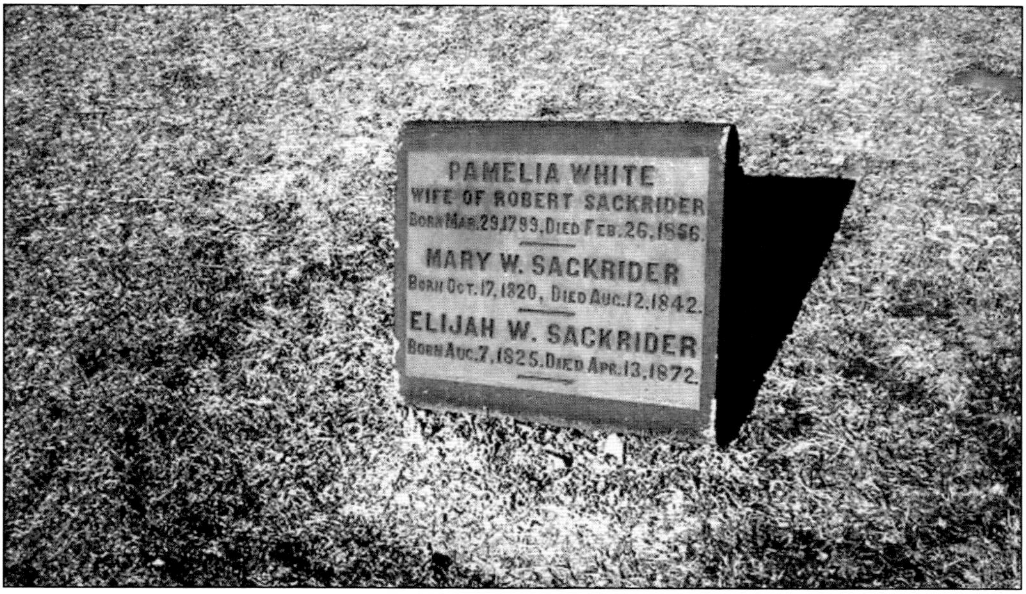

Pamelia White (1799–1856) married Robert Sackrider of Plattsburgh, New York. She came to Cleveland with three children. Their son Elijah White Sackrider (1825–1872) was a Cleveland druggist. After the death of her half-sister Harriet, Pamelia kept house for her brother-in-law Amos Shepard Hutchinson and took care of his two children.

Eleazer Albee Brock was born to David Brock and Philena Albee in Vermont in 1806. Eleazer married Margarita M. Platt, the daughter of Nathaniel C. Platt. They married in Plattsburg, New York, and had seven children. Eleazer was a pioneer businessman in Cleveland. He established and operated the first oilcloth factory as well as a boot and shoe business. Eleazer Brock's family is listed in the 1850 census of Cuyahoga County.

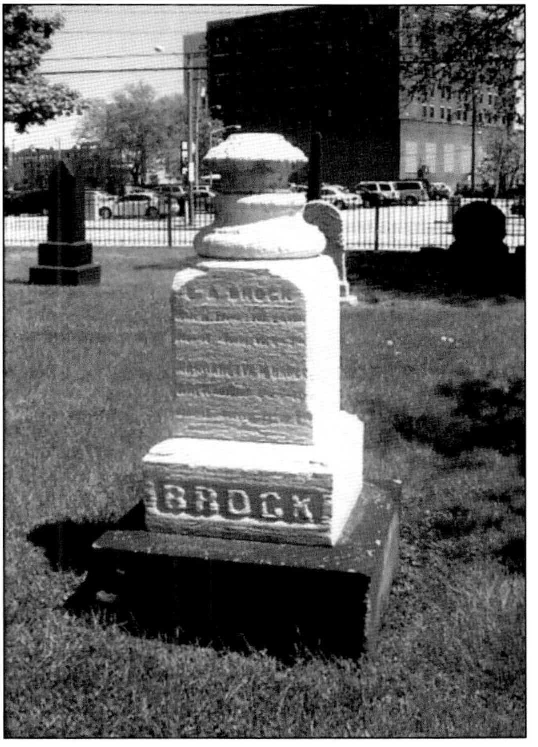

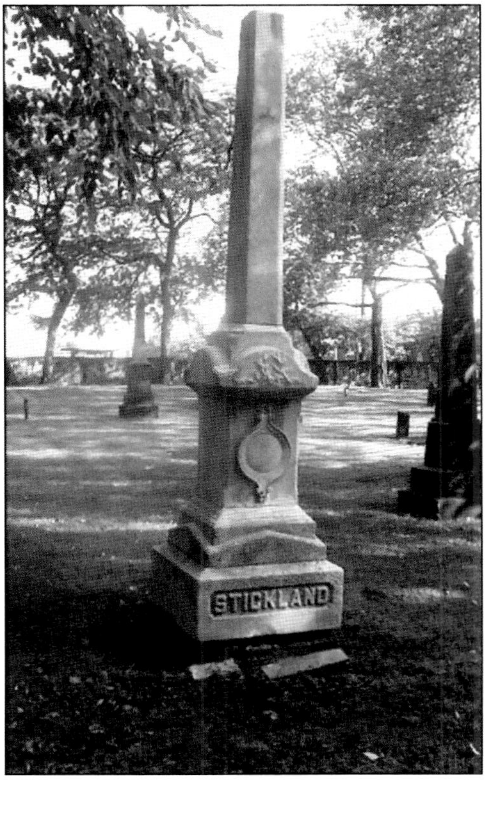

Aaron Stickland (1790–1842) came to Cleveland from Ashford, Connecticut, and opened a drugstore in 1831. In 1833, he made Erastus F. Gaylord a partner. The following year, Erastus's younger brother also came into the partnership. In 1836, Stickland was a councilman elected in the first municipal election in Cleveland. He died in 1842 at the age of 51 and left Erastus in charge of the property and business.

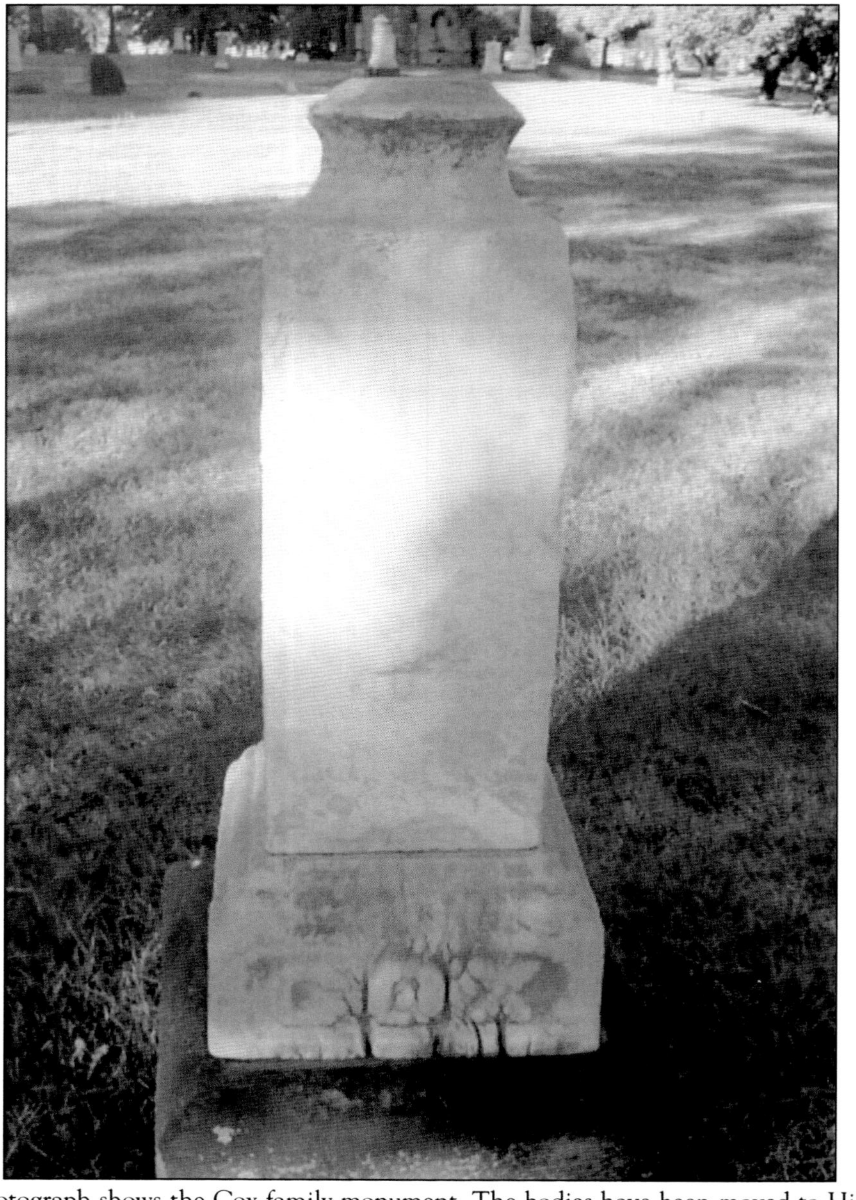

This photograph shows the Cox family monument. The bodies have been moved to Highland Park Cemetery. The first family members buried in Erie Street Cemetery were Charley, 11 months, and Charley, two months. Jacob Dolson Cox Jr. was the son of Gov. Jacob D. Cox Sr., who was governor of Ohio from 1866 to 1868. Before becoming governor, he was a major general in the Civil War, US Secretary of the Interior under Pres. Ulysses S. Grant, dean of Cincinnati Law School, and then became an author of books on the Civil War. Jacob Dolson Cox Jr. started his career in western New York before coming to Cleveland. He borrowed $2,000 from his father to purchase a 50 percent interest in a small twist drill company and then convinced his partner to move the company to Cleveland. At that time, Cleveland was a bustling Great Lakes city with a port. It took Jacob Dolson Cox Jr. 14 years to pay off the $2,000 loan, but eventually Cleveland Twist Drill became a multimillion-dollar company listed on the New York Stock Exchange.

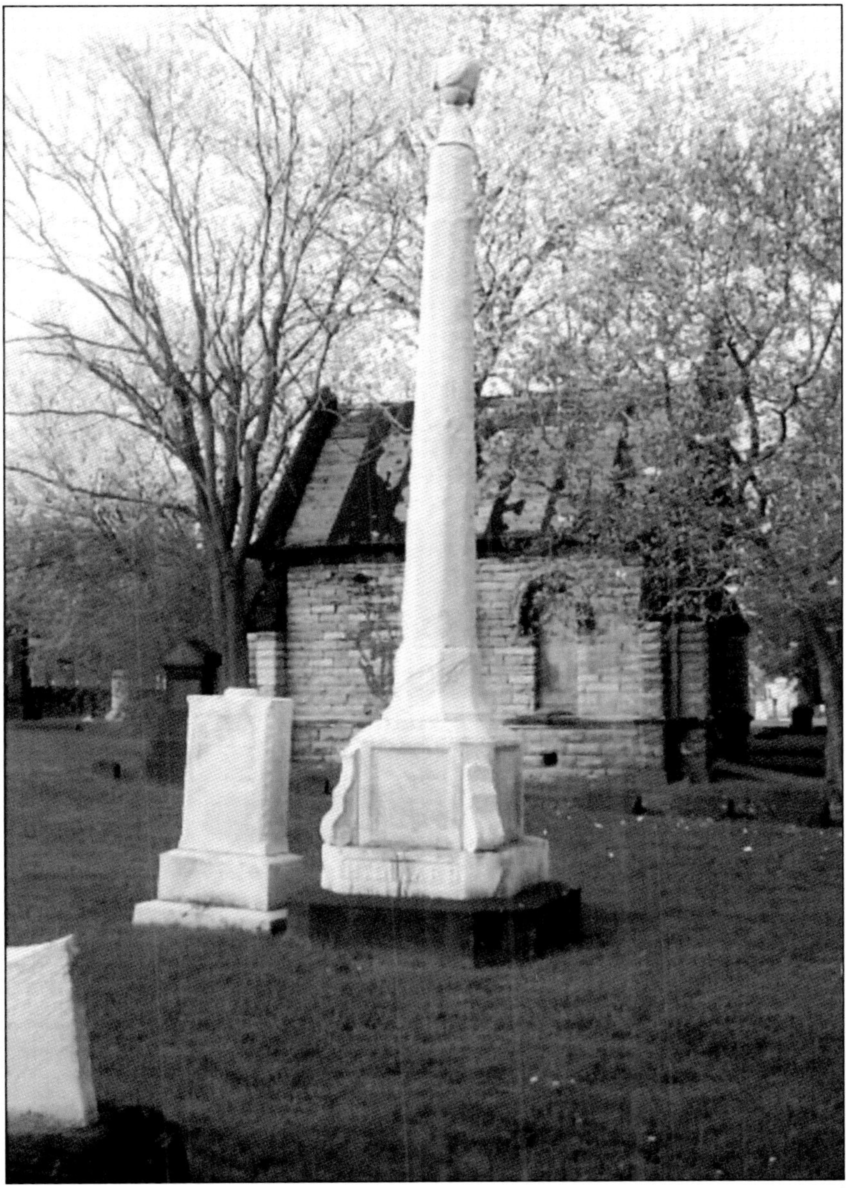

Richard Hilliard, a pioneer merchant, died in 1856. During his life, he left his mark on Cleveland. At a young age he went into the trades as a hat maker and then as a salesman in upstate New York. With the opening of the Erie Canal, he went to work for a man named John Daly, a merchant from the town of Black Water, which today is a neighborhood of Buffalo. Richard became a member of the Daly firm and was sent to Cleveland to start a store and work as the manager. In 1824, Daly left the business in Cleveland, and Hilliard's brother-in-law became his partner in the new firm known as Hilliard and Hayes, a store of dry goods, groceries, and vessel supplies. For two years, he was president of the village council and one of three aldermen in the first city government. He also served as a commissioner of the water works, trustee of Homeopathic College, and a member of the first board of trade. It is said that he was active in everything that affected the growth and prosperity of the city.

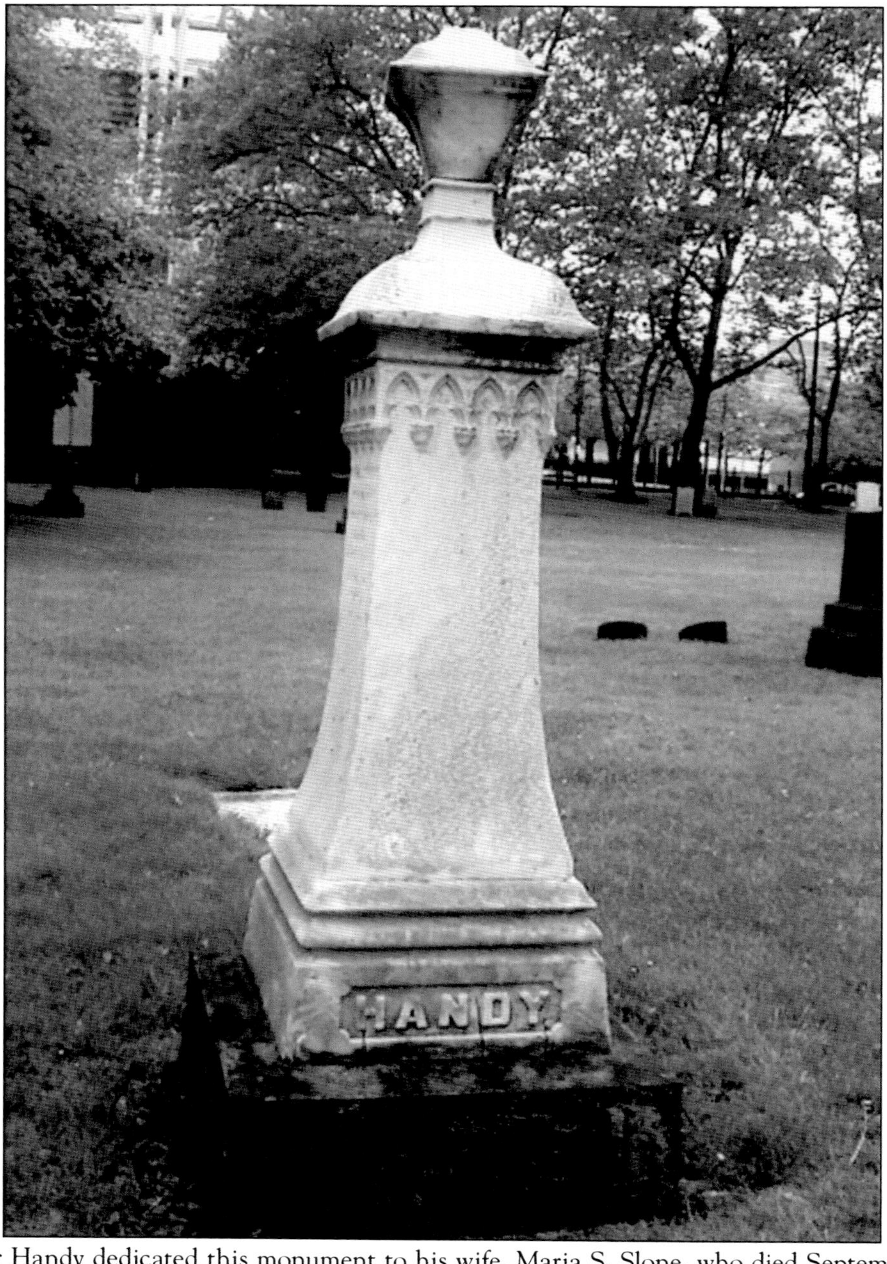

Parker Handy dedicated this monument to his wife, Maria S. Slone, who died September 8, 1848. Urns were first used by ancient Greeks and Romans to hold the ashes of the dead, but used today on a gravestone an urn is a sign of mourning, according to gravestone symbolism. Parker Handy was the first president of the Bank of Commerce, a bank that was chartered in 1845. Parker's brother Truman was also a banker. He started as a cashier in the Commercial Bank of Lake Erie under Leonard Case, president, and went on to a distinguished career. He became the first president of the Clearing House Association, organized to affect a safe manor of exchange between banks and bankers. He also had the distinction of lending young John D. Rockefeller a $2,000 business loan.

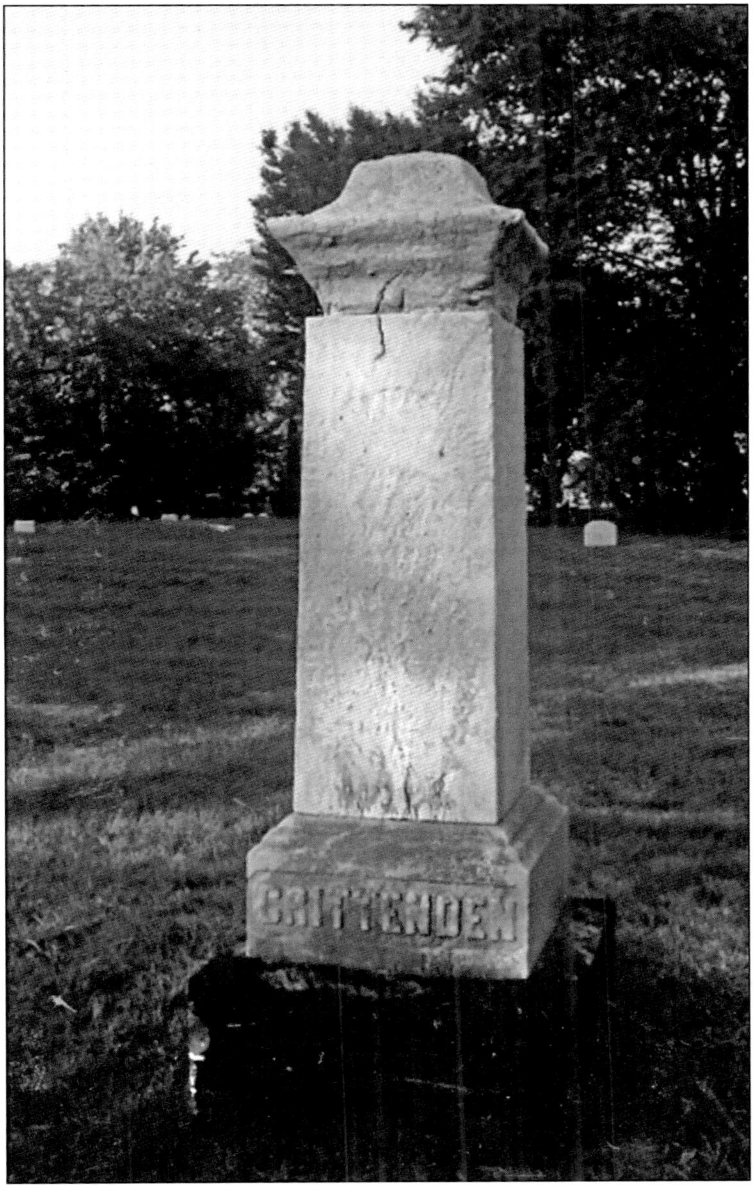

The Crittenden family was a well-known and prominent family of the early days of Cleveland. Newton E. and Joseph H. Crittenden were born in Conway, Massachusetts. Newton came to Cleveland in 1826 and opened the village's first jewelry store in a small brick building that stood next to the Franklin House Hotel on Superior Avenue. It was said he did not have to depend on Clevelanders to fill his store because people from all over the state could be seen shopping there. His business was called the finest jewelry store west of New York. Joseph began a shoe and leather business in 1832 and worked until 1857, when he retired to Brooklyn, New York, where he died. In the 1860s, family members got involved in banking. Cleveland's pioneer First National Bank, the seventh in the nation, was organized in 1863 in the SW Crittenden banking house. By 1868, the Newton E. Crittenden family had moved to Millionaire's Row on Euclid Avenue. A building in Cleveland's historic Warehouse District still carries the Crittenden name.

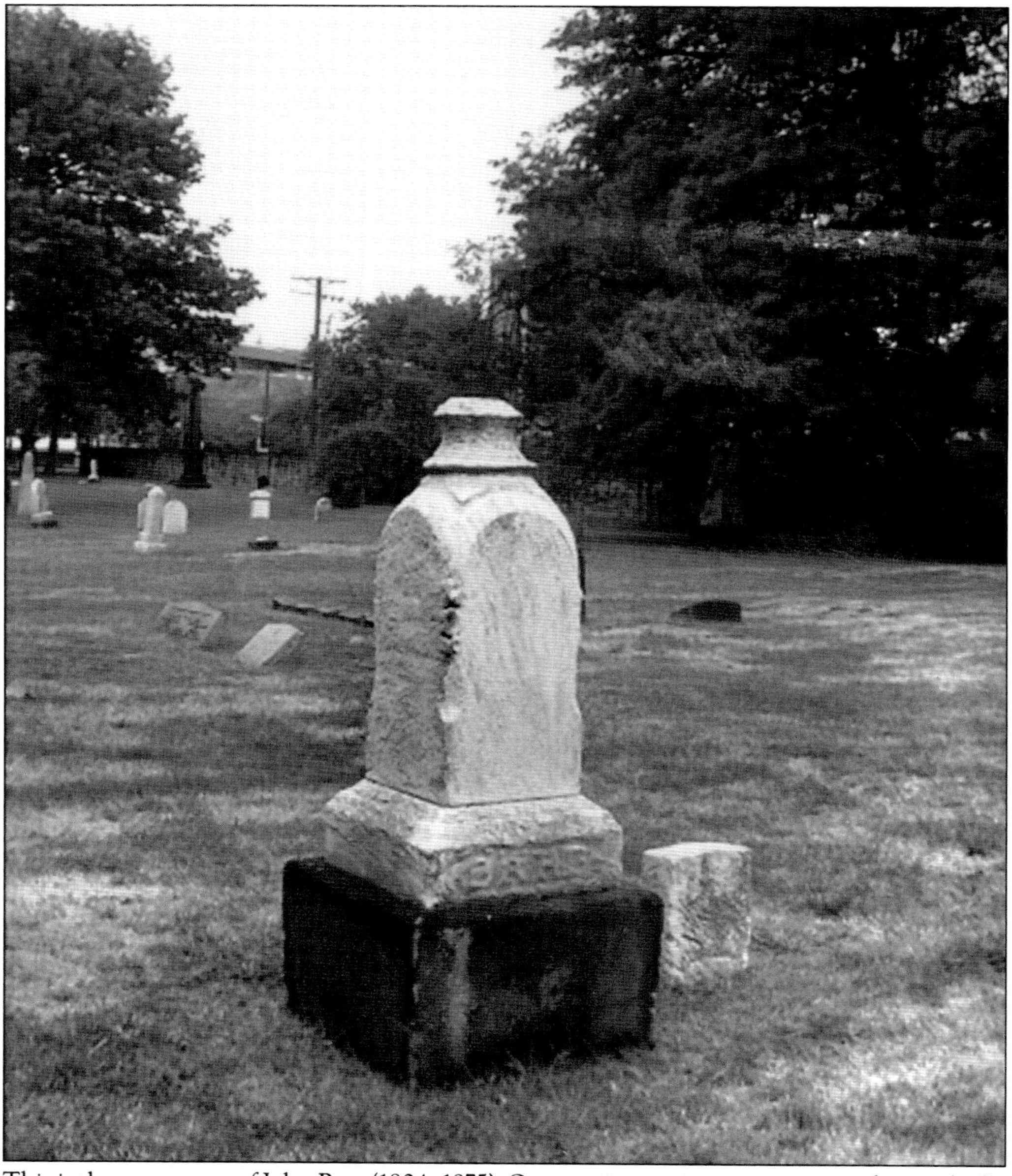

This is the gravestone of John Barr (1804–1875). Once an impressive monument, today it is badly deteriorated. Barr came to the Western Reserve in 1828 and made Cleveland his home. He had a distinguished career as a member of the Cleveland community. He started as a deputy sheriff under Edward Baldwin, and in 1830, he was elected sheriff of Cuyahoga County. His career included membership on the school board, one term as clerk of the common pleas court, and as elected judge of what was called "police court," which was established in 1853. He was a member of the law firm of Stillman, Stetson, and Barr and was active in civic affairs. The Cuyahoga County Historical Society was founded in 1858 with Barr serving as its secretary. This group was the forerunner of the Western Reserve Historical Society. Barr also wrote a short history of Cleveland. He was a proprietor of the Clarendon Hotel, which opened in 1870. One of the organizations he helped to establish was the Lyceum, an association for instruction and entertainment through lectures.

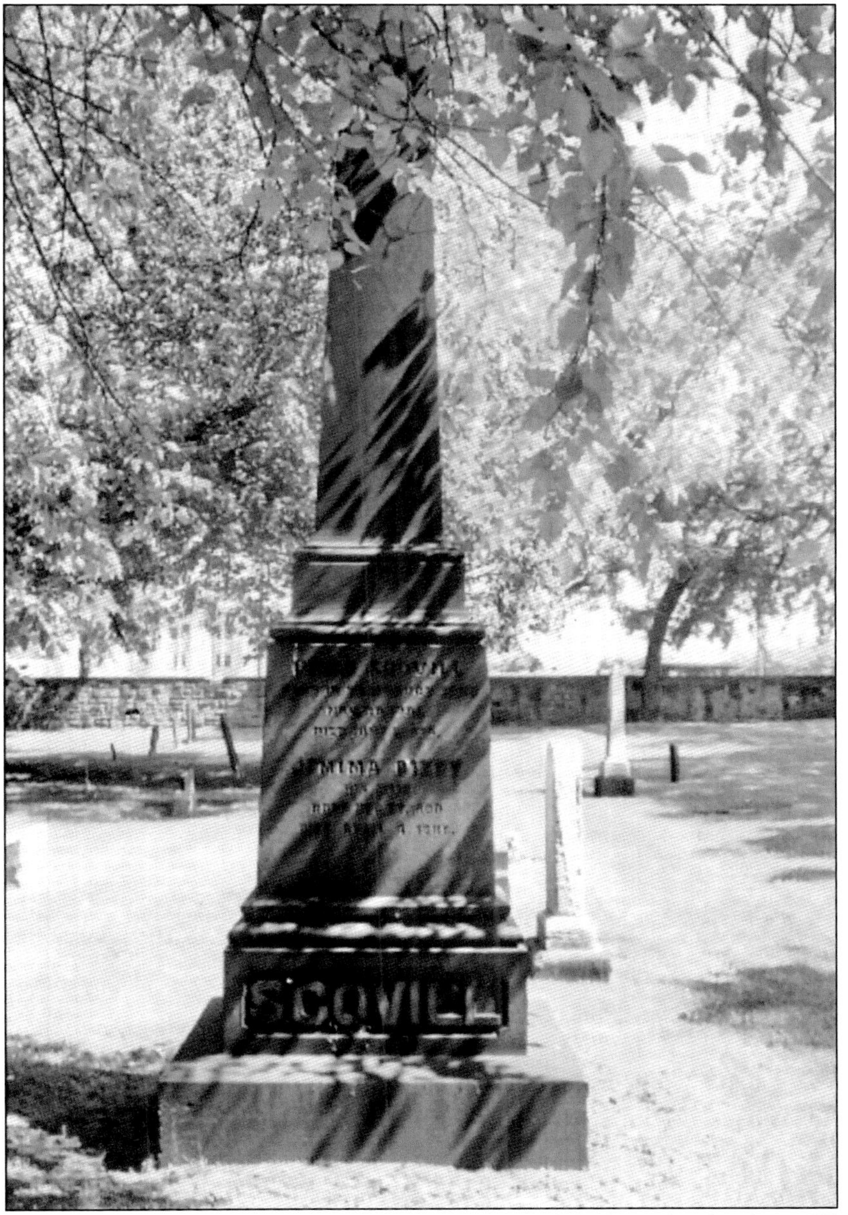

Philo Scovill was born in Salisbury, Connecticut, in 1791 and died in Cleveland in 1875. In 1816, he came to Cleveland by wagon, bringing groceries and other supplies that were needed in the village. He opened a small store. When other stores were opened that provided competition, he went back to work as a carpenter—a trade that was in demand in the growing village. After becoming a successful builder, he saw opportunities in real estate and acquired a large number of properties. In 1826, he built a stagecoach station that became known as the Franklin House Hotel, named after Benjamin Franklin. For years, it was the most popular hotel in Cleveland. Five stagecoach lines were headquartered out of the hotel by 1848. He had a 170-acre farm that encompassed much of the land where Cuyahoga Community College was built. He had a street named after him, Scovill Avenue, which is today called Community College Drive.

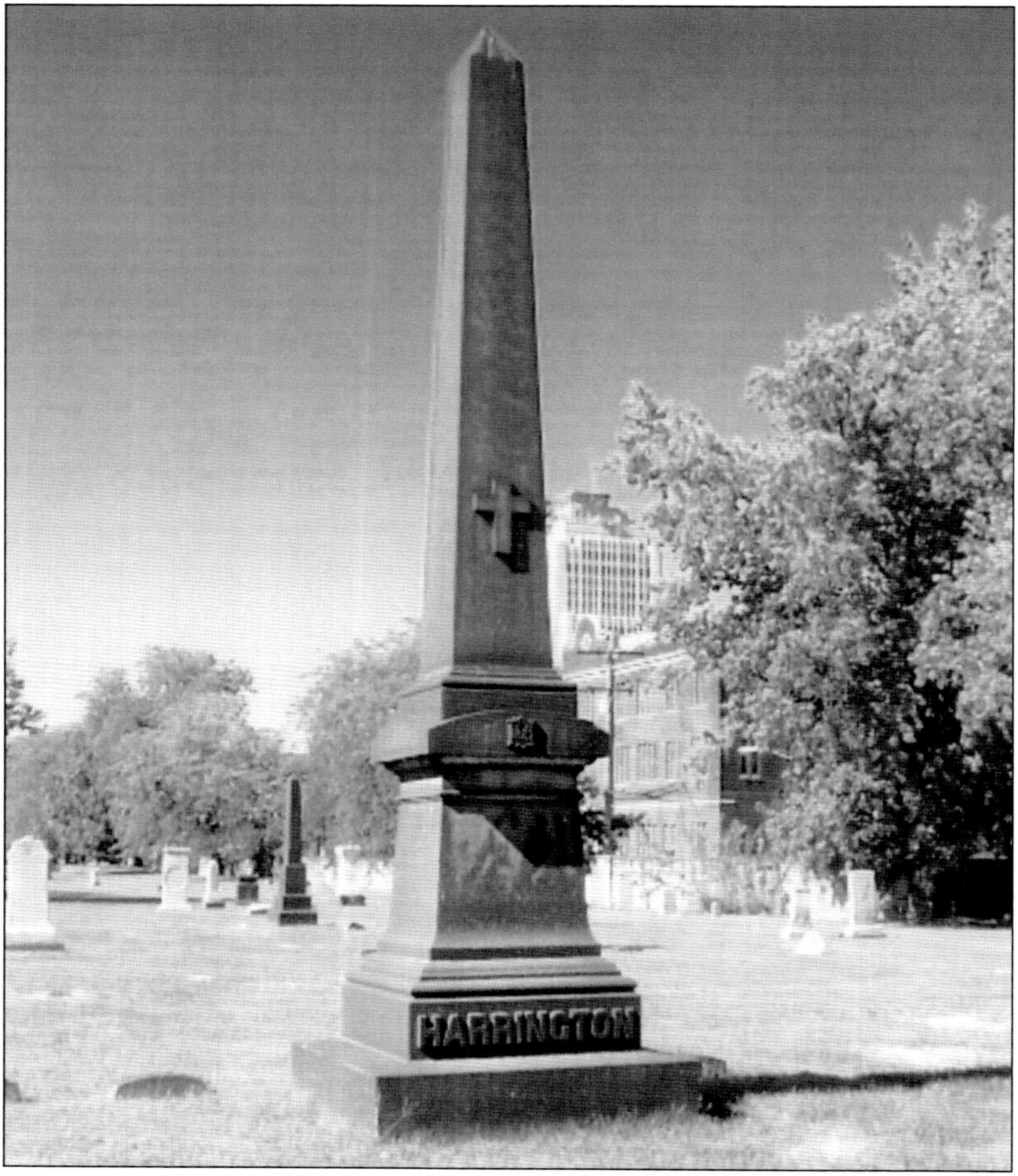

For many years, Benjamin Harrington (1806–1878) and his wife, Chloe (née Prentiss), were the host and hostess of the Franklin House, a hotel built by Philo Scovill in 1826 to accommodate the stagecoach business. It was named after Benjamin Franklin. When Scovill retired, the Harringtons took over operation of the hotel. Both of the Harringtons were from Vermont; Benjamin was born in Shelburne in 1806, the son of a sea captain, and Chloe was from Rutland. The Franklin House was the most popular hotel in those early days. Five stagecoach lines were headquartered out of the hotel. Every morning at 8:00 a.m., one could hear the blast of a bugle and the crack of a driver's whip as a stagecoach made its way to Buffalo (a 40-hour trip), or to Pittsburgh, Beaver Falls, Cincinnati, Columbus, Detroit through Toledo, and Warren, Ohio. Benjamin also became very successful in real estate by constructing commercial buildings. Chloe died in 1873, and Benjamin died in 1878.

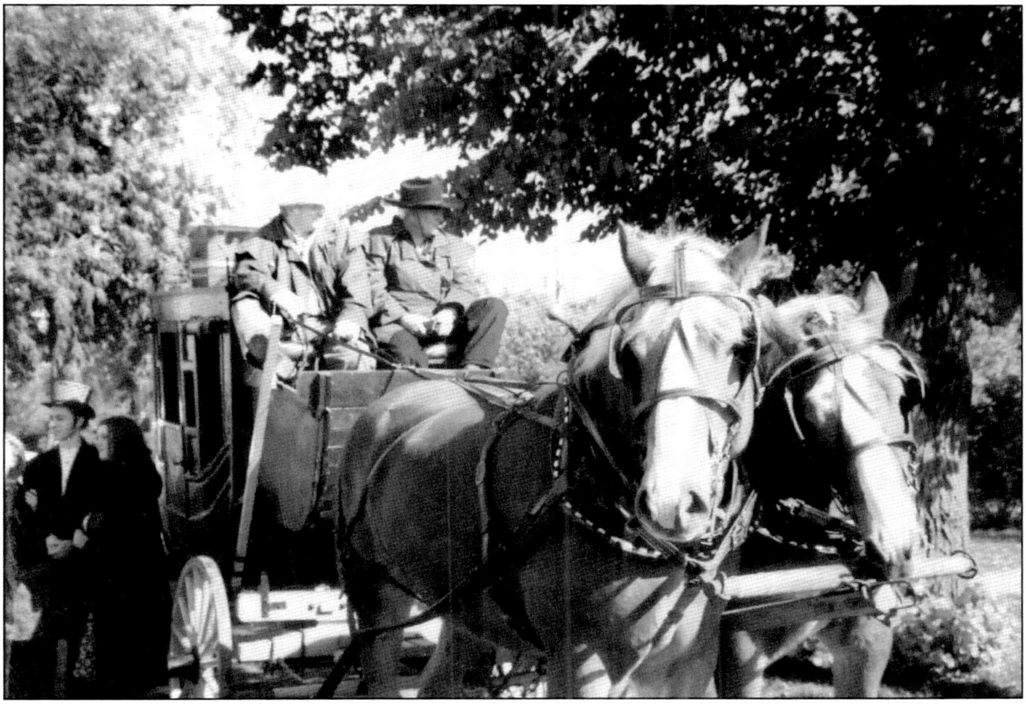

Seen here, a stagecoach waits at Dunham Tavern Museum during a celebration program. This photograph is a good example of what the town would have looked like in the late 1840s with passengers waiting in front of hotels and coach stops. Dunham Tavern was built in 1824. Anyone wanting to experience what life was like in the early days of Cleveland should visit Dunham Tavern.

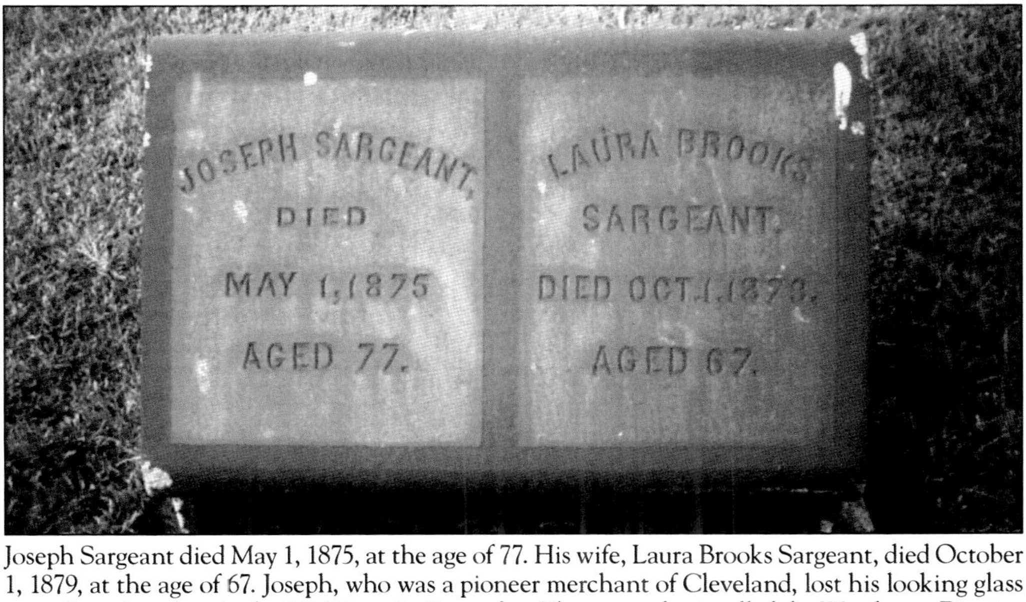

Joseph Sargeant died May 1, 1875, at the age of 77. His wife, Laura Brooks Sargeant, died October 1, 1879, at the age of 67. Joseph, who was a pioneer merchant of Cleveland, lost his looking glass manufacturing plant in the 1835 Superior Street fire. The area today is called the Warehouse District, a Cleveland historic district that has become a housing, dining, and entertainment center.

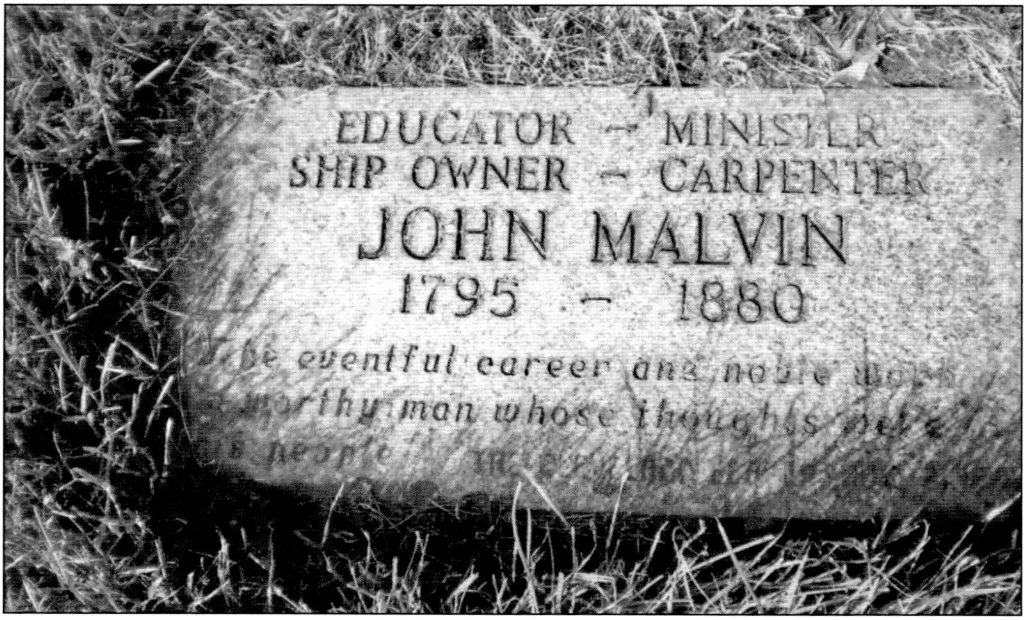

John Malvin (1795–1880) was an educator, minister, ship owner, and carpenter. At the outbreak of the Civil War, he recruited African Americans for service in the Union army. It was not until 1997 that a new gravestone was placed at Malvin's burial site. A dedication program included a tribute by the director of the National Museum of American History of the Smithsonian Institute. The inscription on the stone reads, "The eventful career and noble work of a worthy man whose thoughts were of his people." He is considered one of the most important African American citizens in Ohio's history. This historic marker is located on East Thirtieth Street between Central Avenue and Community College Boulevard. It was erected in 2003 and records Malvin's legacy.

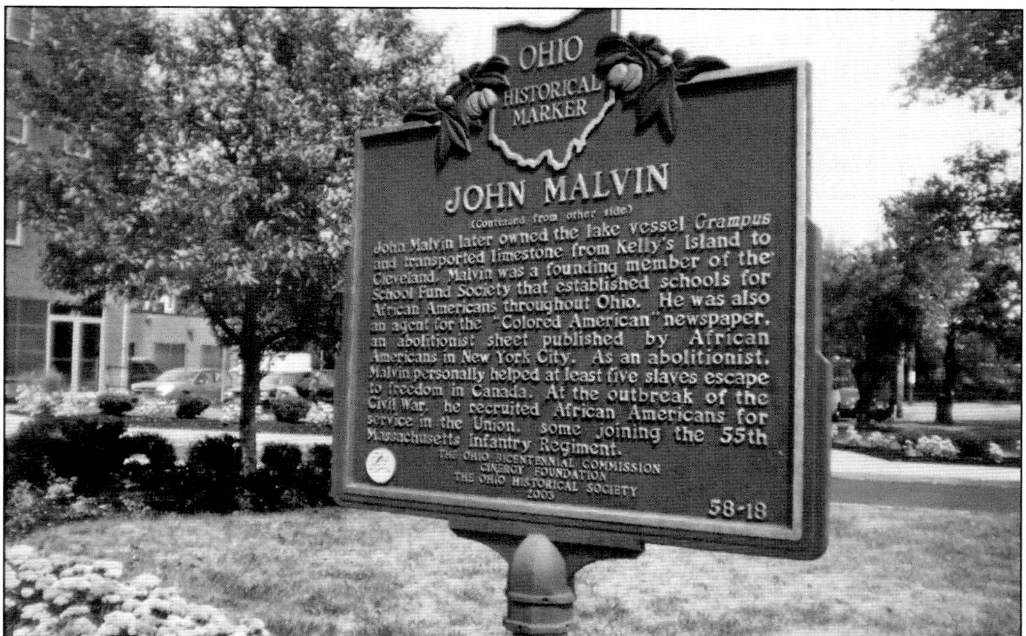

Two

As the City Grows

As Cleveland grew, the land that Erie Street Cemetery occupied became more sought after for expansion and development. An interesting quote attributed to judge Rufus P. Spalding can be found in the annals of the Early Settlers Association from when the cemetery was first opened in 1826: "In riding away from Cleveland in the stage coach I passed the Erie Street Cemetery just then laid out. I recollect it excited my surprise that a site for a burying ground should be selected so far out of town." It was not long after that Cleveland became a boomtown and grew very rapidly.

In 1916, after about 400 bodies had been removed from the Erie Street Cemetery, a number of Cleveland's founding families, with the support of other patriotic and civic organizations, formed the Pioneer Memorial Association. The association's goal was to save Erie Street Cemetery from the fast-encroaching city activities and to establish the cemetery as a hallowed ground worthy of the pioneers buried there. But this action did not end the city's desire to move the cemetery. In 1923 and 1926, Cleveland Chamber of Commerce reports called for the abandonment of Erie Street Cemetery so that a more appropriate place might be found for the interment of the city's founders. Again, there was strong community support to save the cemetery.

A wealth of genealogical information can be found on a reel of microfilm maintained at the Western Reserve Historical Society entitled *Burials and Removals, Erie Street Cemetery 1840–1918*. Also found there are the destinations of the bodies removed between 1905 and 1925. As stated earlier, most of the removals were undertaken because of the expected abandonment of the cemetery by the city. Of special importance are the alphabetical listings of persons buried prior to April 12, 1840, and a complete listing by section and lot of burials from 1840 through 1918. In 1840, Erie Street Cemetery was replotted, and a record of lots and burials was begun. No register had been kept prior to that time.

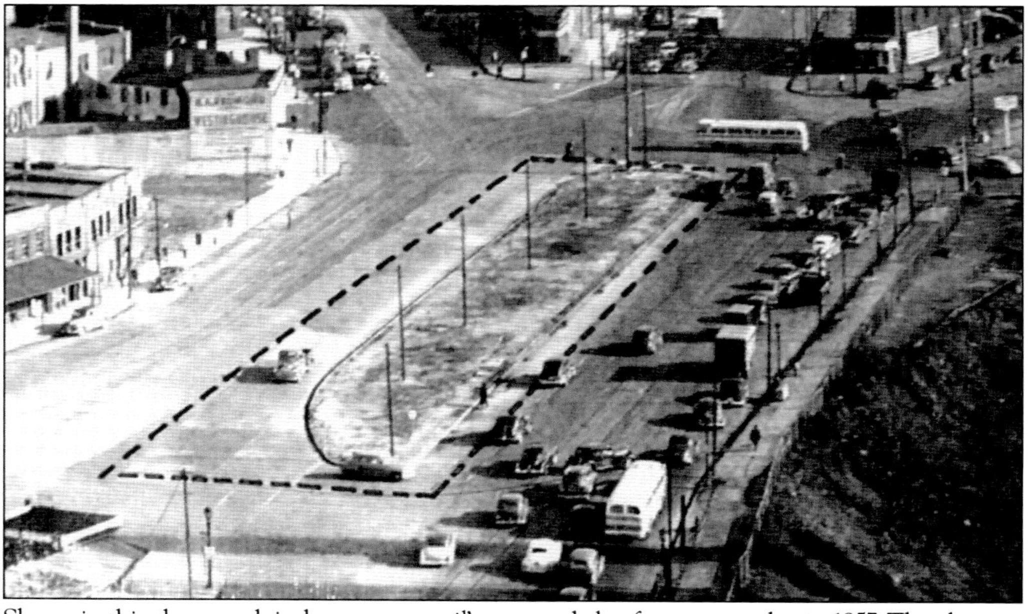

Shown in this photograph is the town council's approved plan for a new market in 1857. The plan was to move the Michigan Street market to a new site that would be called Central Market. The property was purchased for about $1,500. (Cleveland State University, Cleveland Press Collection.)

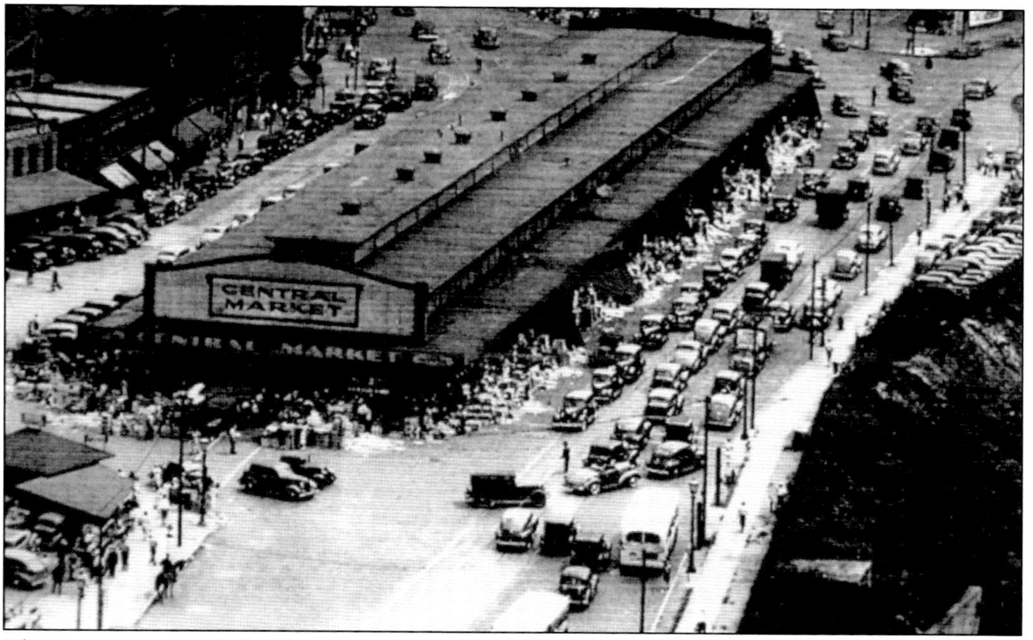

The new Central Market became very successful and was a threat to the Erie Street Cemetery because of the market's possible expansion. Mayor Tom L. Johnson and his administration favored the expansion that would take over Erie Street Cemetery, but public opposition saved the cemetery. The Early Settlers Association organized the opposition with a petition drive that was submitted to the town council. The petitioners prevailed, and Erie Street Cemetery survived another threat. (Cleveland State University, Cleveland Press Collection.)

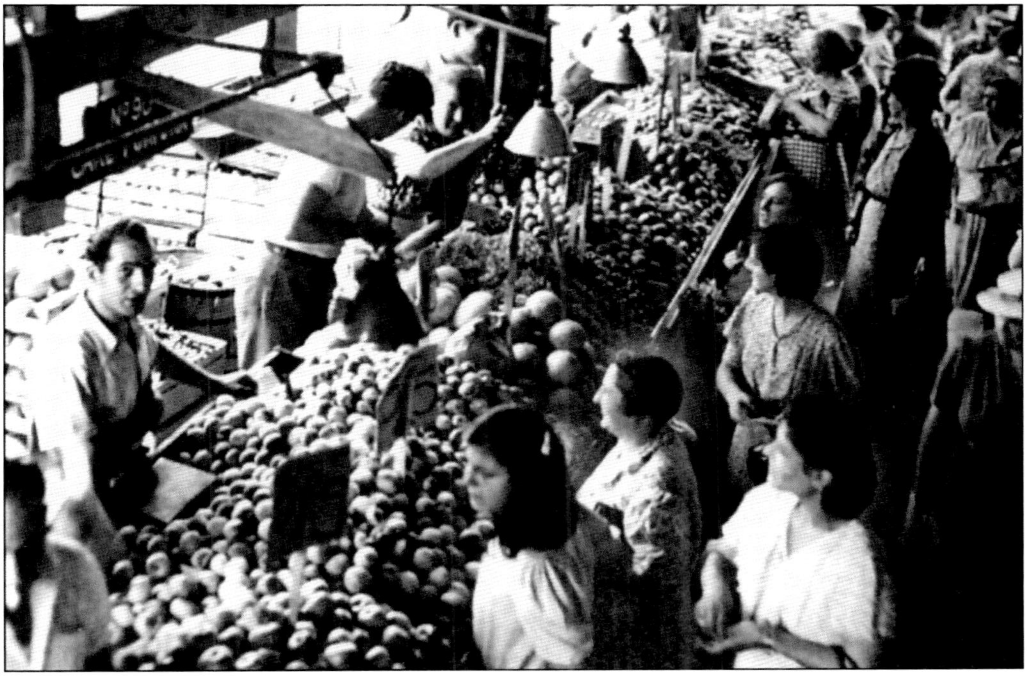

As stated in the *Encyclopedia of Cleveland History*, "The public market is an institution in Cleveland." The first market in Cleveland was established in 1929 on Ontario Street, south of Public Square near what was the Ontario Street Cemetery, Cleveland's first cemetery. The Central Market drew large crowds of shoppers until it burned down in 1949. The following spring, tenants reopened the Sheriff Street Market building and renamed it the New Central Market. The New Central Market remained in business until 1988, when it was razed for the Gateway Project. The project included the construction of Jacob's Field, now known as Progressive Field, the home of the Cleveland Indians. These photographs show shoppers and merchants during the heydays of the Central Market. (Cleveland State University, Cleveland Press Collection.)

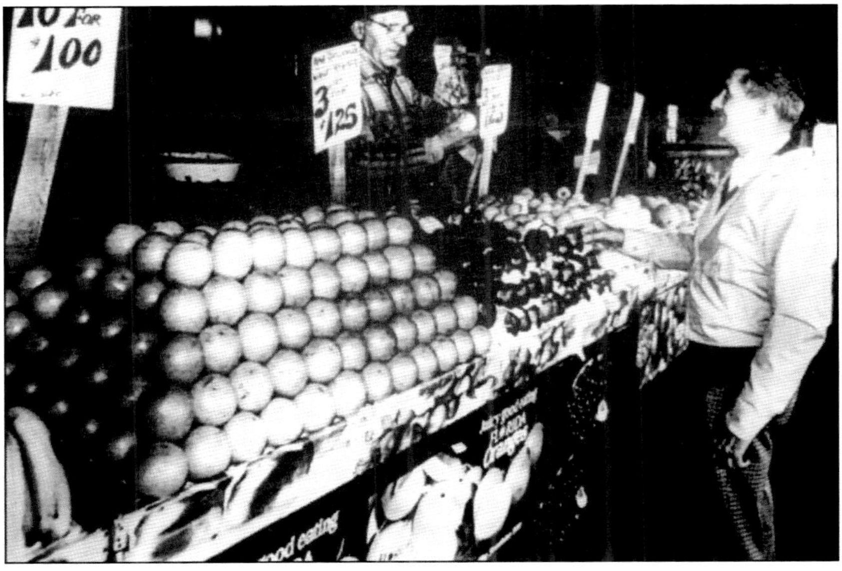

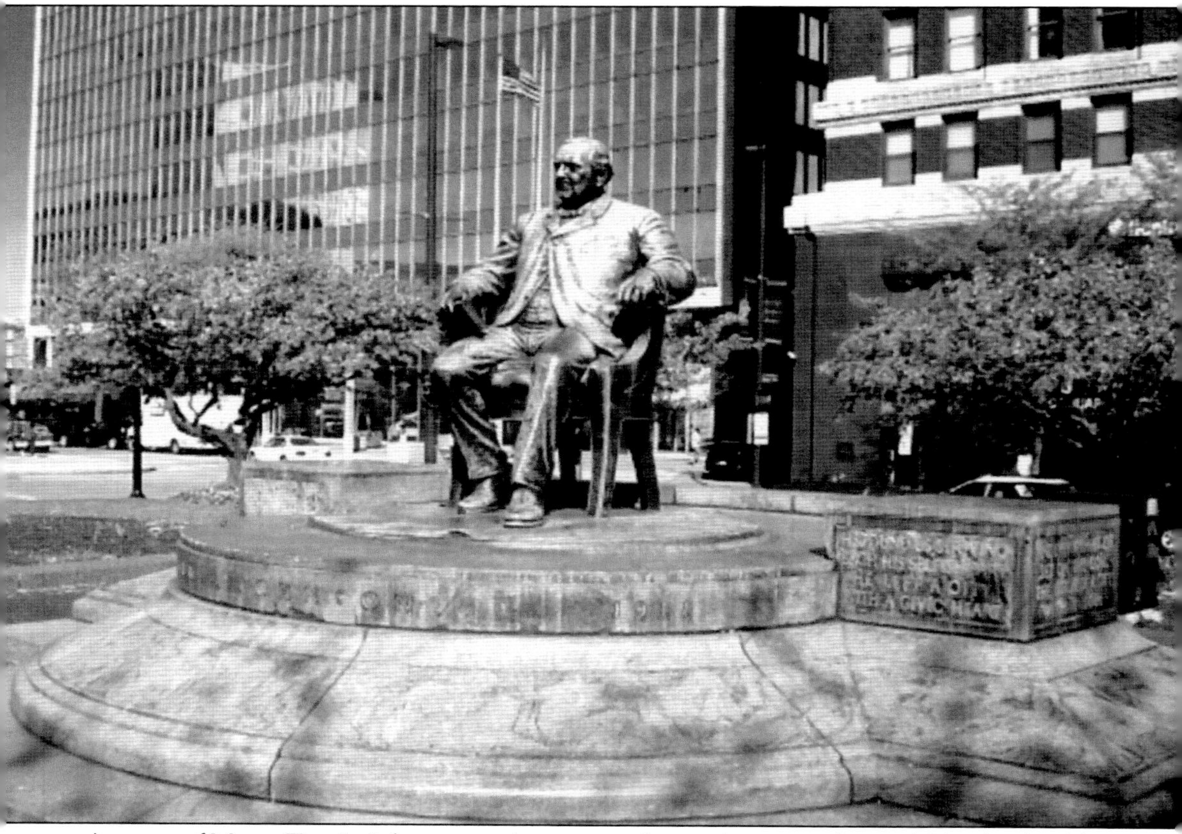

A statue of Mayor Tom L. Johnson can be seen on the northwest quadrant of Cleveland Public Square. Johnson (1854–1911) was the 35th mayor of Cleveland, in office from 1901 to 1909. He also served two terms in Congress before becoming mayor of the city. The statue depicts Johnson holding Henry George's book *Progress and Poverty*. Johnson's father was a Confederate general who fought in the Civil War. After the war, former Confederates could not find work. This caused Johnson to go to work at a very young age to raise money for the family, a hardship that helped mold his character. As Mayor Johnson developed Highland Park Cemetery in 1904, he suggested those buried at Erie Street Cemetery be moved to Highland Park Cemetery. His plan was to use the land of Erie Street Cemetery for a road and streetcar turnaround. It was not a popular idea and may have played a part in his defeat for reelection. In 1909, he lost the election to Herman C. Baehr.

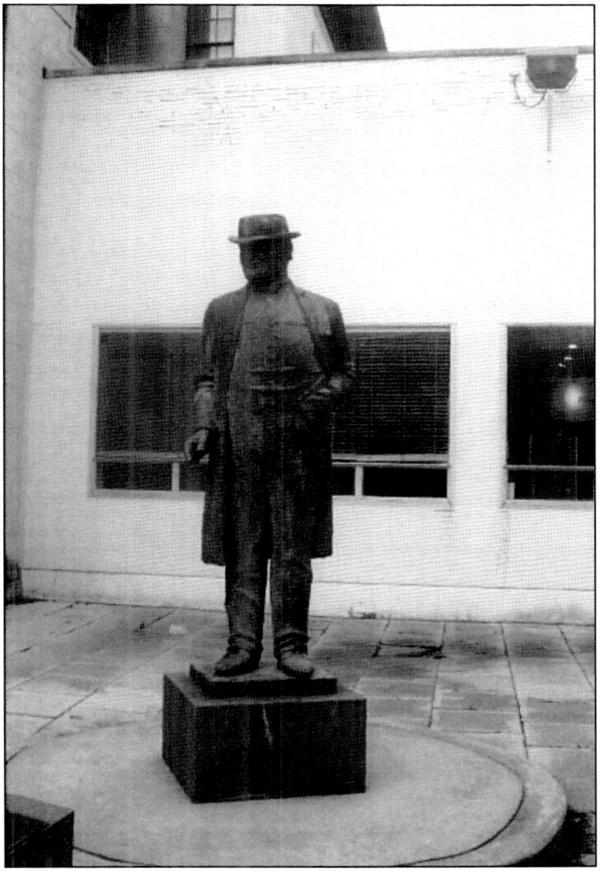

Tom L. Johnson (1854–1911) not only sits on Public Square but also stands near the back entrance to the Western Reserve Historical Society. He was mayor from 1901 to 1909. The statue was crafted by Cleveland's outstanding sculptor, William M. McVey, and was dedicated in October 2002. This is one of the last works of McVey. The statue is on permanent loan from Case Western Reserve University in memory of professor David D. Van Tassel (1928–2000), a historian, author, teacher, and trustee of the Western Reserve Historical Society.

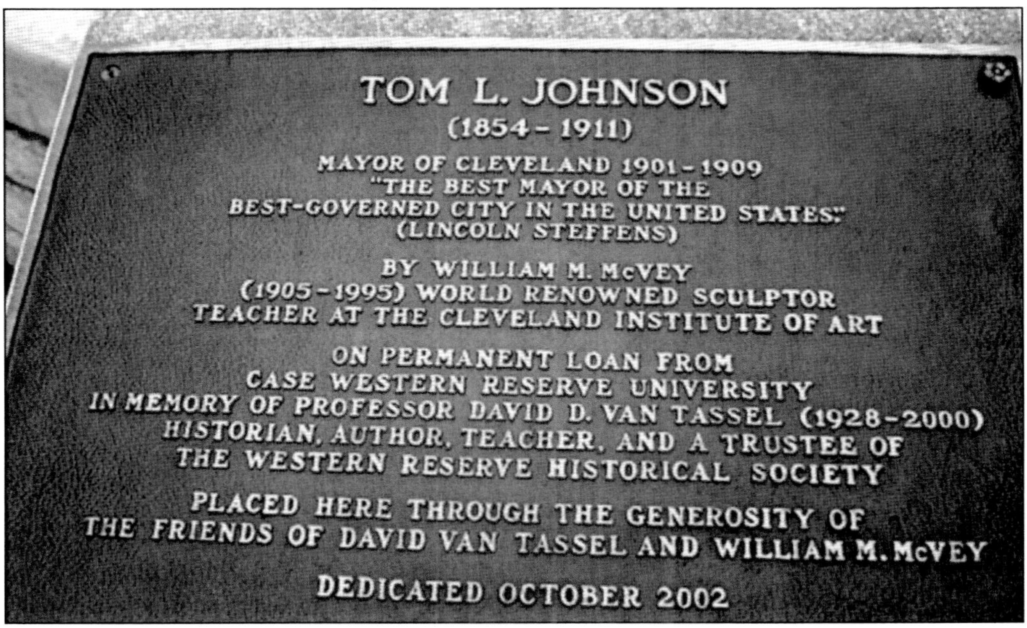

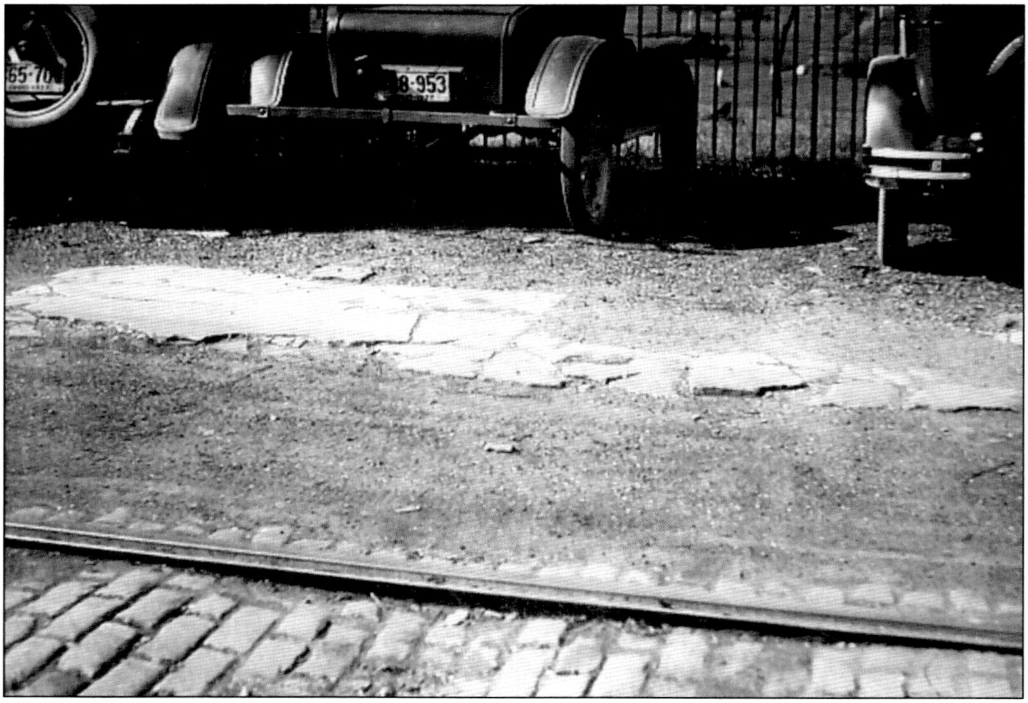

By the turn of the 19th century, streetcars operated to Erie Street Cemetery. In the photograph below, a streetcar turnaround does not look very attractive, which is why Mayor Tom L. Johnson's idea of using the grounds of Erie Street Cemetery for a streetcar turnaround was rejected by the people of Cleveland. (Cleveland State University, Cleveland Press Collection.)

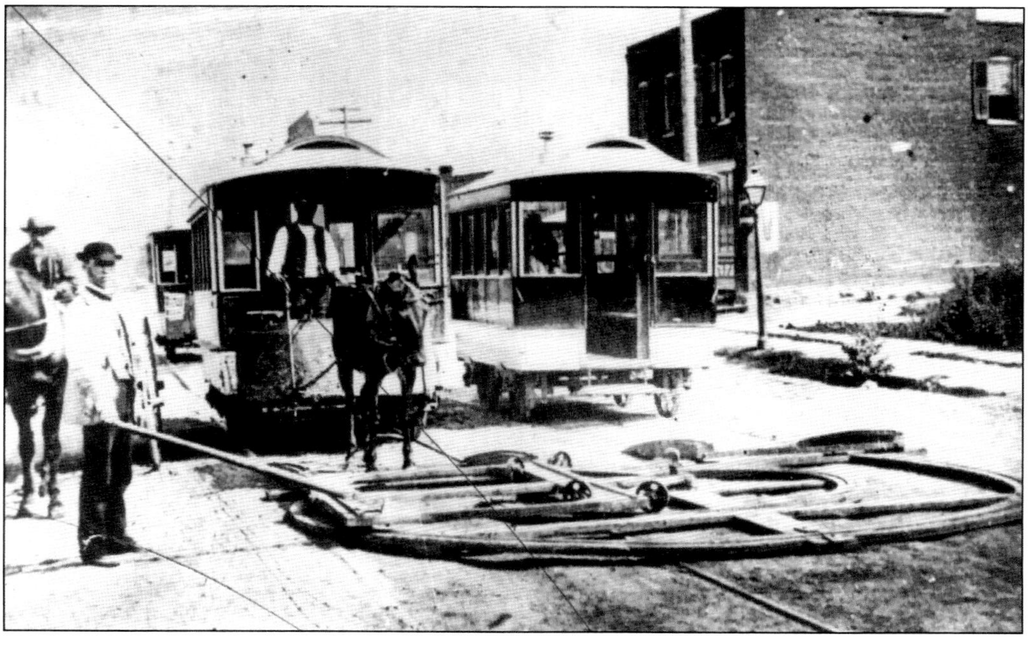

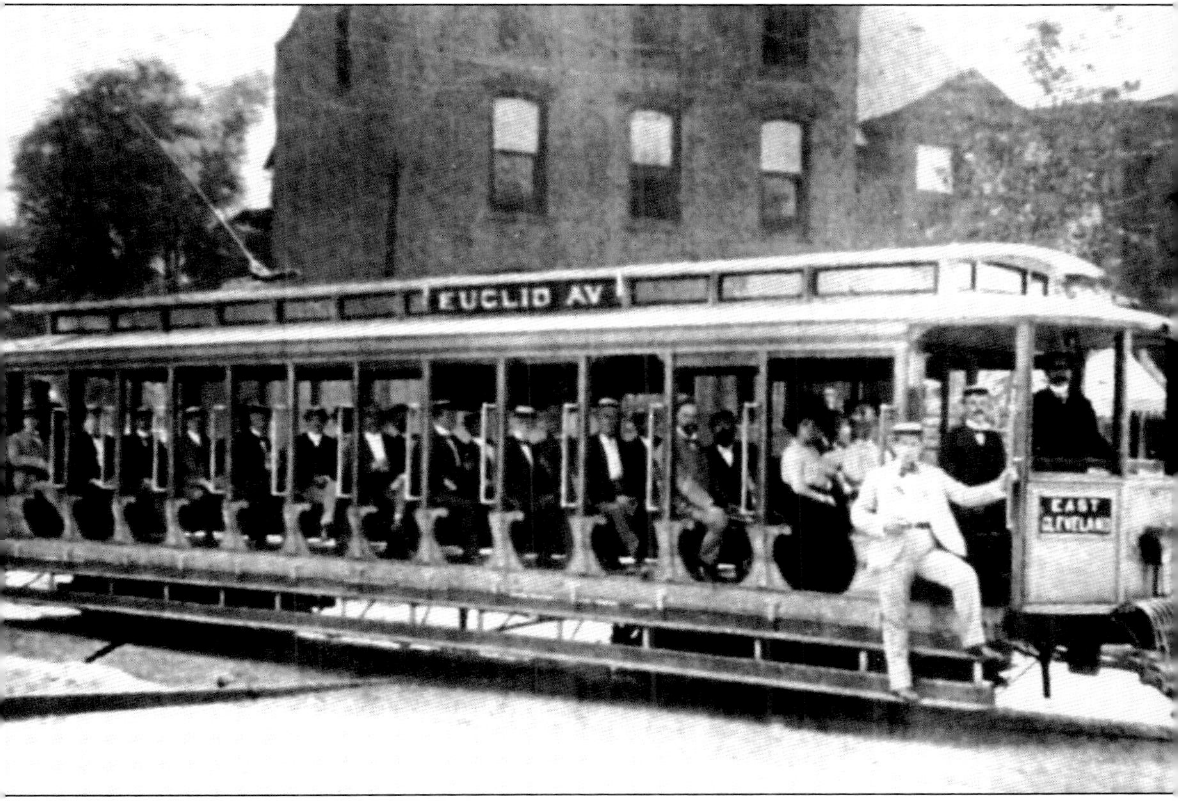

Cleveland went from the horse-drawn streetcar of the 1860s to the electric-powered streetcar at the turn of the century. As seen here, well-dressed men and women went off to work by streetcar, not in a chauffeured-driven car. The automobile changed that just a few years later. This photograph was taken in 1901. The day fare for the streetcar was 5¢, and the night fare was 10¢. Tom L. Johnson based much of his political career on the street railway system. He wanted to reduce fare to 3¢. Erie Street Cemetery almost became a casualty because Johnson wanted to use the land of the cemetery for a streetcar turnaround since the Central Market was just across the street. Looking closely, just behind the front of the streetcar, one can see the other means of transportation of the day, the bicycle.

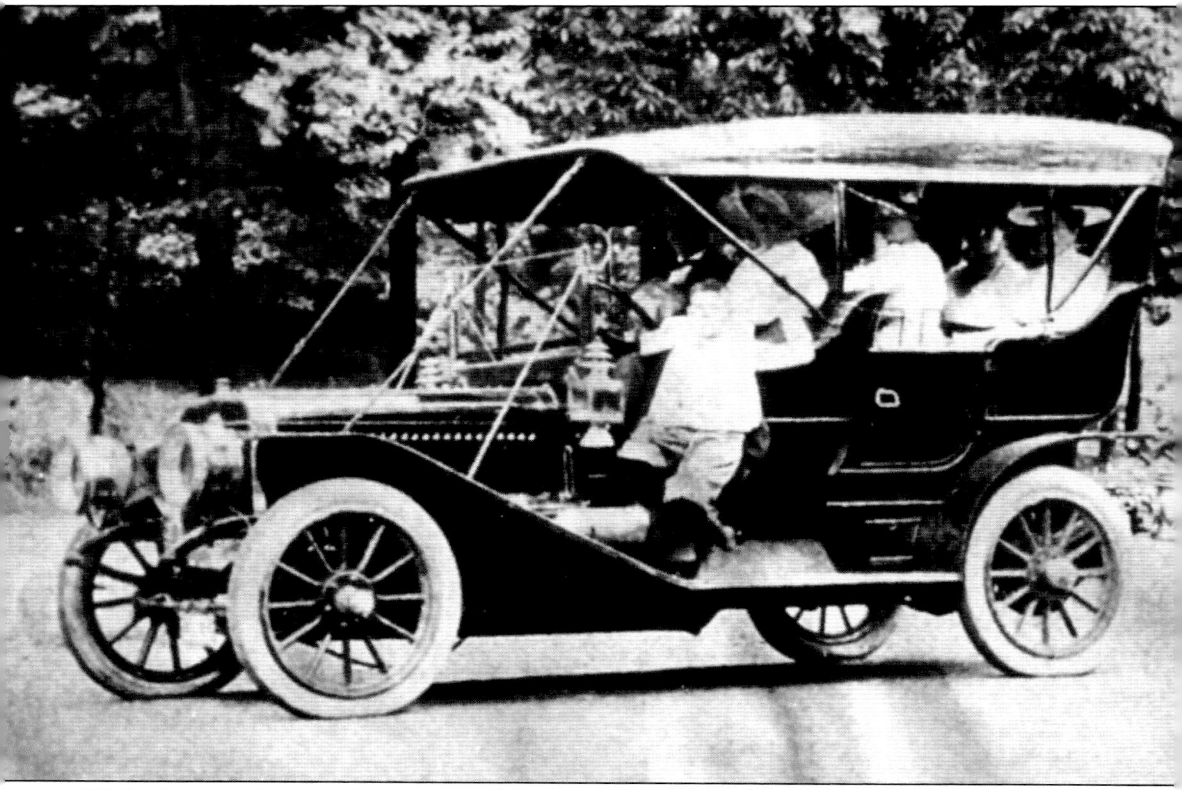

With the introduction of the automobile, many families had the opportunity to get together for a Sunday drive and pay respects to deceased family members or founders of the city. This is a photograph of the Henry H. Taylor family members in their new car. Taylor was one of the first elders of the Windermere Presbyterian Church that was organized in 1896. He became Cleveland postmaster in 1923. Even before the turn of the 20th century, Cleveland was a leader in the automobile industry. Windsor T. White, and his younger brothers, Rollin and Walter, built White steam cars. Walter C. Baker built electric cars in the 1890s. More can be learned about the part Cleveland played in the automobile industry by visiting the Automobile and Aviation Museum of the Western Reserve Historical Society. The first Cleveland automobile show opened on February 1, 1904 at Grays Armory. The armory building shadows over Erie Street Cemetery, and its members, the Cleveland Grays, the city's militia, played a significant role in Cleveland history. (Western Reserve Historical Society.)

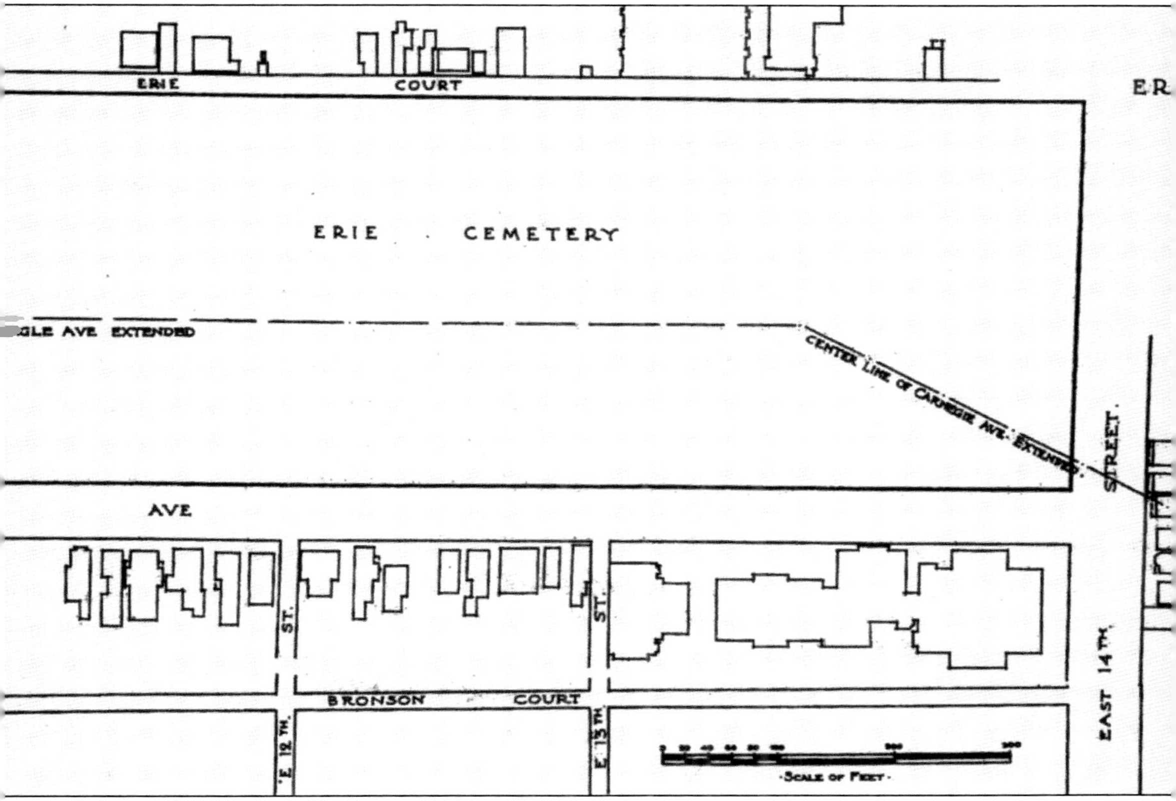

This map shows the plans of Eagle Avenue running through the Erie Street Cemetery to a centerline of a Carnegie Avenue extension. The plan for the street was to connect Carnegie Avenue with a proposed Huron-Lorain Bridge. This was a plan developed by the City Plan Commission in November 1920 during the term of Mayor William S. Fitzgerald. At the time, the city offered a $500 prize for the best plan for the use of the land after the road was extended. It was part of the effort to gain public support for the abandonment of Erie Street Cemetery. Public opposition brought an end to the plan. (City of Cleveland Archives.)

O. P. VAN SWERINGEN, Chairman
MORRIS A. BLACK, Vice Chairman
F. F. PRENTISS,
H. M. FARNSWORTH,
WILLIAM G. MATHER,
RICHARD HARBURGER, Executive Secretary, 435 City Hall.
ROBERT H. WHITTEN, Special Plan Adviser.

CITY PLAN COMMISSION

CITY OF CLEVELAND

W. S. FITZGERALD
MAYOR

WILLIAM B. WOODS
ALEX BERNSTEIN
FLOYD E. WAITE
DUDLEY S. BLOSSOM
A. B. SPROSTY
THOMAS S. FARRELL
CLARENCE METCALF
Ex-Officio Members
FRANK R. WALKER, General Plan Adviser

$500 PRIZE COMPETITION

Subject: THE FUTURE USE OF ERIE STREET CEMETERY

A COMPETITION OF IDEAS — OPEN TO ALL

FOR THE BEST SUGGESTION A CASH PRIZE OF $500
WILL BE AWARDED BY THE MEMBERS OF
THE CITY PLAN COMMISSION

DETAILS AND RULES OF COMPETITION

Erie Street Cemetery covers about 9 acres in the heart of Cleveland's business district. It has long since practically ceased to be used as a burial ground and many bodies have been removed. Most of the City's early settlers were interred there.

RESTRICTION OF USE

It is essential, in veneration of the pioneer citizens who founded and first developed Cleveland, that any future use of their burial place be combined with a memorial in their honor. It is further deemed necessary that Erie Street Cemetery should be preserved largely as an open breathing spot in the downtown congested district so as to assure the maximum inspiration, enjoyment and benefit to the greatest number of Cleveland's inhabitants and visitors.

CARNEGIE AVENUE EXTENSION THROUGH CEMETERY

Carnegie Avenue is planned to be extended downtown to connect with the proposed Huron-Lorain Bridge. This will give Cleveland a through thoroughfare for rapid vehicle traffic, second to none in the

(Rules continued on page four)

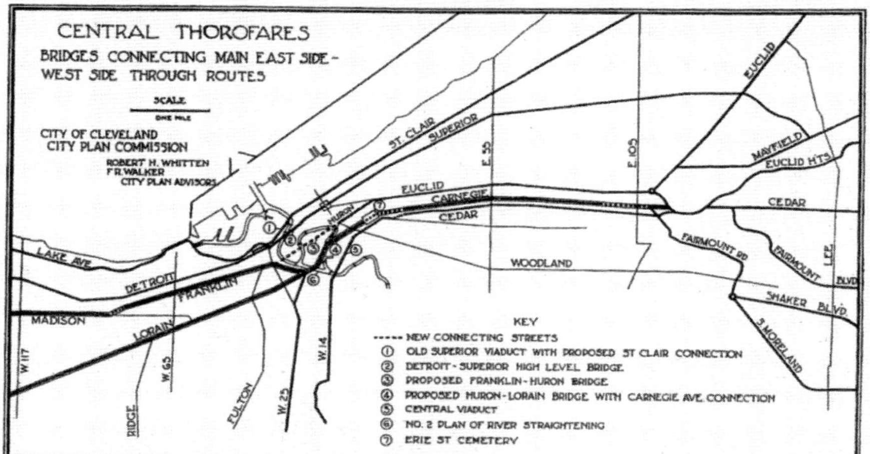

For citizens who feel they "can't fight city hall," Erie Street Cemetery is a poster child for disproving that belief. The effort to close and remove the bodies from Erie Street Cemetery began under Mayor Tom L. Johnson's administration when Highland Park Cemetery was opened in 1904. Consequently, the records for burials of Erie Street Cemetery were transferred to Highland Park Cemetery where they can be found today. The effort to move the cemetery continued through the administration of Mayor William S. Fitzgerald. In 1920, there was a competition for ideas from citizens for the reuse of the cemetery. The City Plan Commission offered a $500 prize for the best suggestion, but public concern for preservation of the cemetery prevailed. Pressure for the reuse of Erie Street Cemetery land began again in later years. The restoration of the cemetery in 1939 and 1940 was undertaken by community groups that stopped proposed suggestions for reuse of the land for a period of time. Restoration efforts continue today. (City of Cleveland Archives.)

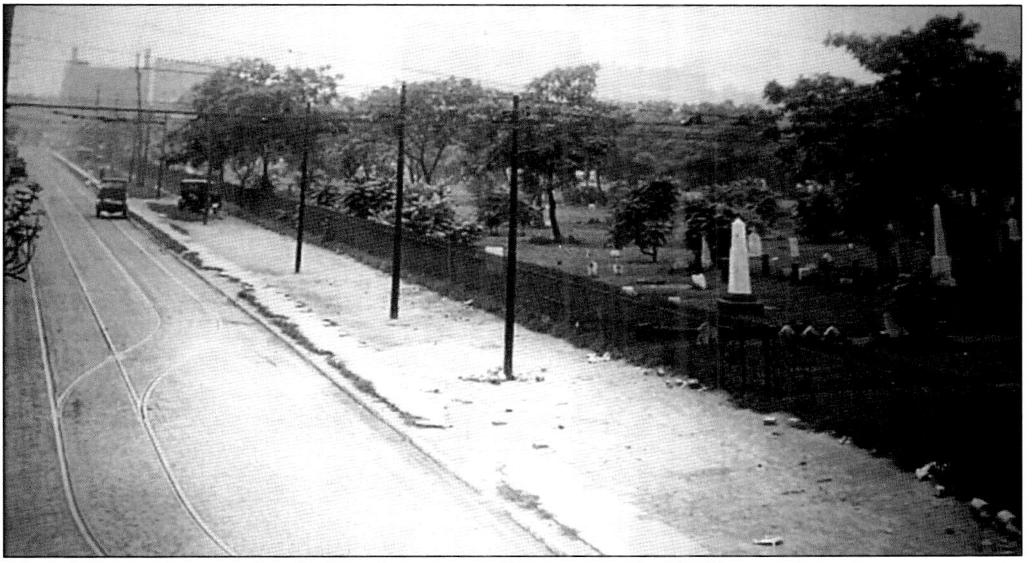

This photograph was taken before the stone wall was erected in 1939 to enclose the cemetery. As reported in the 1941 annals of the Early Settlers Association, $239,000 was raised to build the wall and restore the cemetery. (Cleveland State University, Cleveland Press Collection.)

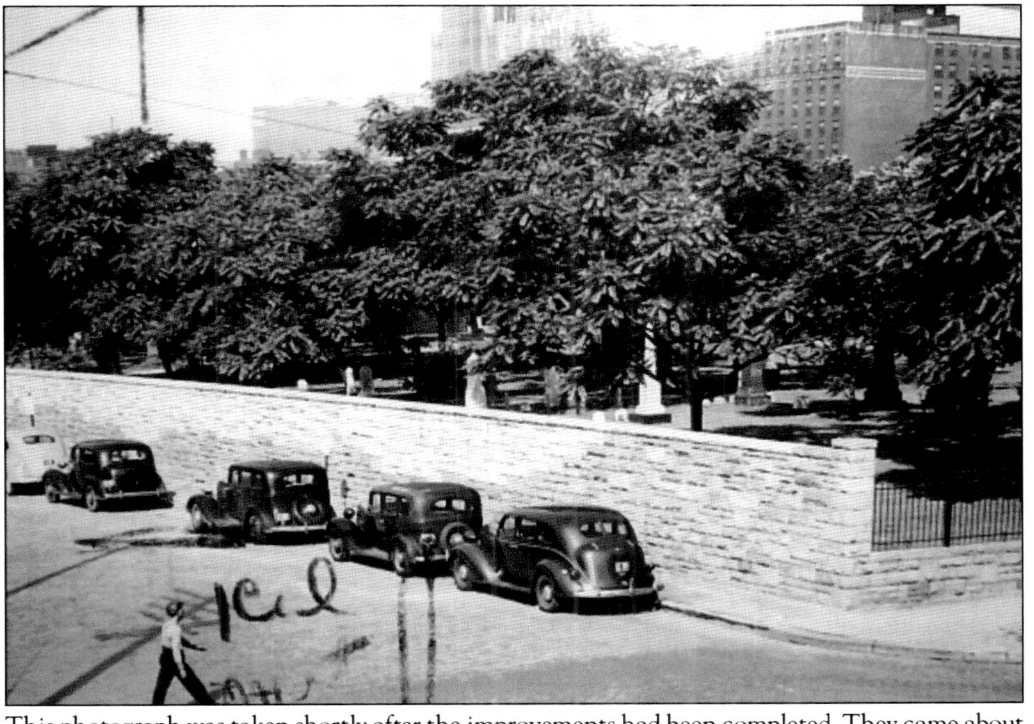

This photograph was taken shortly after the improvements had been completed. They came about due to the efforts of the Early Settlers Association and a number of other organizations, such as the Daughters of the English Empire, Erie Street Memorial Association, Cleveland Indians baseball team, and the heirs of Judge Kingsbury, one of the settlers who came to the Western Reserve with Lorenzo Carter. (Cleveland State University, Cleveland Press Collection.)

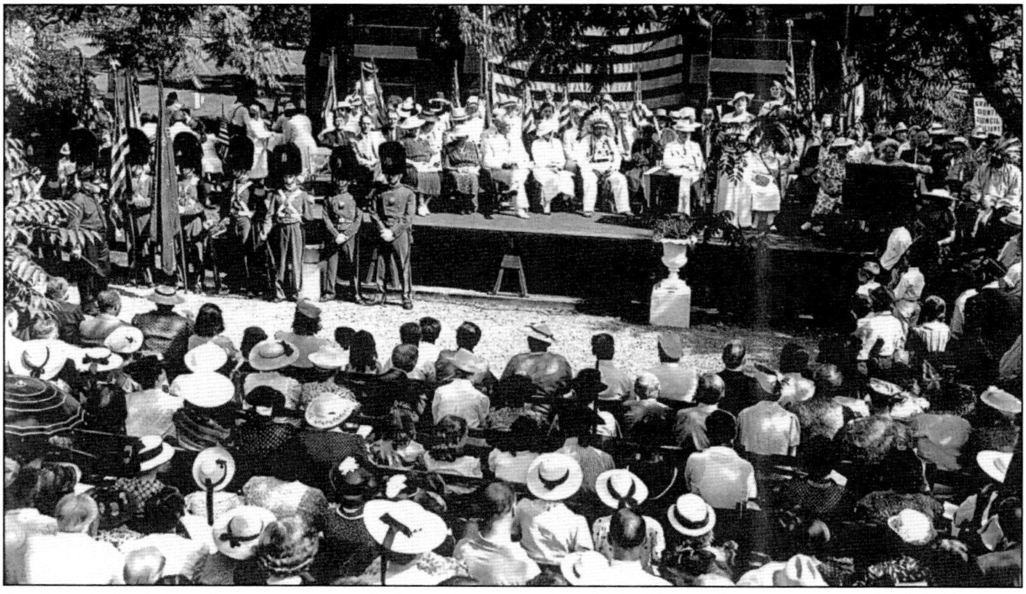

Civic-minded Clevelanders assembled on the grounds of Erie Street Cemetery on July 23, 1940, to celebrate the restoration of the cemetery. The years 1939 and 1940 were a time of unprecedented progress in the city. Parades and festivals were very much a part of the time. The men in uniform are members of the Cleveland Grays, Cleveland's Home Guard. (Cleveland State University, Cleveland Press Collection.)

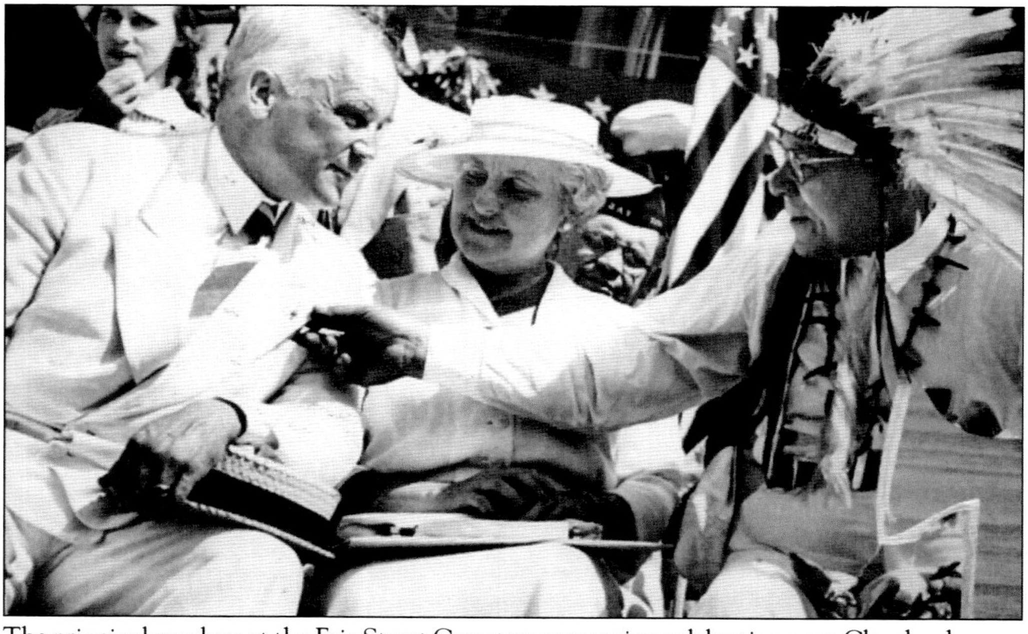

The principal speakers at the Erie Street Cemetery restoration celebration were Cleveland mayor Harold Burton (1888–1964), Congresswoman Frances Bolton (1885–1977), and Chief Thunderwater (1865–1950). Bolton was a member of Congress from 1940 to 1969. Burton was mayor of Cleveland from 1935 to 1940. He was then elected to the US Senate and later appointed to the Supreme Court by Pres. Harry Truman. (Cleveland State University, Cleveland Press Collection.)

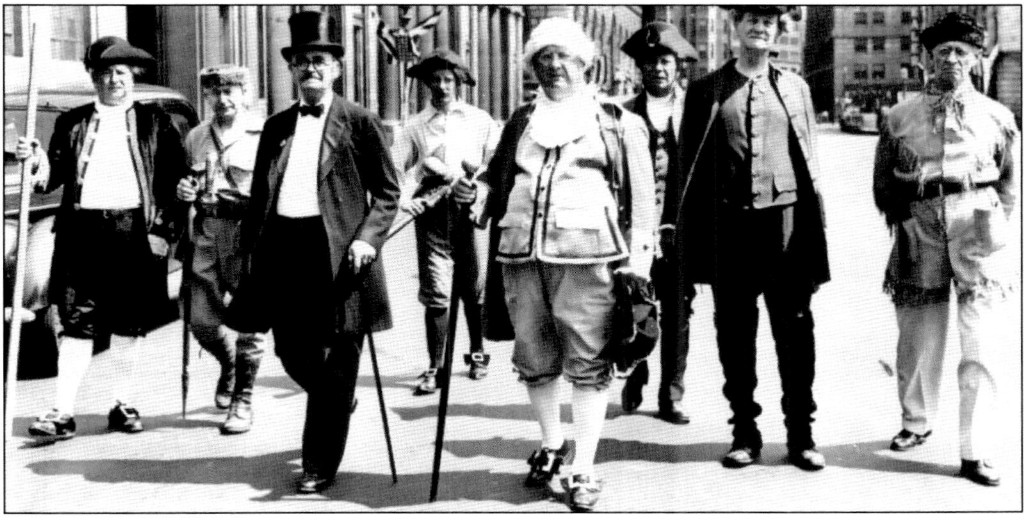

Early Settlers Association (ESA) members lead a parade from ESA headquarters to Erie Street Cemetery to join in the July 23, 1940, celebration. The association raised $239,000 for cemetery improvements that included a stone wall and a wrought iron gate around the cemetery grounds. (Cleveland Public Library.)

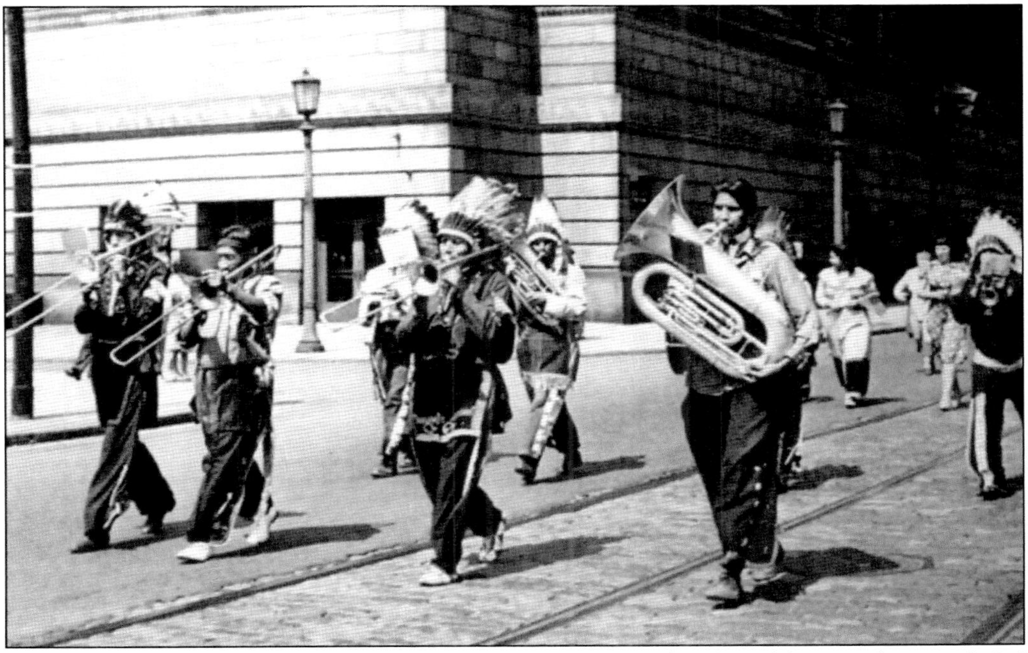

A Seneca American Indian band from Akron, New York, joined in the celebration that concluded at Erie Street Cemetery on July 23, 1940. Akron, New York, is adjacent to the Tonawanda Reservation of the Seneca Nation. Akron is a village in Erie County, New York. It is part of the Buffalo-Niagara Falls metropolitan area. (Cleveland Public Library.)

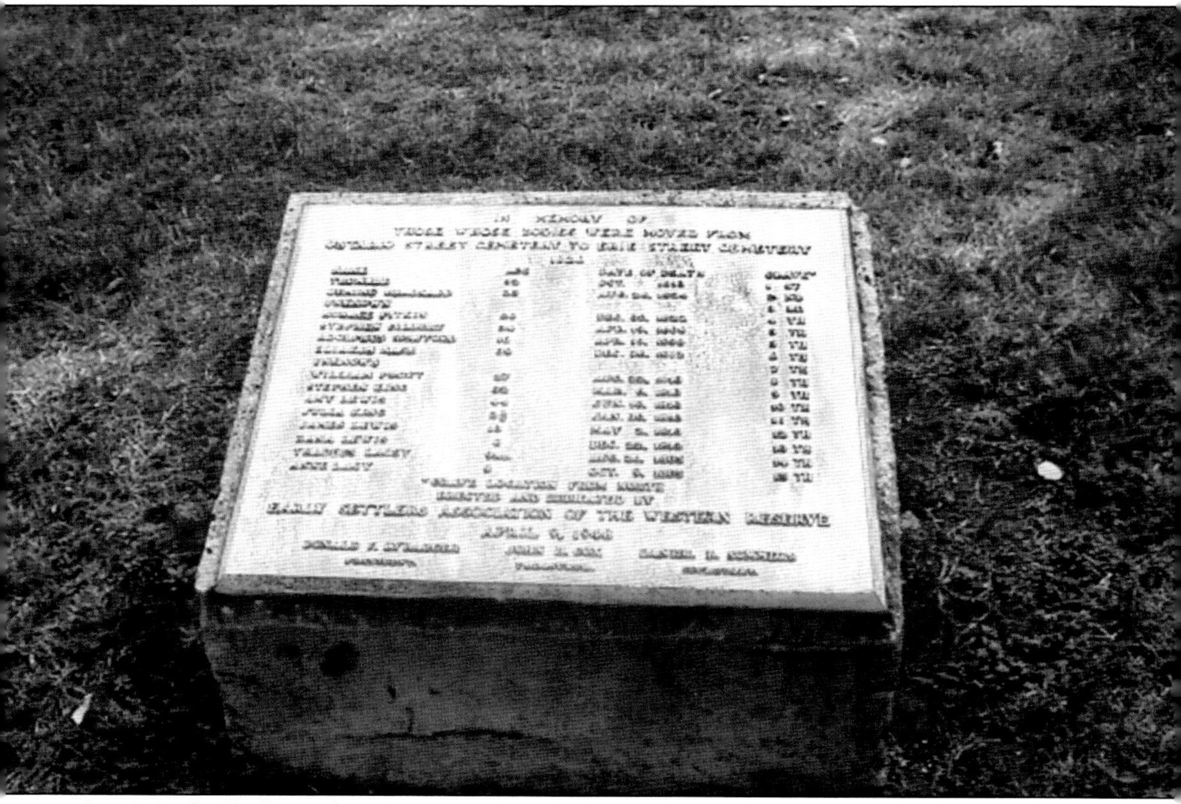

In 1948, the Early Settlers Association placed a marker in Erie Street Cemetery in memory of those people whose bodies were moved from Ontario Street Cemetery to Erie Street Cemetery. The inscription on the marker reads from left to right the individual's name, age, date of death, and grave location. The inscription reads as follows, beginning with the first name: "Trumble, age 32, died in October 1813; Deming Brainard, age 25, died August 28, 1824; unknown; Horace Pitkin, age 20, died December 20, 1822; Stephen Gilbert, age 34, died April 19, 1808; Adolphus Spafford, age 16, died April 19, 1808; Eliakim Nash, 39, died December 28, 1812; unknown; William Prout, age 27, died August 22, 1813; Stephen King, age 32, died March 6, 1813; Amy Lewis, age 44, died June 10, 1813; Julia King, age two-and-a-half, died January 30, 1813; James Lewis, age 13, died May 2, 1813; Rana Lewis, age eight, died December 22, 1812; Thadeus Lacey, age nine months, died August 21, 1805; and Anne Lacey, age nine, died October 9, 1805." Their bodies are buried just below the marker.

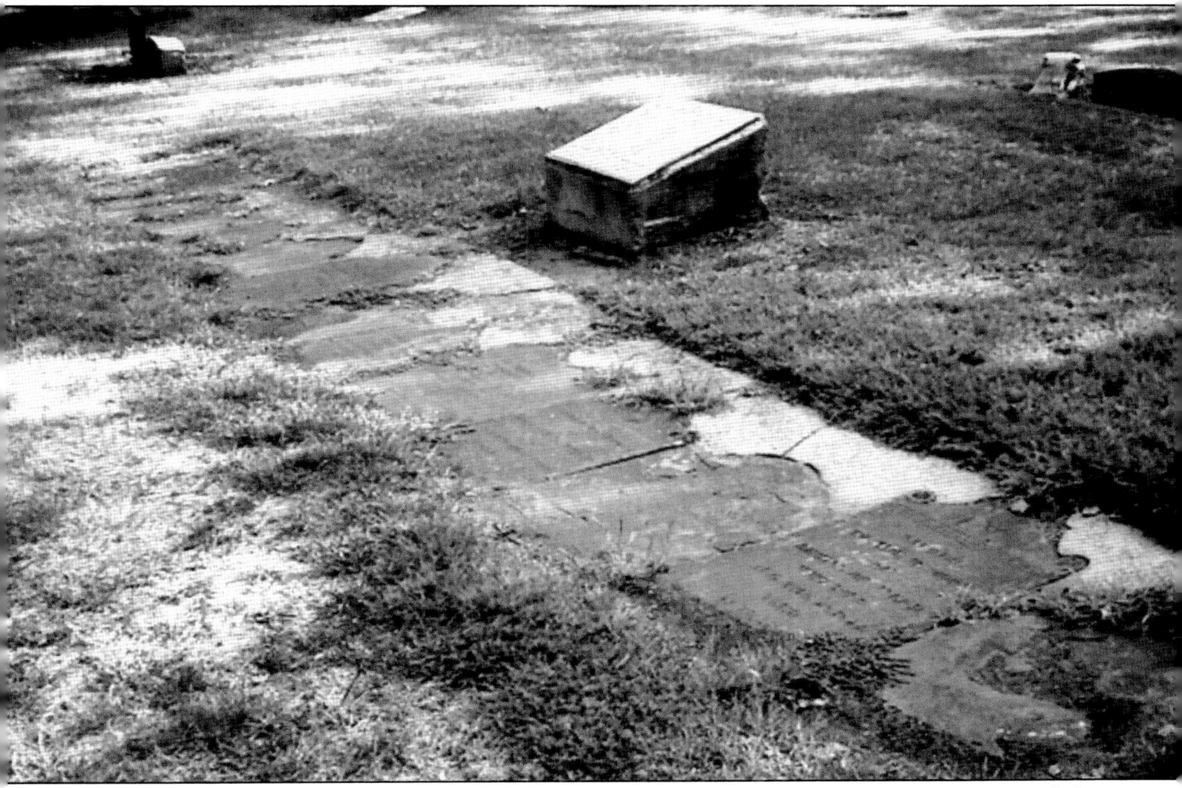

Just in front of the 1948 marker placed by the Early Settlers Association in memory of the bodies moved from the Ontario Street Cemetery is what was called "mortuary roll," the original headstones of those people moved to Erie Street Cemetery. The headstones bear dates from 1805 to 1825 and the names of many of the early settlers of Cleveland. The names represented are Perry, Gilbert, Spafford, Lacey, Kelley, Case, Mills, Cowles, Merwin, Weddell, and Brainard. Some of the stones still can be read, such as Deming Brainard, William Prout, Amy Lewis, Stephen Gilbert, and Adolphus Spafford. Gilbert and Spafford drowned in Lake Erie on April 19, 1808. Another stone that is readable is that of Eliakim Nash, which states, "Died December 28, 1812 of a 'malignant fever' at 39 years old."

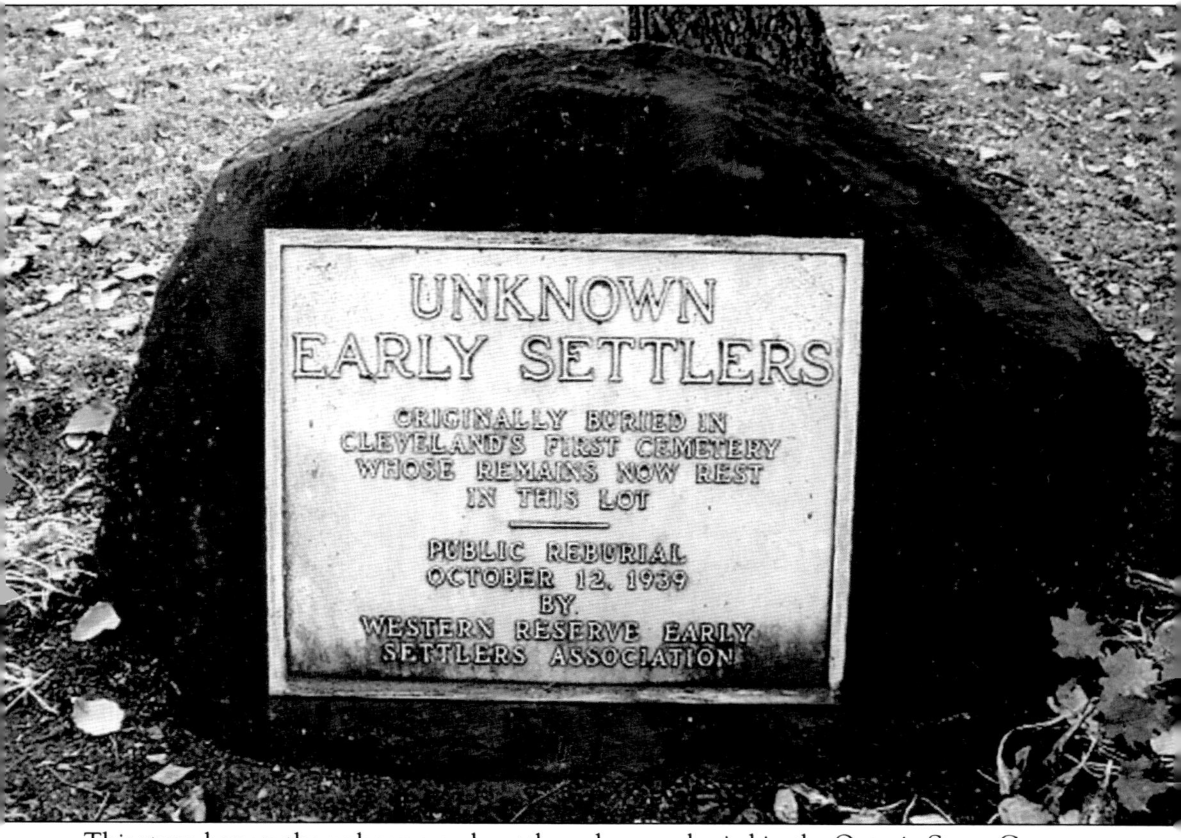

This stone honors the unknown early settlers who were buried in the Ontario Street Cemetery and were later moved to the Erie Street Cemetery for reburial on October 12, 1939. The stone and the ceremony were made possible by the Early Settlers Association of the Western Reserve. The inscription reads, "Unknown Early Settlers originally buried in Cleveland's first cemetery whose remains now rest in this lot." The courage and determination of those first settlers who came to the Western Reserve should be remembered. It was a struggle to make a better life for their families and to make their lives meaningful. Their courage and determination can best be described by this statement, "I dare you to sacrifice a life predetermined with guided direction and ease for a path of unknown challenges and choice—bestowed the freedom to fail and grow—thus experiencing the gift of life."

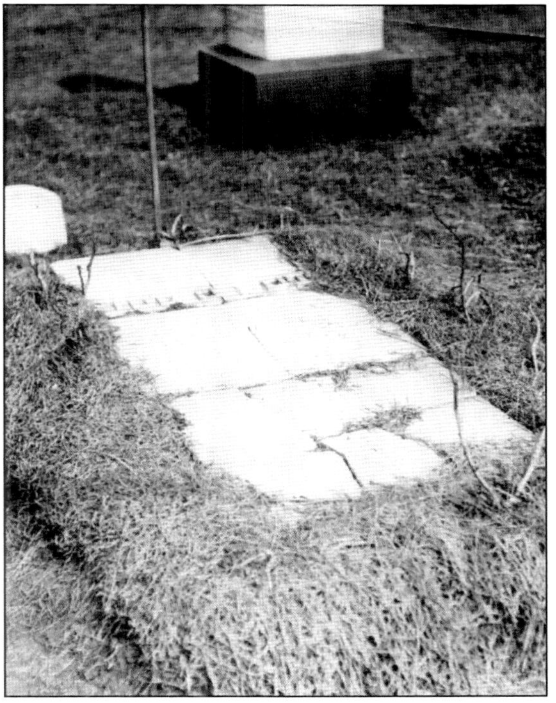

The original Joc-O-Sot, a Sauk chief, gravestone can still be seen in the cemetery today. When the new stone was placed, the first marker was not removed and efforts were made to improve and protect it. It is a tribute to those early settlers who honored Joc-O-Sot and developed admiration for him even though he fought against the Americans in the Black Hawk War. These two photographs depict the gravestone over time. The Early Settlers Association originally had plantings of corn (maize) around the gravestone to honor his Indian heritage, but over the years maintenance was neglected. (Cleveland State University, Cleveland Press Collection.)

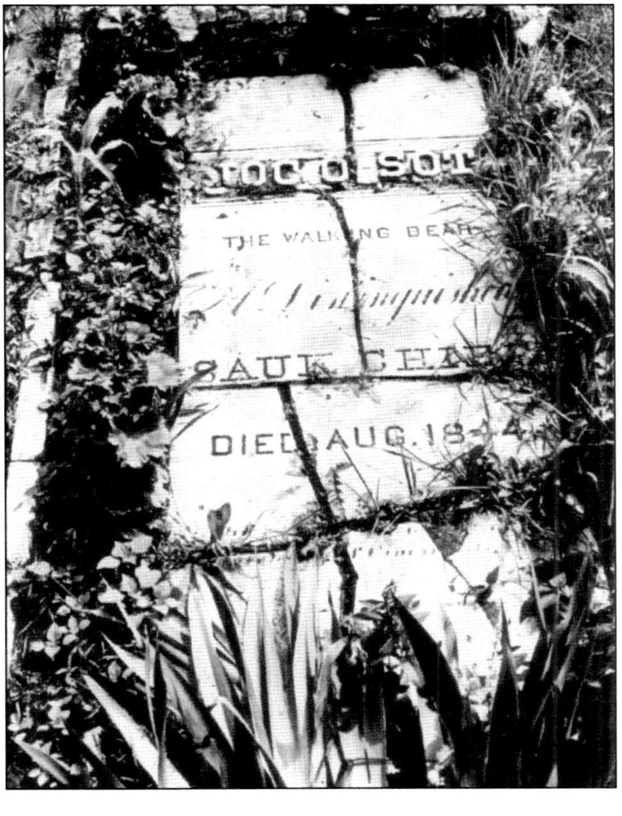

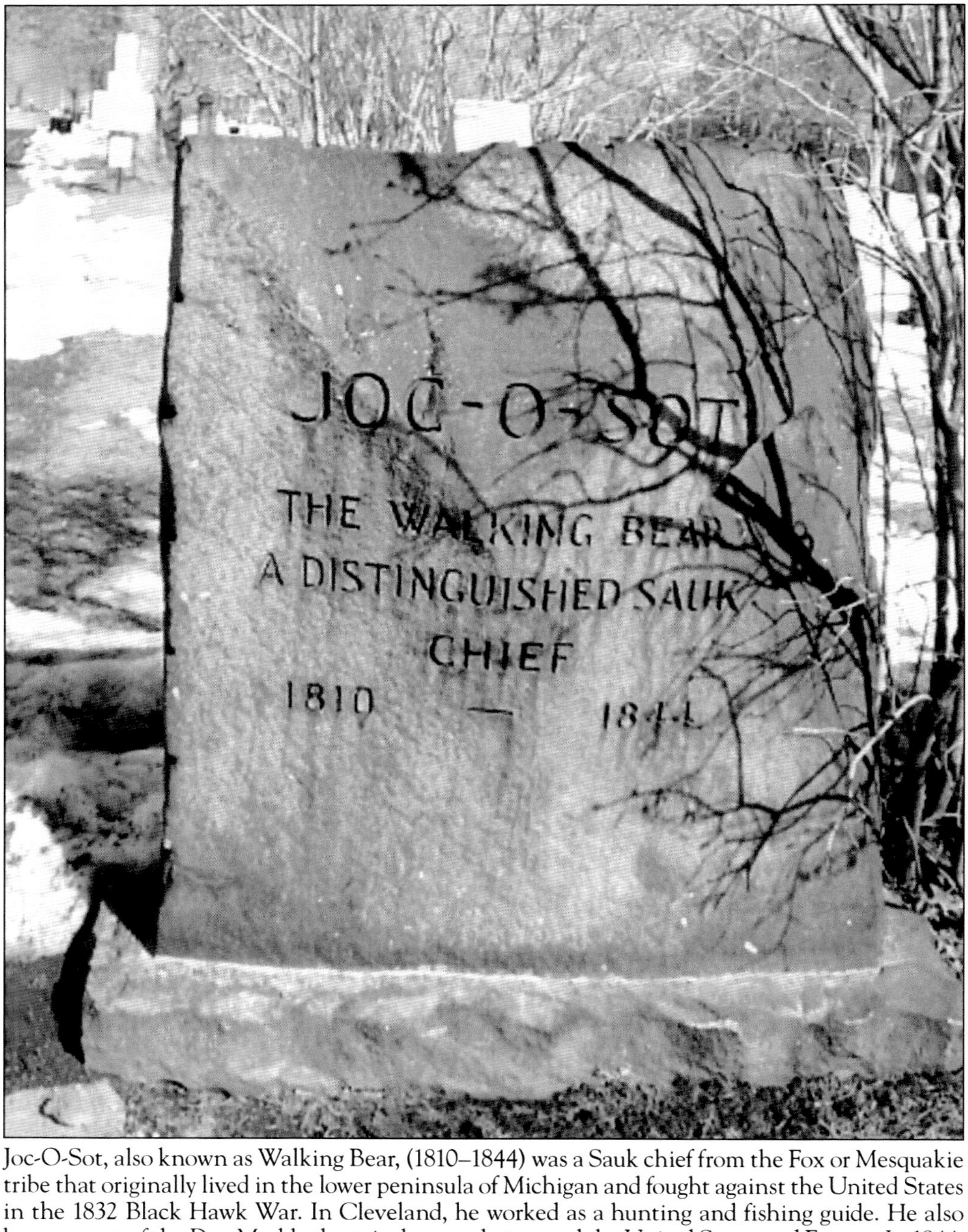

Joc-O-Sot, also known as Walking Bear, (1810–1844) was a Sauk chief from the Fox or Mesquakie tribe that originally lived in the lower peninsula of Michigan and fought against the United States in the 1832 Black Hawk War. In Cleveland, he worked as a hunting and fishing guide. He also became part of the Dan Marble theatrical group that toured the United States and Europe. In 1844, after a successful European tour, the group was received by Queen Victoria, who commissioned a full-length portrait of Joc-O-Sot. While on tour, he fell ill from an old bullet wound. He then came back to Cleveland to see his friend Dr. Horace A. Ackley. Joc-O-Sot never reached the doctor's office; he died on what was called Stockley's Pier, cared for by Dr. Ackley. He never lived long enough to return to his tribal home. He died on September 3, 1844, and funeral services were held at Cleveland's Second Presbyterian Church.

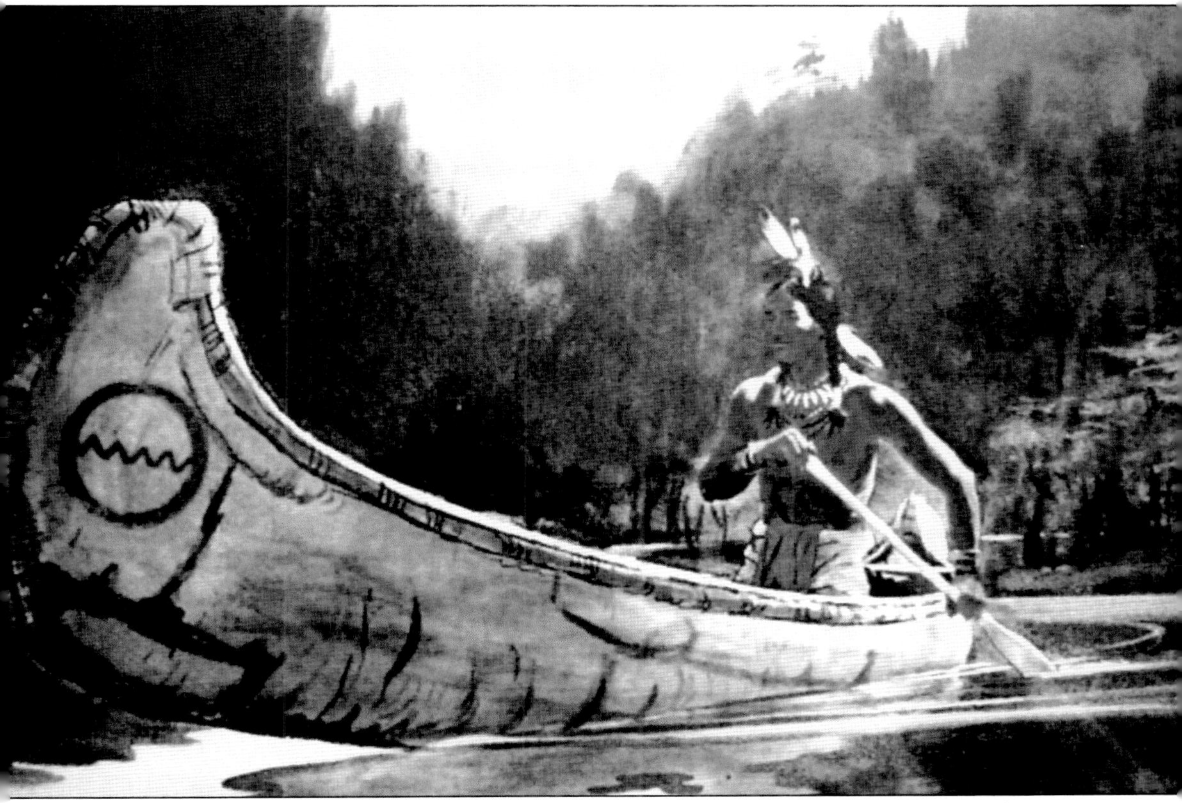

The Black Hawk War was fought in 1832 in what was then the Michigan Territory, today's state of Wisconsin. The war was called the Black Hawk War after a war chief named Black Hawk, who fought with the British against the US Army. He was chief of the Sauk, Fox (Mesquakie), and Kickapoo tribes. Abraham Lincoln and Jefferson Davis distinguished themselves in the Black Hawk War, which helped their political careers. The war began on May 14, 1832, and ended in August of that year after a victory by the US Army. Gen. Winfield Scott signed a treaty with the Indian tribes to end the war. This photograph is from a painting of Joc-O-Sot canoeing on the Cuyahoga River. After fighting in the Black Hawk War, Joc-O-Sot made his way to Cleveland and began leading hunting and fishing trips. He died at the age of 34 on September 3, 1844. His gravestone reads, "The Walking Bear A Distinguished Sauk Chief." (Early Settlers Association.)

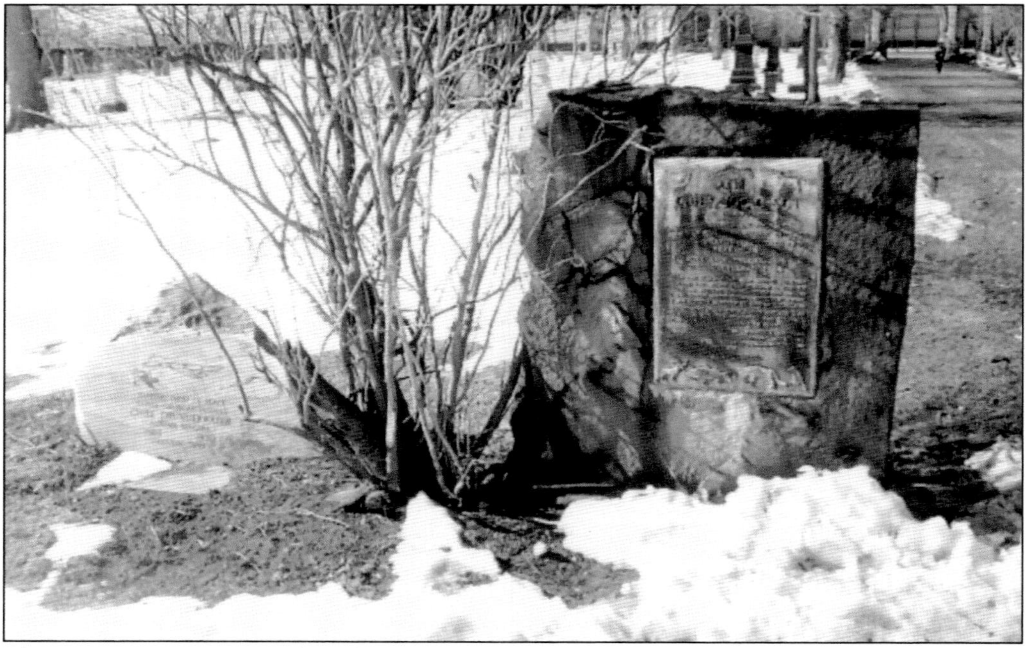

There are two American Indians buried in Erie Street Cemetery, Chief Thunderwater and Joc-O-Sot. Chief Thunderwater (1865–1950) was active in Cleveland civic affairs and was a member of the Early Settlers Association of the Western Reserve. He became a spokesman for the valuable role tribesman played in early pioneer life in the Western Reserve. He toured North America and Europe in Buffalo Bill's Wild West Show, and throughout his life, he was a Cleveland celebrity. His tombstone reads, "Supreme Chief of Peace North American Indians."

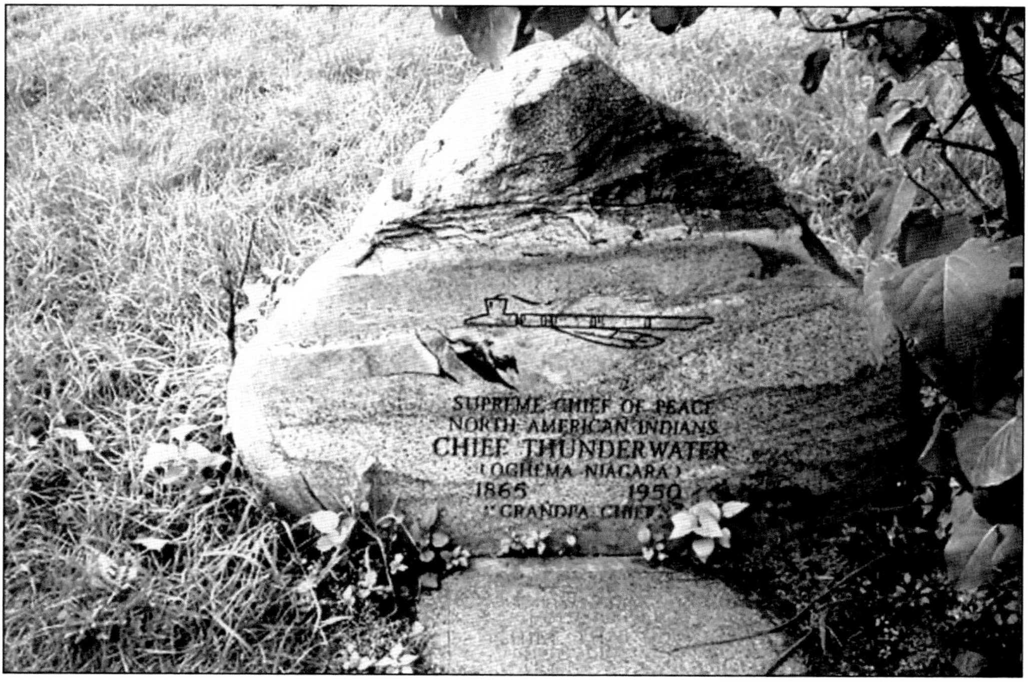

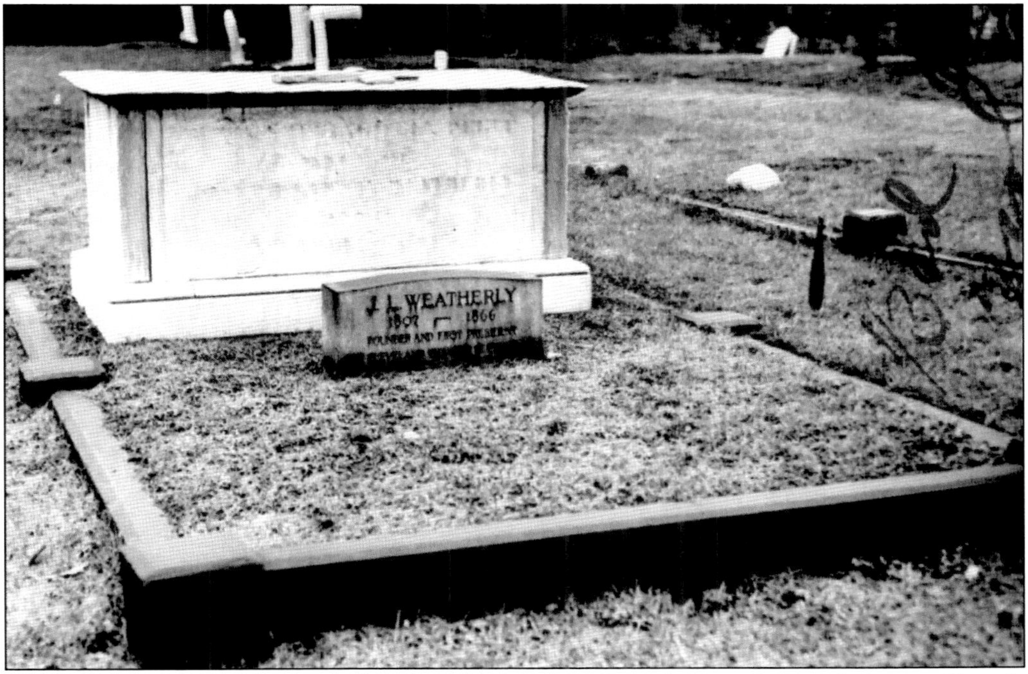

On July 20, 1940, the Cleveland Chamber of Commerce erected a new stone at the grave of Joseph L. Weatherly, founder and first president of the parent organization of the chamber of commerce, the Cleveland Board of Trade, which was organized in 1848. The new stone can be seen here in front of the old weathered stone. (Cleveland State University, Cleveland Press Collection.)

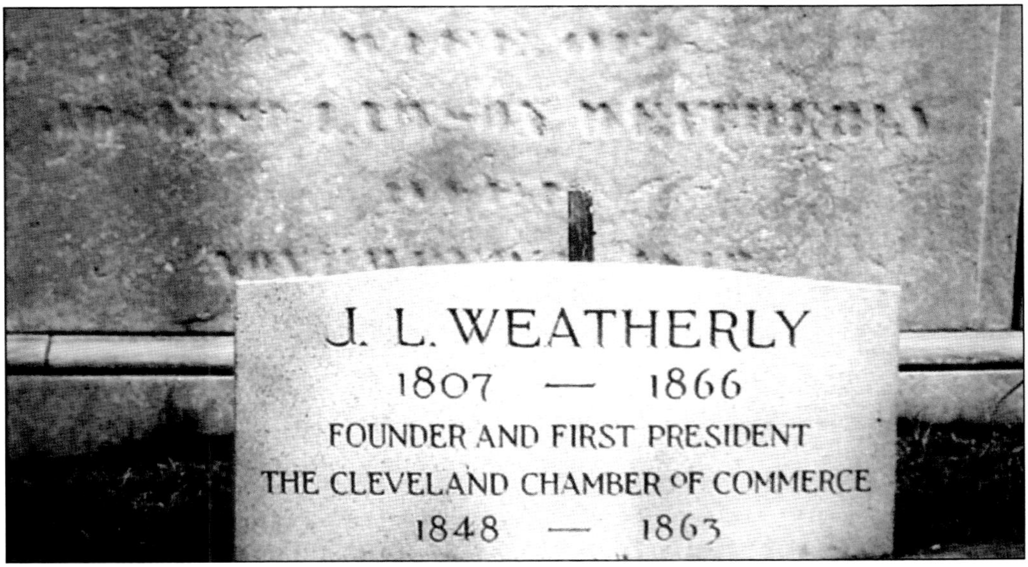

The Joseph L. Weatherly gravestone is pictured here as it appears today. He was very active in Cleveland civic affairs. In May 1836, city council passed an ordinance to establish a fire department, and in 1840, Weatherly became chief of what was called the Hook and Ladder Company. Cleveland's first fireboat was named the *JL Weatherly* in his honor. In 1846, he served as president of the Cleveland Board of Underwriters.

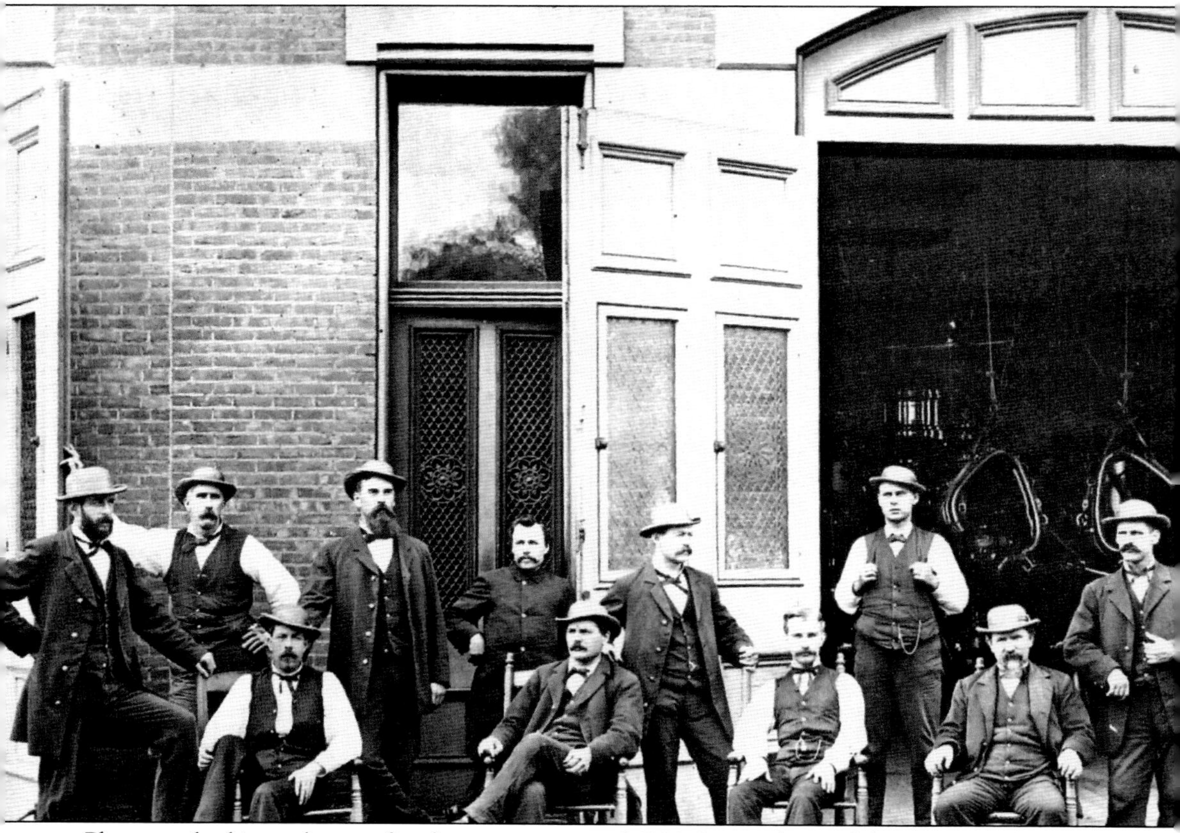

Photographed is a volunteer fire department around 1890. It is made up of the movers and shakers of the town. In those early days of the city, one was not considered a good citizen unless he volunteered for the fire department. Prominent citizens like H.L. Noble, J.L. Weatherly, James Barnett, and Jabez W. Fitch were all members of the volunteer fire department. By the 1880s, fire had taken a heavy toll on Cleveland. With the city's rapid growth in industry and population, the fire department was unable to meet the demands for service and often had to turn to neighboring cities for assistance. (Early Settlers Association.)

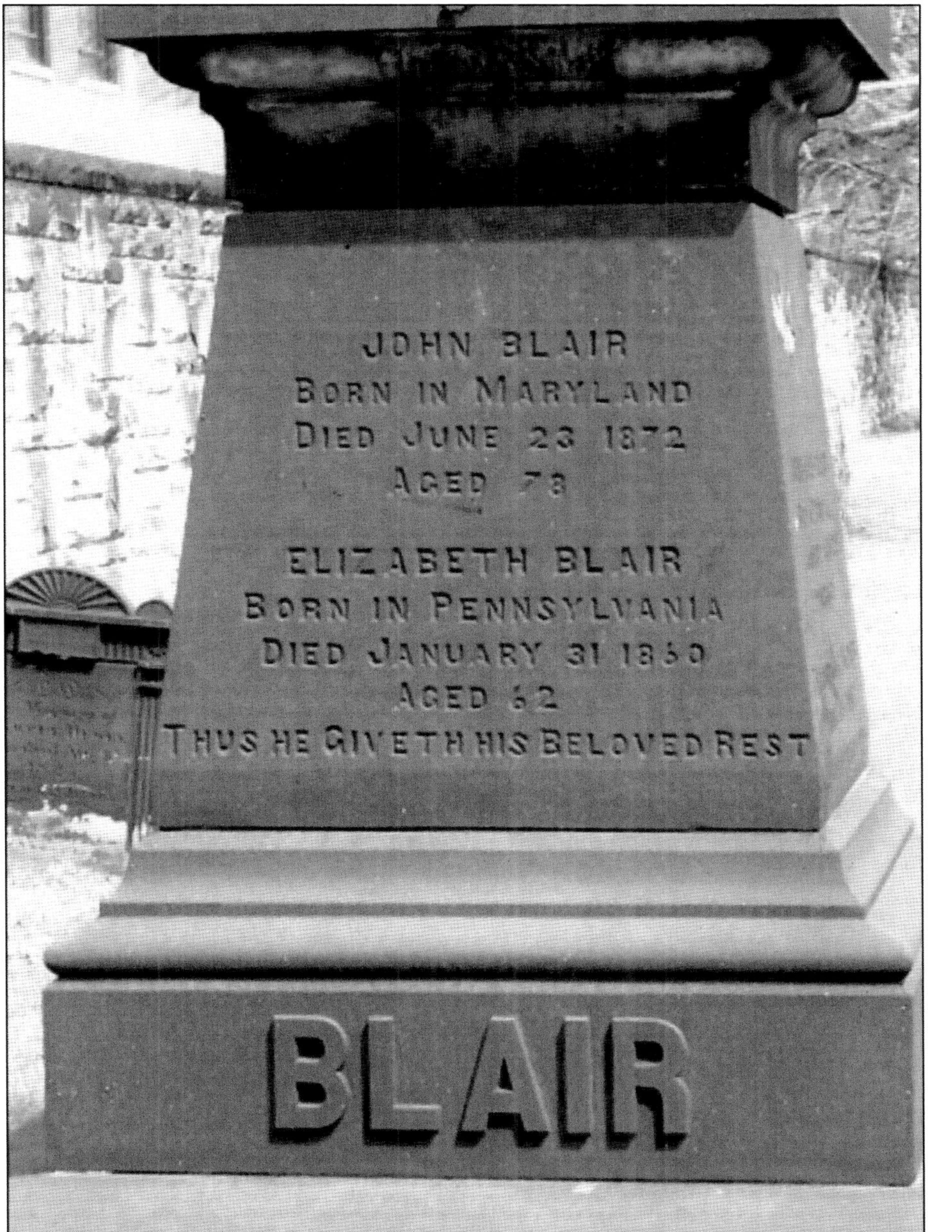

John Blair came to Cleveland in 1819 from Maryland when he was 26 years old and was said to have only $3 in his wallet. He married 22-year-old Elizabeth Holm from Wilkesburgh, Pennsylvania. The couple boarded at the Carter Tavern for a short time until John built a warehouse along the Cuyahoga River. He traded with the Indians and farmers and became very successful. In 1827, when the canal opened, John built a boat that carried passengers along the canal. The name "John Blair" can be found on the incorporation papers for the city of Cleveland in 1836. He was one of three election judges. The couple had six children. Elizabeth died in 1860 at the age of 63; John lived for 12 more years.

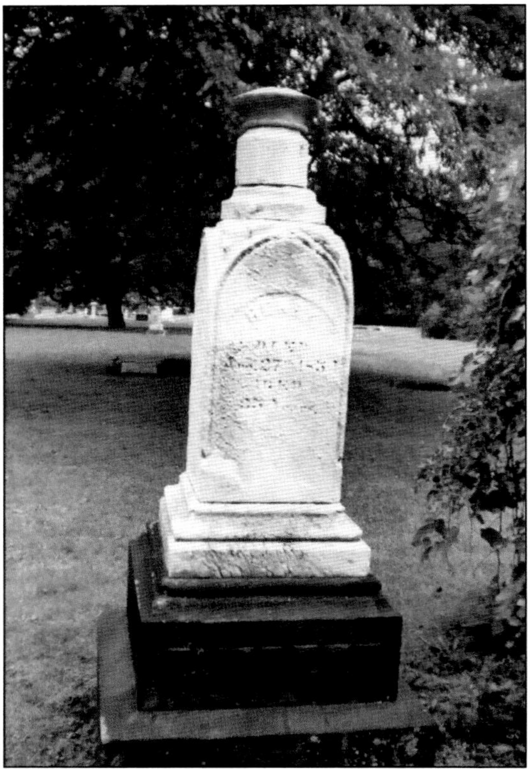

This is the gravestone of Dr. Henry Everett (1819–1854). His brother Sylvester came to live with him at the age of 12. Sylvester went on to become a Republican leader, banker, railroad executive, and one of Cleveland's most prominent citizens. Henry went into medical practice with Dr. Isaac H. Marshall, who was a soldier in the War of 1812. Their office was located on Brownell Street next to Erie Street Cemetery.

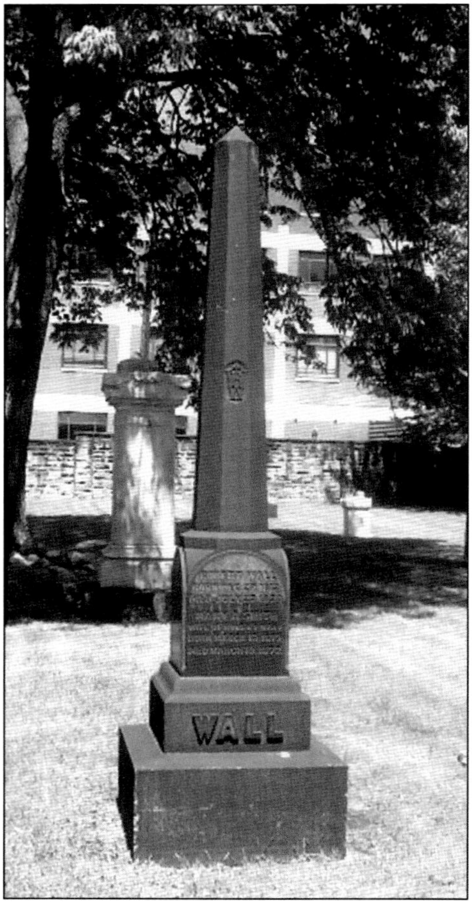

The following is from the cemetery records at the Cleveland Necrology File of the Cleveland Public Library: "Robert Wall died suddenly at this residence at 69 Bolivar on Wednesday evening at 7:40 on July 27, 1874." Today, the residence of the deceased is not published because it becomes an invitation for home burglary.

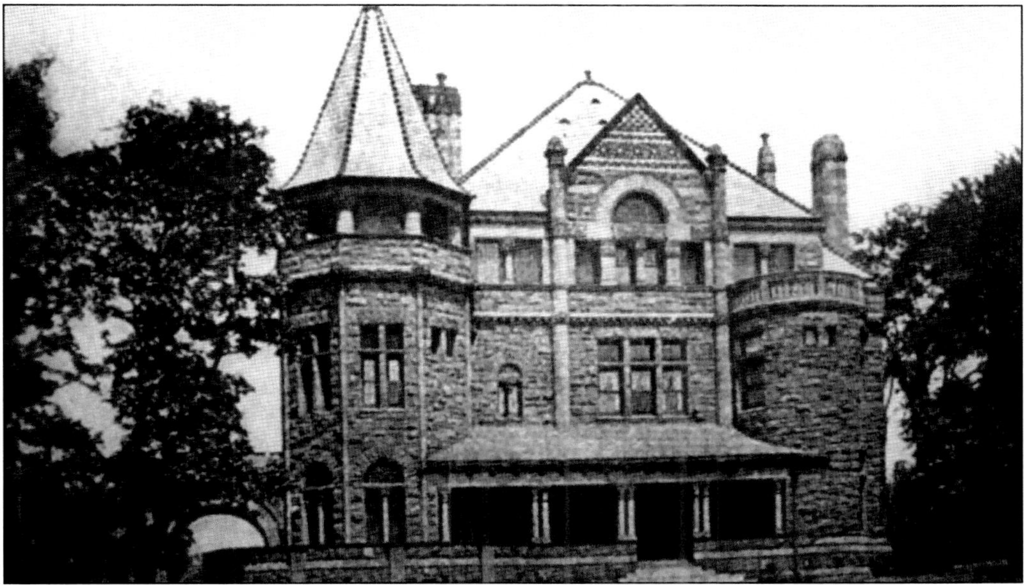

The first settlers went from living in log cabins in the wilderness to building some of the most beautiful homes in the nation. The Sylvester T. Everett home (above) was one of those that made up Millionaire's Row on Euclid Avenue. The Everett family hosted many of their famous friends in their Euclid Avenue home, including guests like Presidents Lincoln, Grant, Harrison, Hayes, McKinley, Roosevelt, Taft, and Harding and Andrew Carnegie, as reported in Ella Grant Wilson's *Recollections of Euclid Avenue*. The Everett home stood near the T.S. Beckwith residence (below) that still stands today at 3813 Euclid Avenue and was built by Col. Anson Stager in 1863. Stager was superintendent of the military telegraph system and manager of Western Union. Beckwith was a dry goods merchant who purchased the Stager home and lived in it until 1907. In 1913, it became the University Club; it stands today as Myers University Club.

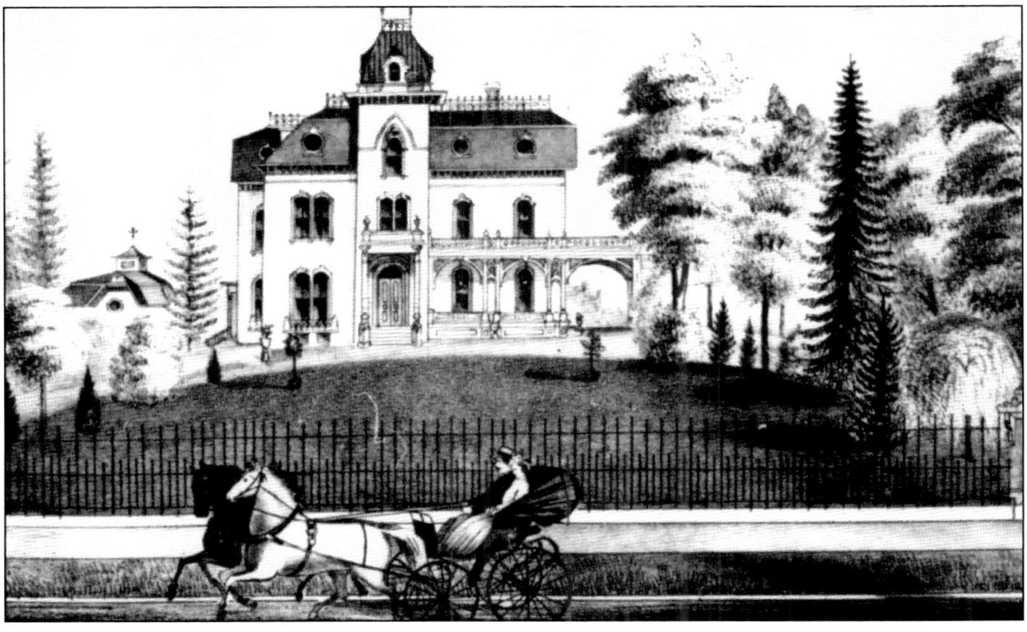

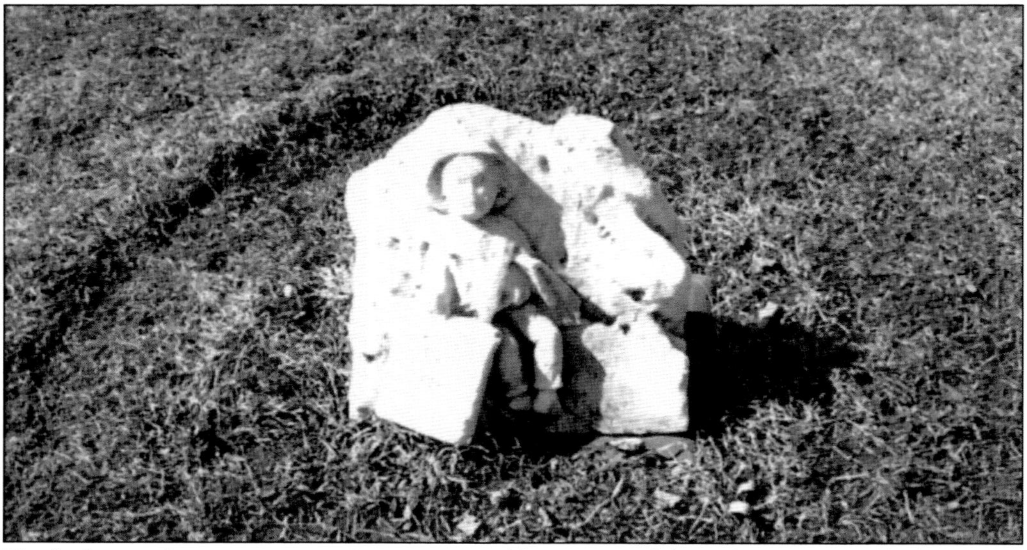

The little paperboy gravestone is for an 11-year-old newspaper delivery boy named Alfred Williams who died in 1900. His death was reported as suicide by poisoning. His fellow newspaper boys raised the money for the gravesite. He was an orphan who came to Cleveland from Pennsylvania with a man who put on glass-blowing exhibitions. Joseph Carabelli of Carabelli Monuments donated the stone with an inscription that reads, "He was a newsboy without father, mother, or home and buried by his newsboy comrades."

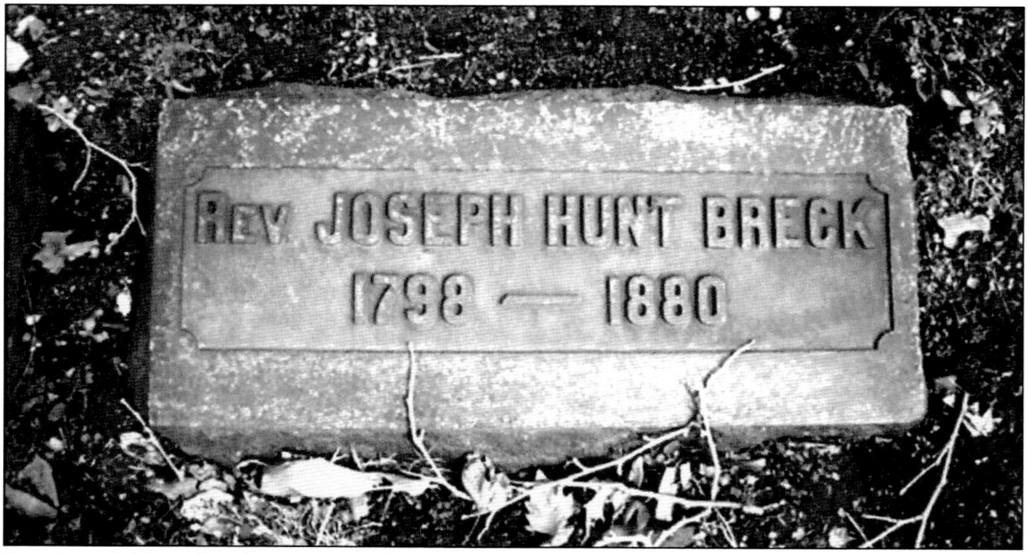

Rev. Joseph Hunt Breck was a preacher for the First Congregational Church from 1829 to 1833. The church was organized by the Connecticut Missionary Society in 1813 in Brecksville, Ohio. Many preachers had to travel long distances to reach small congregations throughout the Western Reserve. The First Congregational Church did not have a regular minister until 1840. Brecksville is named after the Breck family.

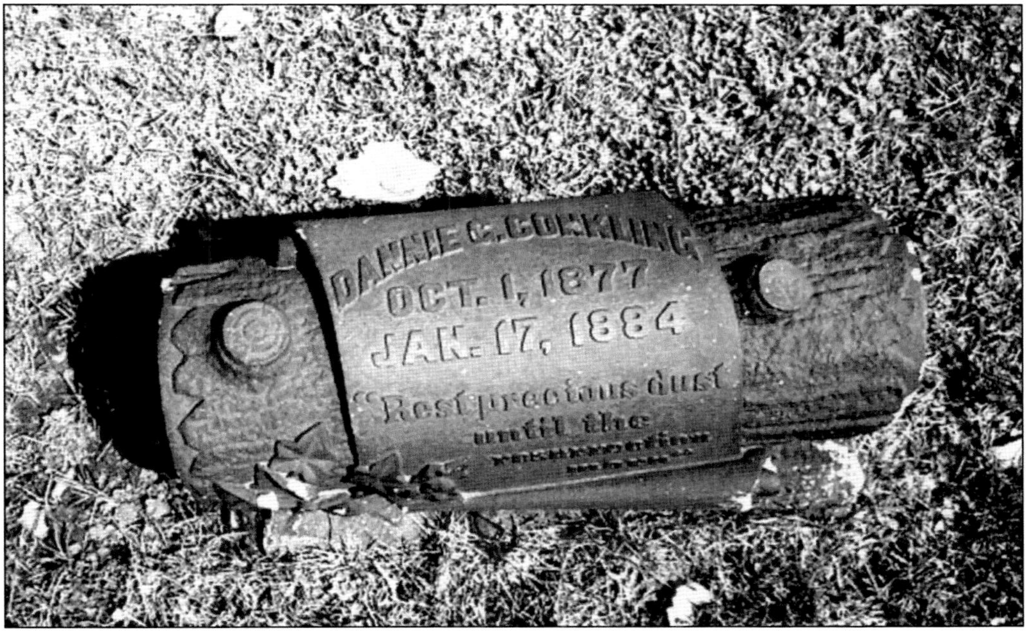

The Dannie G. Conkling (October 1, 1877–January 17, 1884) gravestone reads, "Rest precious dust until the Resurrection Day." Those curious about gravestone symbolism would find the Conkling gravestone an interesting one. A tree trunk symbolizes the brevity of life. Dannie was only seven years old.

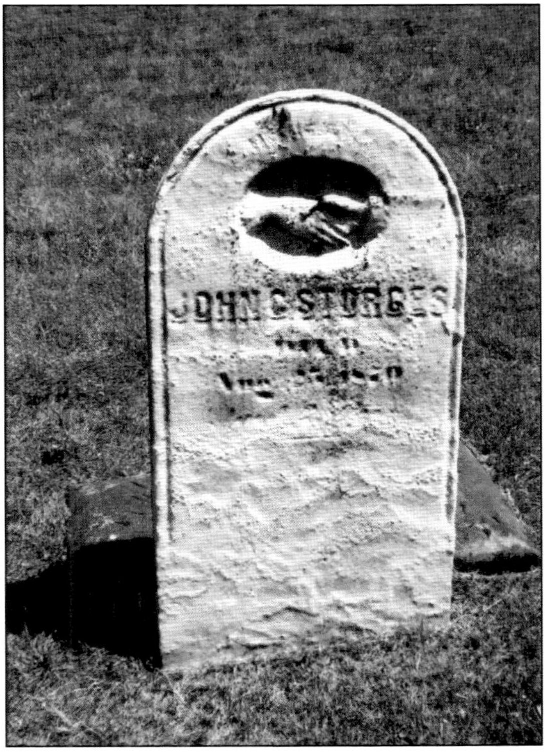

This stone has a very expressive symbol that takes on different meanings depending on the positioning of the hands and the arrangement of the fingers. The handshake on the John C. Sturgess gravestone usually signifies a welcome into the heavenly world or farewell to earthly existence. If it is a marriage symbol, typically one cuff will look masculine and the other feminine.

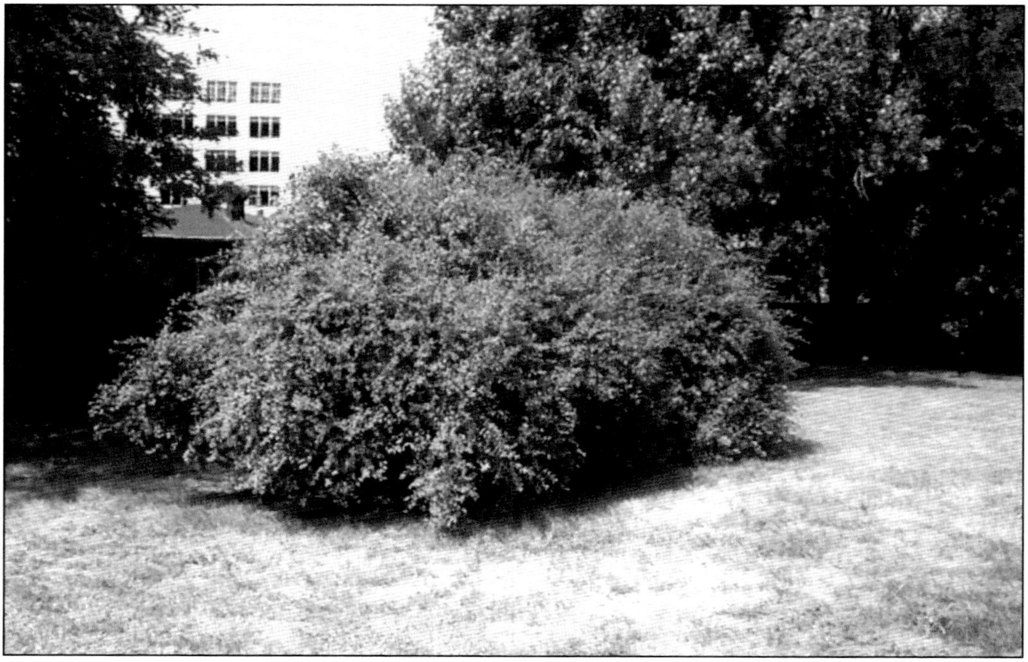

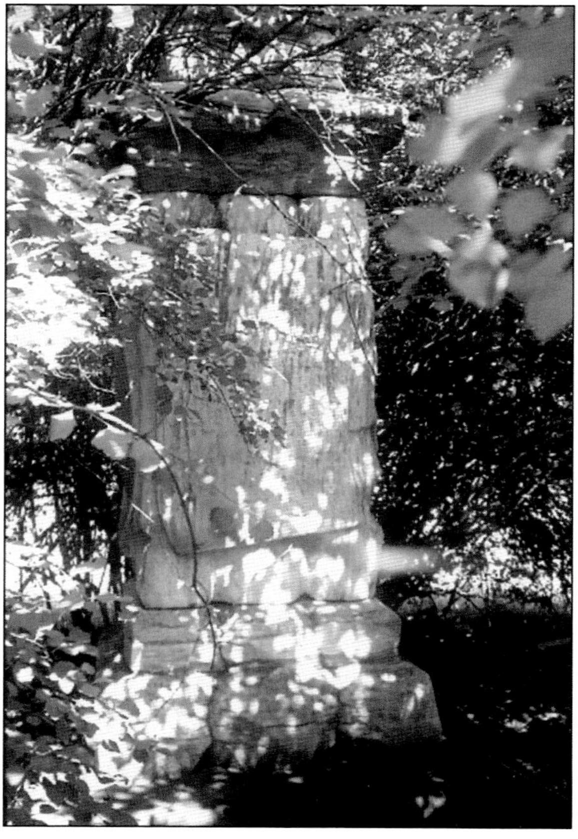

Madison Tilley (1809–1887) is another important Clevelander whose stone, located in section four, lot six, cannot be read today. A community leader and businessman, he was born into slavery but escaped to Ohio and came to Cleveland as a boatman and teamster. It was reported that by 1840 he was one of only five African Americans in the city who owned taxable property. He was an excavating contractor who owned 20 wagons, 40 horses, and had an integrated workforce, at times employing 100 men. His gravestone is under a large bush, making it difficult to photograph.

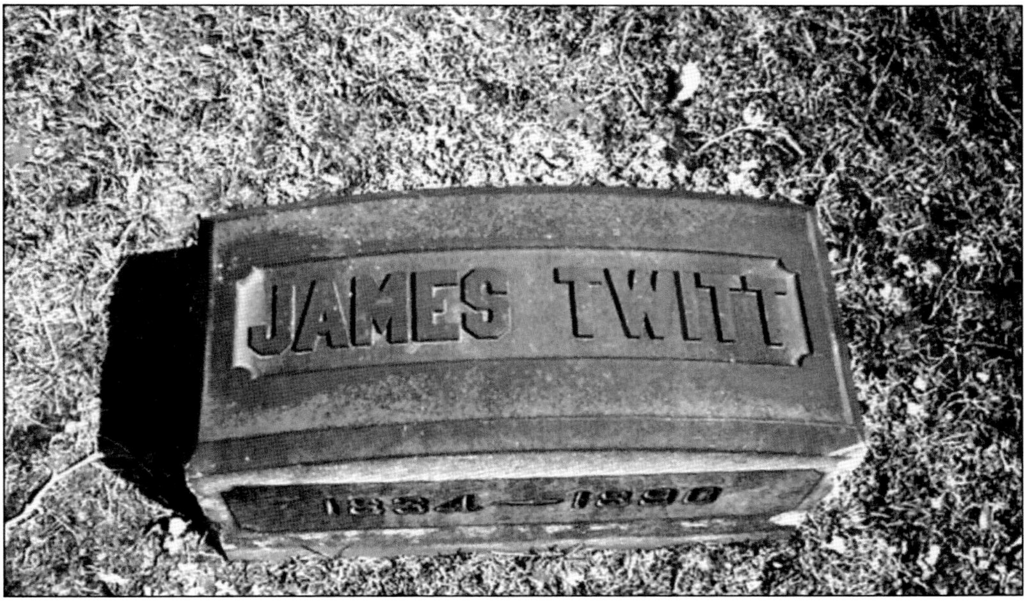

James Ellis Twitt (1834–1890) was born in Whiting, Indiana, a town located on the shores of Lake Michigan in the Chicago metropolitan area. Twitt spent his productive years in Cleveland. He was the husband of Bessie Dowes Twitt. Funeral services were held at the residence of his sister Mrs. W.P. Agnew.

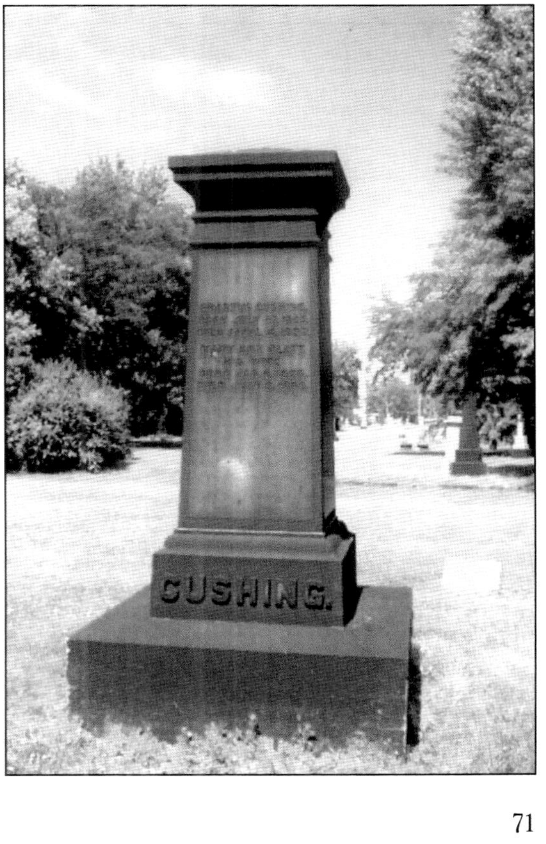

Erastus Cushing (1802–1875) came from a family of physicians. Cushing practiced medicine in Massachusetts for 10 years before coming to Cleveland in 1835 where he became a leader in the medical field. He married Mary Ann Pratt (1806–1868). Their son Henry was also a doctor, and he organized the Society for Medical Sciences of Cleveland. Cushing's grandson Dr. Harvey W. Cushing became a professor of brain surgery at Johns Hopkins, Harvard, and Yale. He won a Pulitzer Prize and was inducted into Cleveland's Hall of Fame.

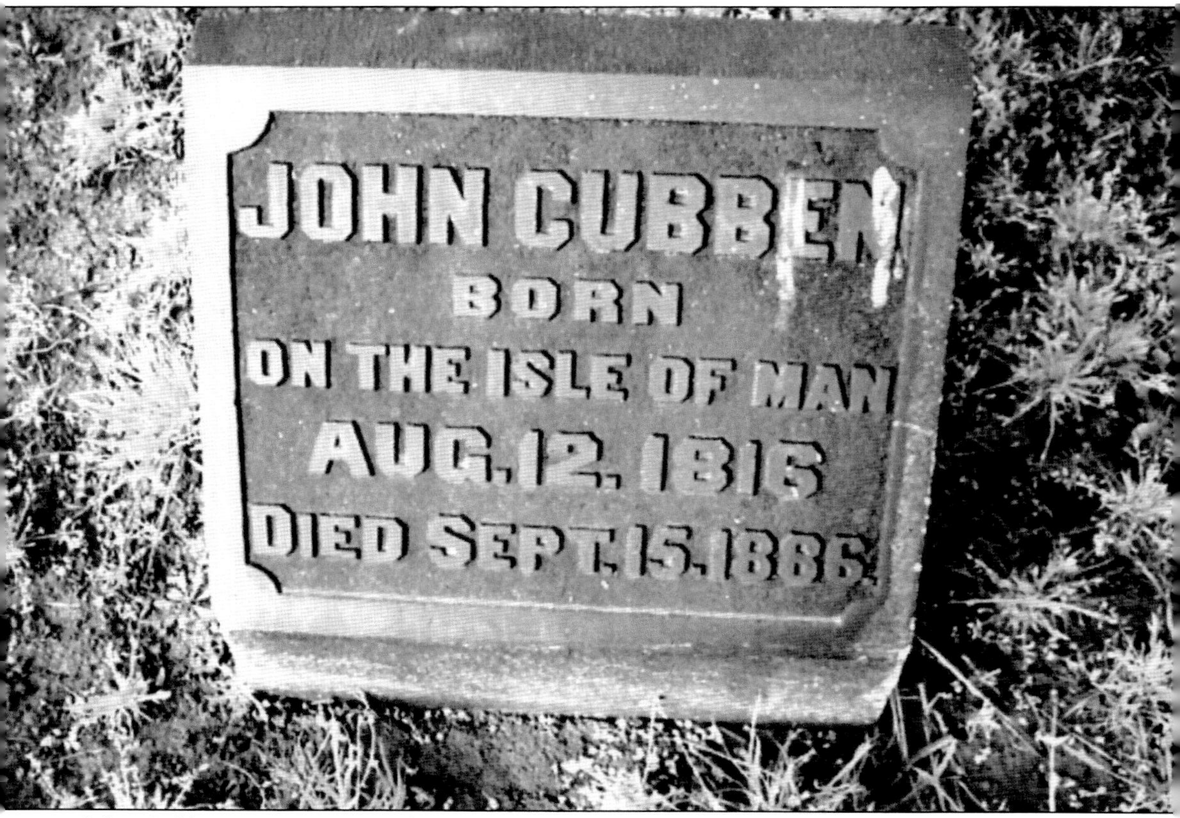

John Cubben's gravestone reads, "Born on the Isle of Man Aug. 12, 1816, Died Sept. 15, 1886." The Isle of Man is a self-governing British Crown dependency located in the Irish Sea between the islands of Great Britain and Ireland. Manx was once the language of the Isle of Man, and the inhabitants of the isle are called Manx. Cleveland is reported as having the largest number of Manx people and those descended from Manx of any place in the United States. Manx immigration to America came in the mid-1920s. The Mona's Relief Society was organized to aid those immigrating from the Isle of Man to Ohio in 1851. An excerpt from the magazine *Éllan Vannin*, which is Manx for "Isle of Man," states, "Three families left the dear little Island, and, after a voyage of seven weeks in sailing vessel, landed in New York. Thence by way of the Erie Canal and Lake Erie, they reached Cleveland, which was then a small town of only six hundred inhabitants, in May of 1826."

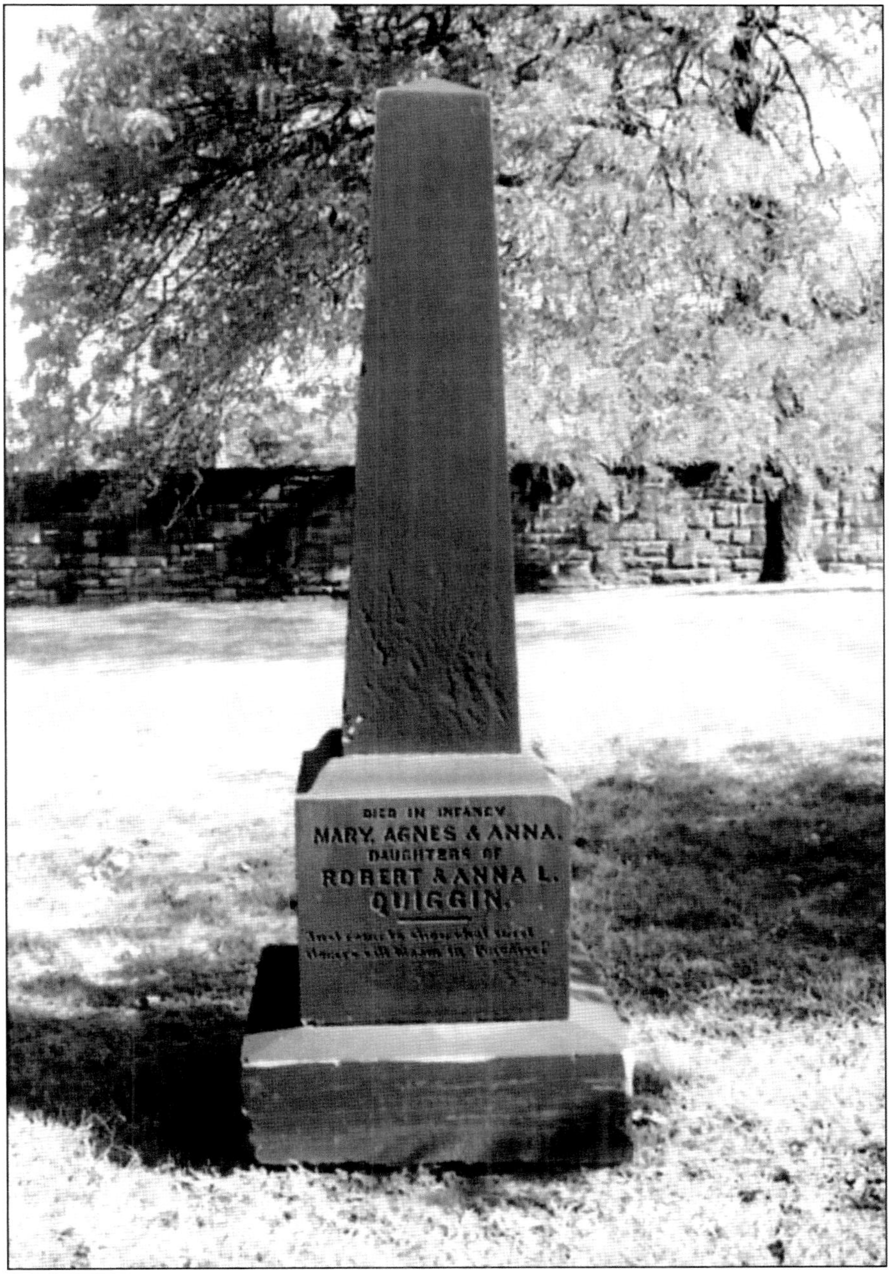

The Quiggins came to Cleveland from the Isle of Man. They lived in an area that is now around Union Avenue and Kinsman Road. The area started as a small community, but by 1926 Cleveland was quoted as having the largest number of Manx people, more than any other place in the United States. The Irish immigrants came to Cleveland because of the work available on the Ohio Canal. In the 1850s, a group called the Mona Relief Society was formed to provide aid to Manx settlers from the Isle of Man. The word "Manx" comes from the island's symbol of three bent legs, which originates from the legend that Manannan, a sea deity in Irish mythology, repelled an invasion by transforming into three legs and rolling down a hill to defeat the invaders.

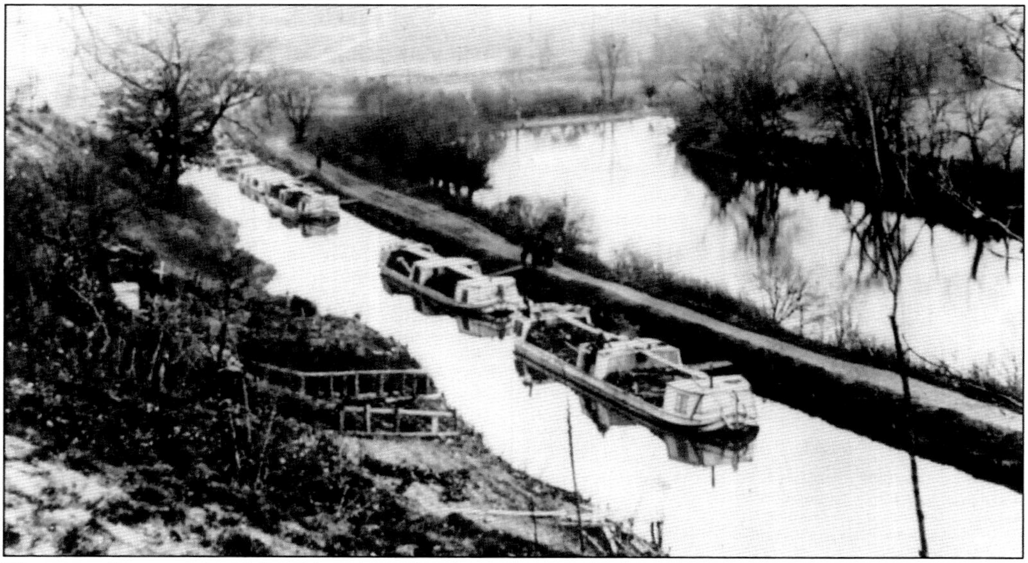

This is a photograph of the Ohio Canal as boats line up before entering the city to unload freight. Both the canal and Cuyahoga River can be seen in this image. The canal era began in the 1820s, and the last lock of the canal reached the Cuyahoga River in Cleveland in 1828. Cleveland became a boomtown. The canal boats were operated by both private individuals and companies, which were subject to tolls charged by the canal builders. There was space for freight, cabins in front, and a saloon or dining room in the back of the boats. Boats were usually drawn by two horses led by crew members. The crew consisted of a captain, two steersmen, drivers, and a cook. The canal era lasted until the late 1870s when the railroad took over to transport freight and passengers because it was faster and more comfortable. Many of those early settlers who came to work on the canal were Irish Catholics, and they were buried in Erie Street Cemetery. Fr. John Dillon, Cleveland's first Catholic priest, came to serve their religious needs and is also buried there. (Early Settlers Association and Cleveland Public Library.)

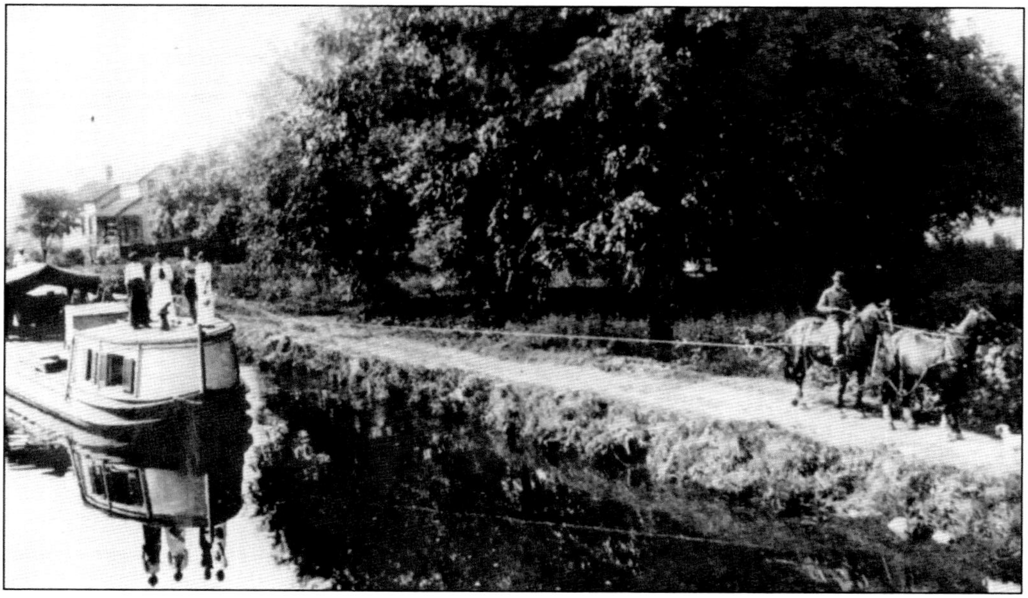

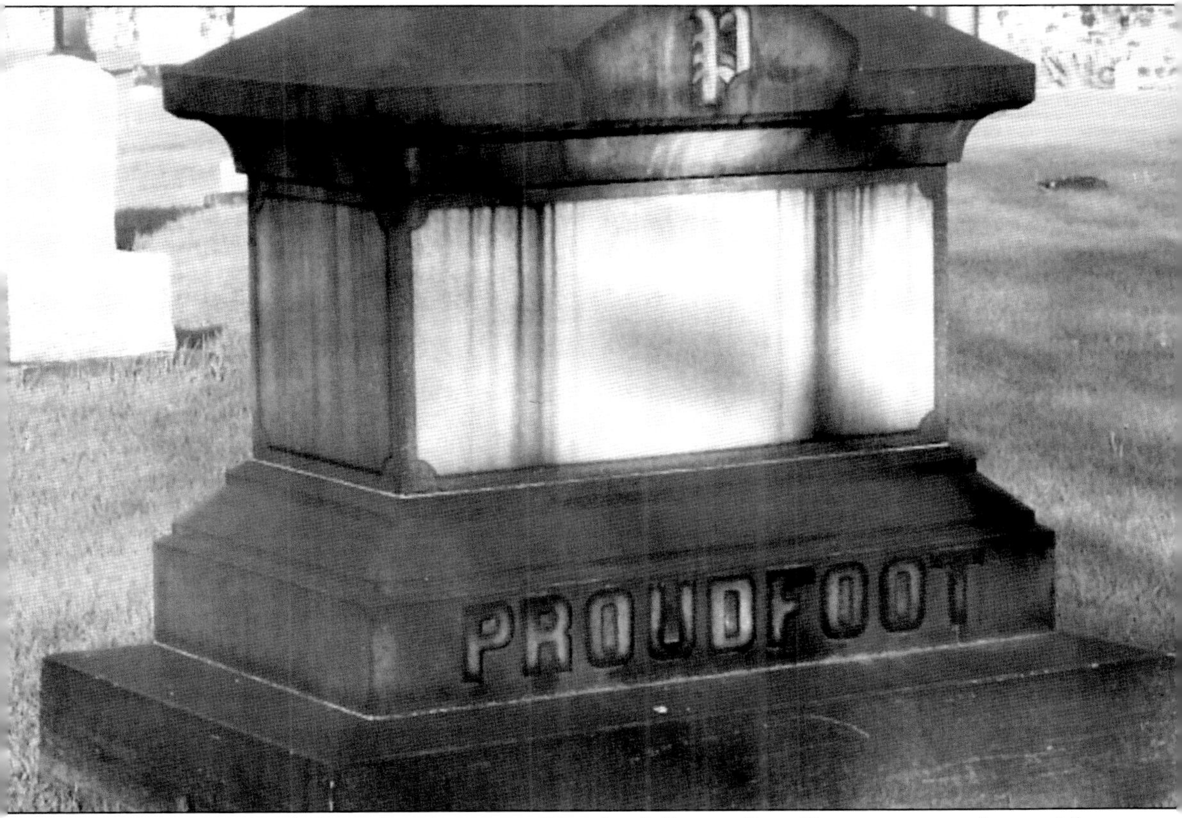

The Proudfoot family has a long history in Cleveland. George Proudfoot was an employee of the Connecticut Land Company who came to the Western Reserve as part of the Moses Cleaveland surveying party. James Proudfoot was a painter-poet and treasurer of the St. Andrew's Society, a group organized in May 1846 "to assist Scottish immigrants who lacked in worldly gear." The St. Andrew's Society was a Presbyterian denomination that was said to give liberally of their skills and abilities to industry and the professions. William Proudfoot served in the navy during the Civil War. There is a large group of Proudfoot family members buried in Erie Street Cemetery, including Joseph (1798–1853), James D. (1807–1864), Ada (1840–1887), Elizabeth M. Brew (1829–1898), James (1851–1864), Jane (1836–1890), James John (1849–1852), Mary Jane (1853–1854), William (1831–1874), William Wallace (1853–1864), Mary R. (d. 1885), and Mary Proudfoot Shotterd (d. 1920).

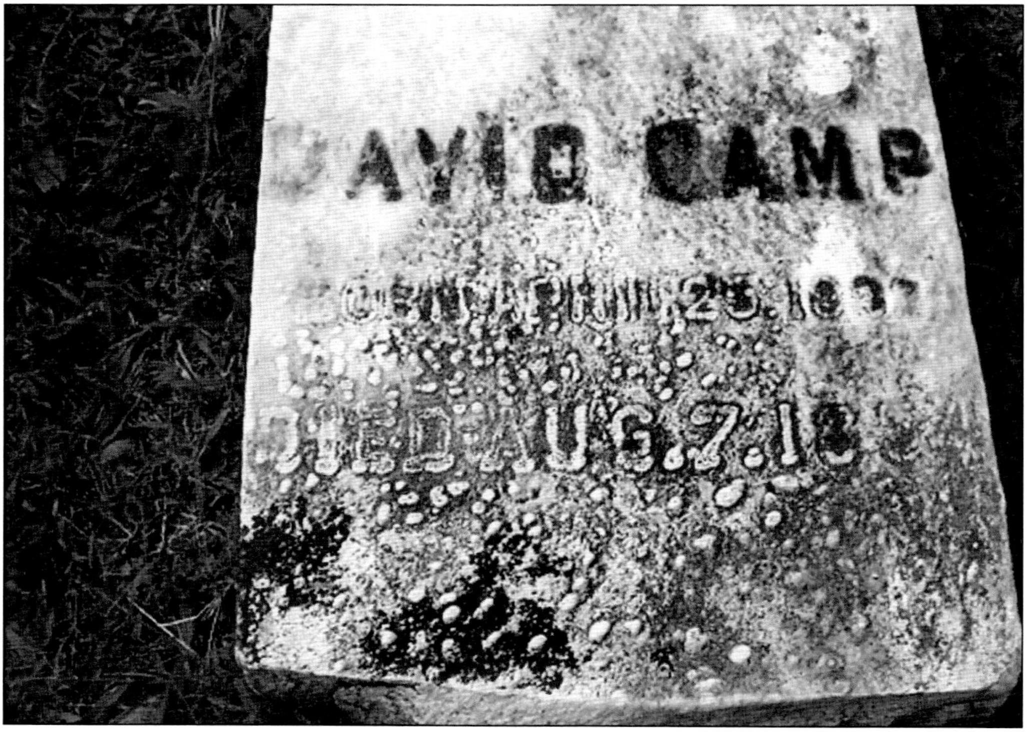

David Camp, who died on August 7, 1854, was one of 100 people who died in the explosion and fire on the steamship *Erie*, which took passengers from Buffalo to Cleveland. The *Erie* was considered one of the finest steamships, but it highlighted the difficulties in the early history of shipping on the Great Lakes. Camp's is one of the many stones that is very difficult to read due to weathering and age.

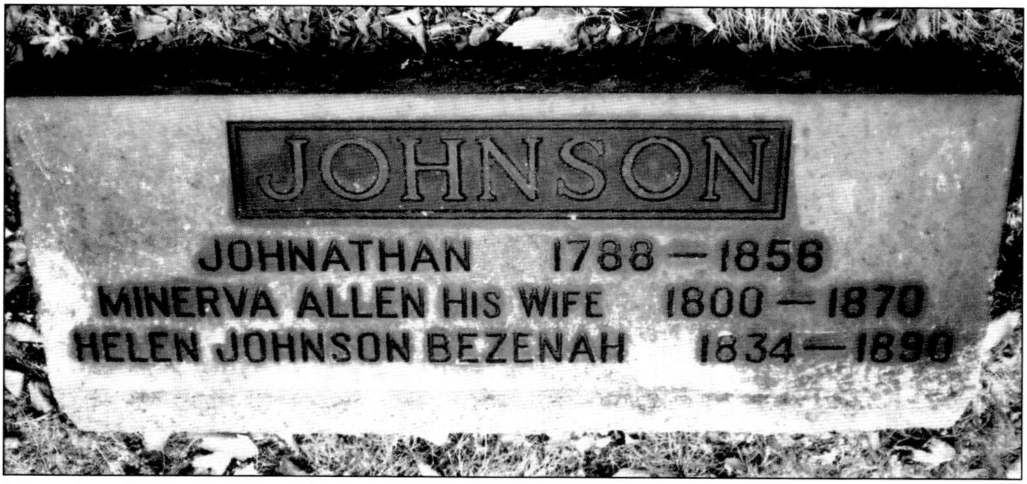

Johnathan Johnson was a lake captain from a family of lake captains. He commanded a small boat called the *Mercator*. He owned 60 acres of land on what is today East Thirty-fourth and Fortieth Streets and Euclid Avenue, and extended to Central Avenue. He married Minerva Allen on February 24, 1821. Minerva was said to have had a fine voice and was much in demand to perform at social events.

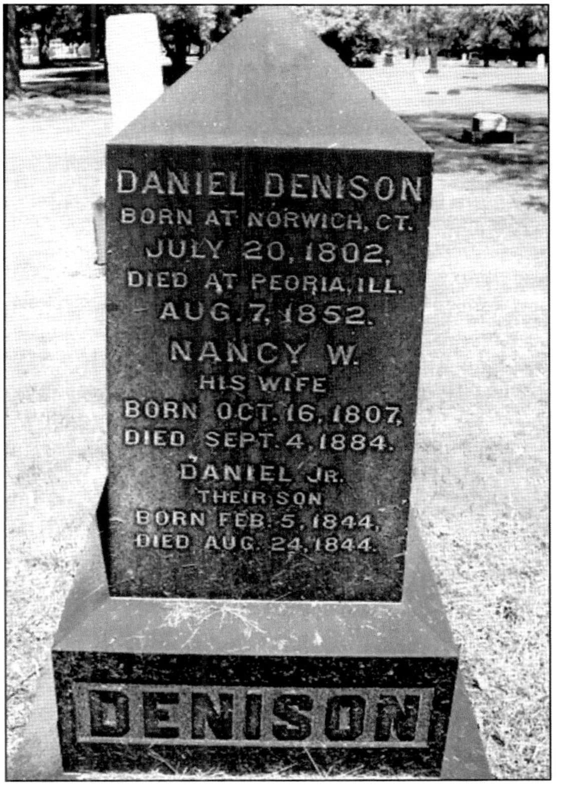

Daniel Denison was born at Norwich, Connecticut, on July 20, 1802, and died in Peoria, Illinois, on August 7, 1852. Nancy (née Williams), his wife, was also born in Norwich on October 16, 1807, and died September 4, 1884. Their son Daniel Jr., who is buried with them, was born on February 5, 1844, and died in that same year. It is unknown what Daniel was doing in Peoria, but he may have been there on a business trip because in the 1850s Peoria was a boomtown alive with many new industries. Unfortunately, Daniel came down with typhoid fever and died in Peoria. It was the oldest settlement in Illinois, and in 1843, Peoria became a world leader in distilleries and other industries. Below is the Denison gravesite on a winter day.

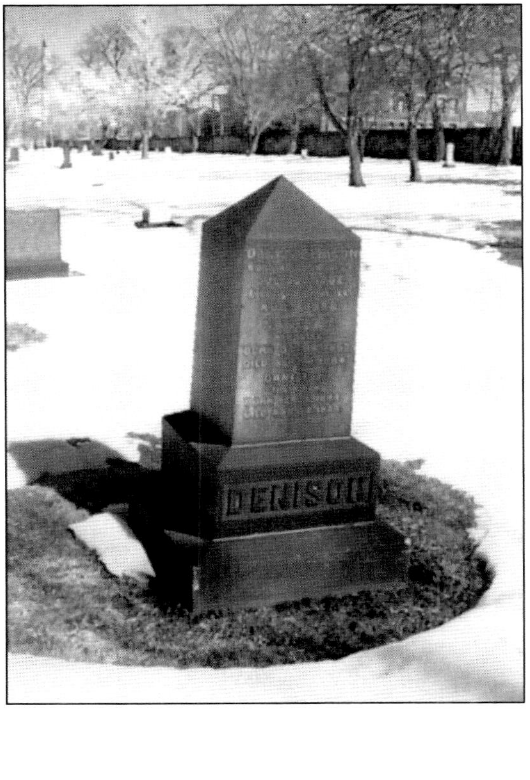

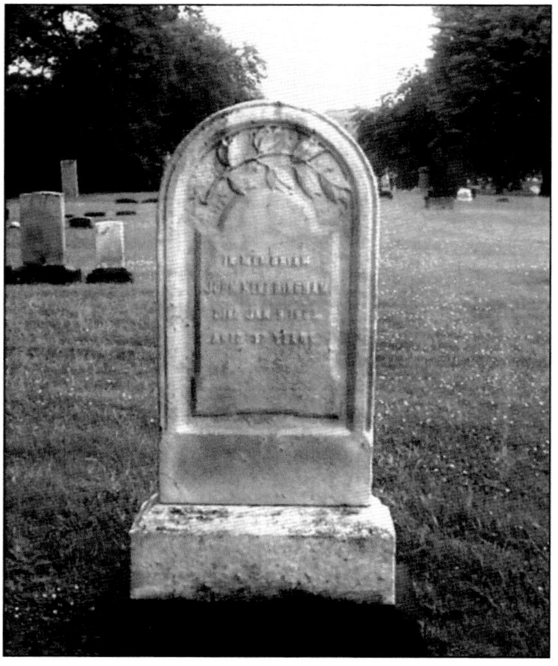

John Kent Bingham died in 1863 at the age of 37, according to the Cleveland Necrology File. His gravestone is well preserved. During the 1800s, the use of floral symbolism became very popular. This must mean that he died in the prime of his life since the flowers are in full bloom.

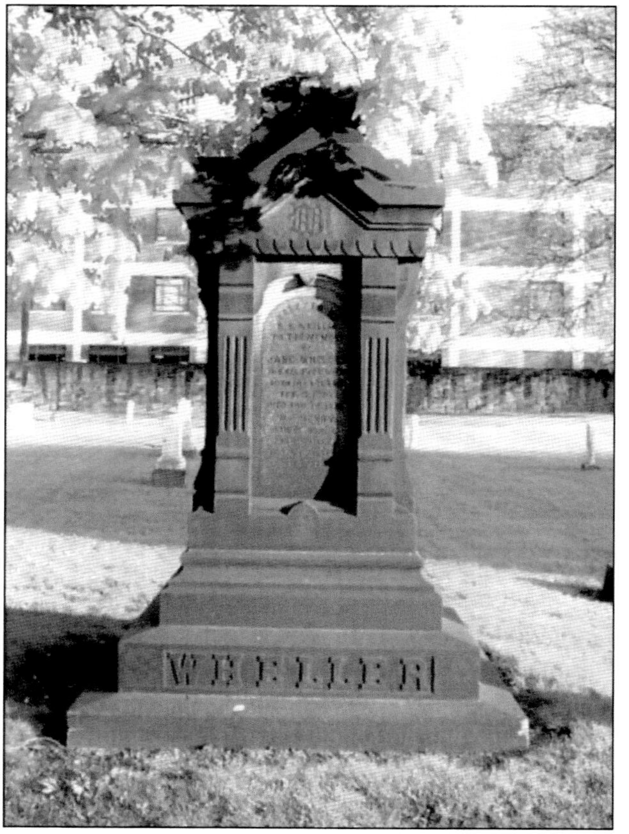

B.S. Wheller erected this beautiful monument to the memory of his wife, Jane Wheller, who was born in England in 1800 and died in Cleveland in 1886, and to his son Henry, who died when he was only nine weeks old.

In 1837, Josiah A. Harris purchased the *Gazette* and *Herald* newspapers, combined them, and changed the name to *Herald and Gazette*. It was a Whig paper and became the chief source of local news. The name of the paper changed again to the *Herald* in 1843. Harris eventually published two newspapers, the *Cleveland Herald* and the *Cleveland Daily Herald*. For nearly 40 years, he was editor and publisher of the *Cleveland Herald*. It was reported that Harris was editor-in-chief, the city editor, financial editor, commercial editor, mailing clerk, and bookkeeper. He served as Cleveland's mayor in 1847 and in 1849 was one of the incorporators of the Society for Savings Bank. He retired in 1857 to a farm in Rocky River where he raised grapes. He died in 1876 at 67 years old. (Cleveland Public Library and Early Settlers Association.)

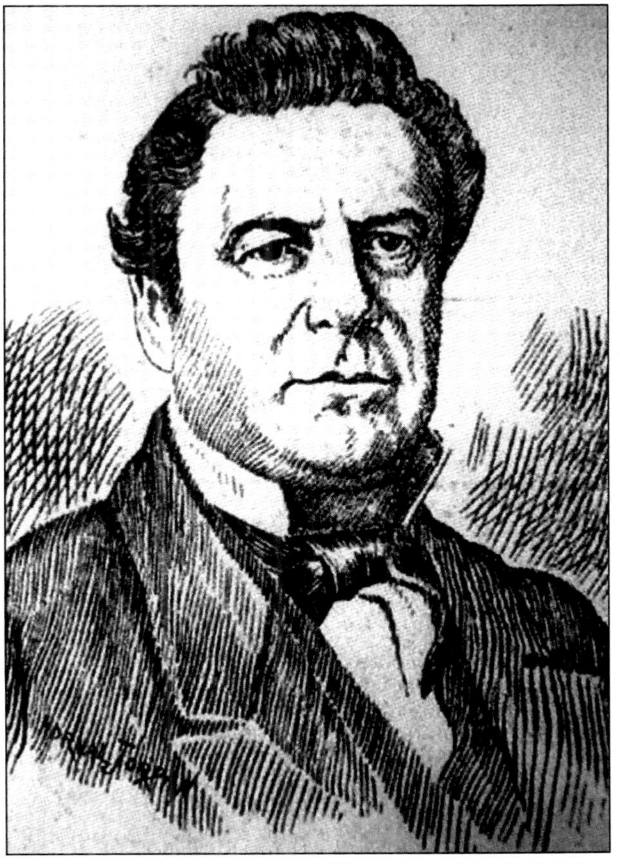

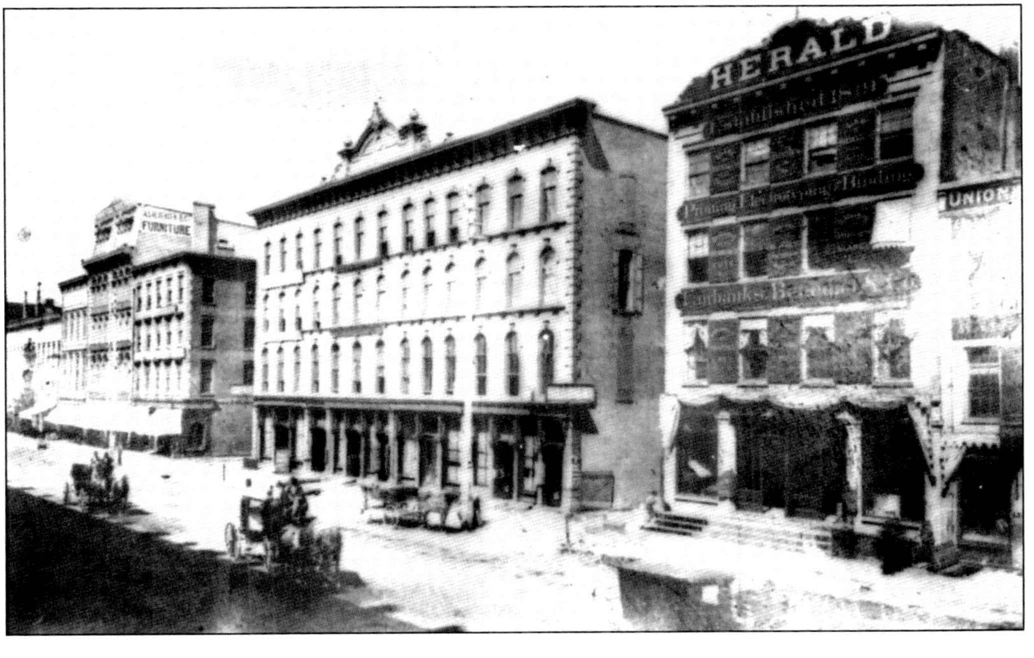

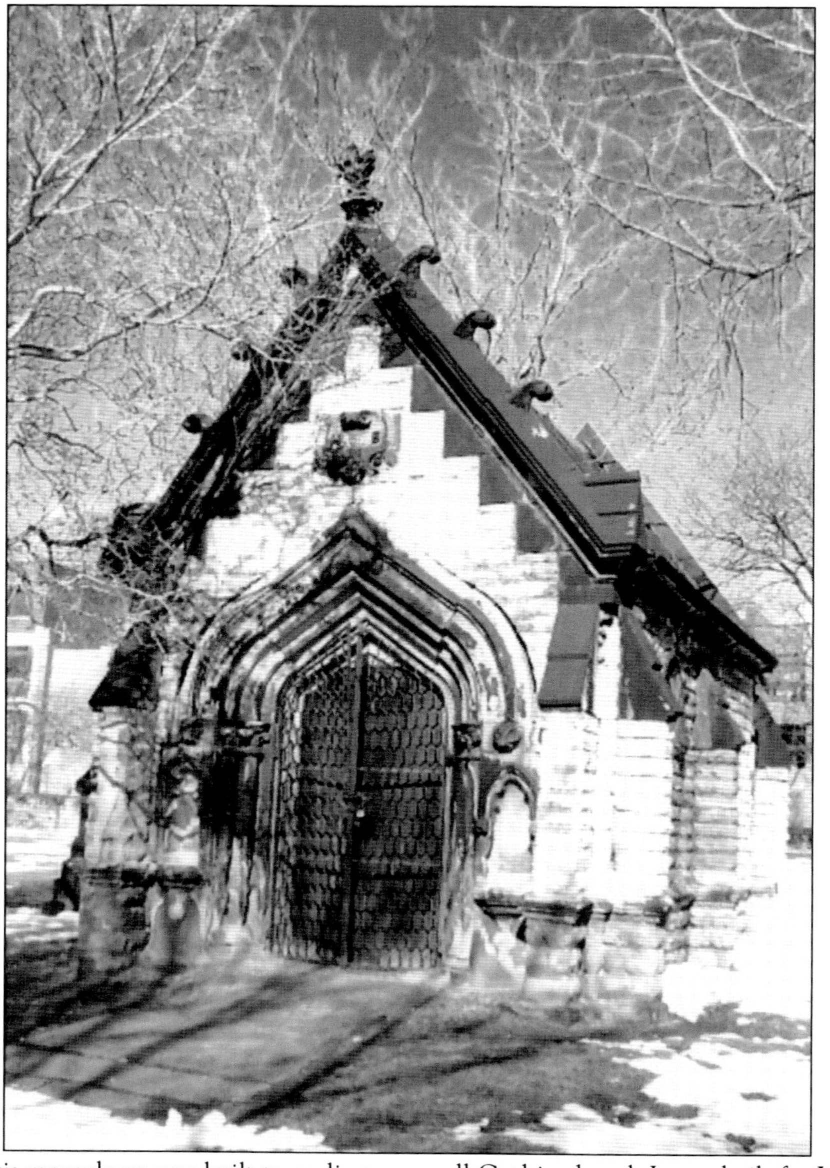

The Harris mausoleum was built to replicate a small Gothic chapel. It was built for Josiah A. Harris (1808–1876). He was the son of Judge Josiah Harris and Charity Messenger Harris of Becket, Massachusetts. Judge Josiah Harris was a very influential Clevelander. He was Cleveland's first postmaster and sheriff. It was said that he was a man who everyone would turn to when they were in financial distress. His son Josiah A. Harris married Ester Race in 1830, and they had four children. In 1832, Josiah A. Harris was elected sheriff of Elyria, Ohio, and also revived Elyria's first newspaper, a weekly called the *Ohio Atlas and Elyria Advertiser.* He sold the paper and moved to Cleveland from Amherst, Ohio. During the Civil War, Ester became a member of the Sanitary Commission, which packed boxes, clothing, and other needs for sick and wounded soldiers. She also was active in many other charities. There is a bas-relief of her on a bronze panel in the Soldiers' and Sailors' Monument on Cleveland Public Square. The mausoleum is now vacant, and the family remains were moved to Lake View Cemetery. (Early Settlers Association.)

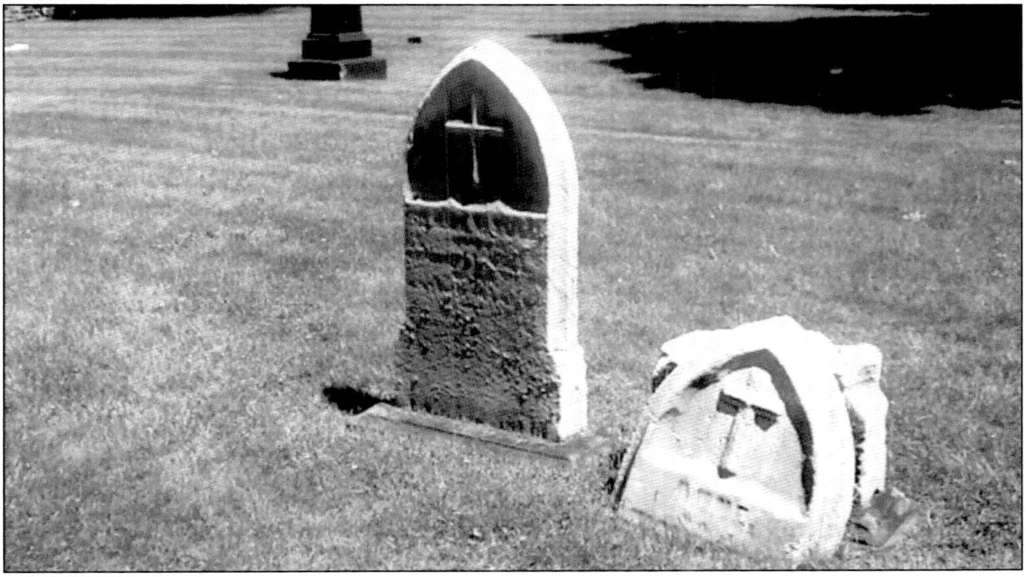

All that can be read on these two stones is the name "Anne." All other lettering has been lost over the years except for the cross that is a lasting Christian message of love, faith, and goodness, according to cemetery symbolism. By the 1860s, almost all the plots were sold, but today there are many open sites because of the fear that the cemetery would be closed.

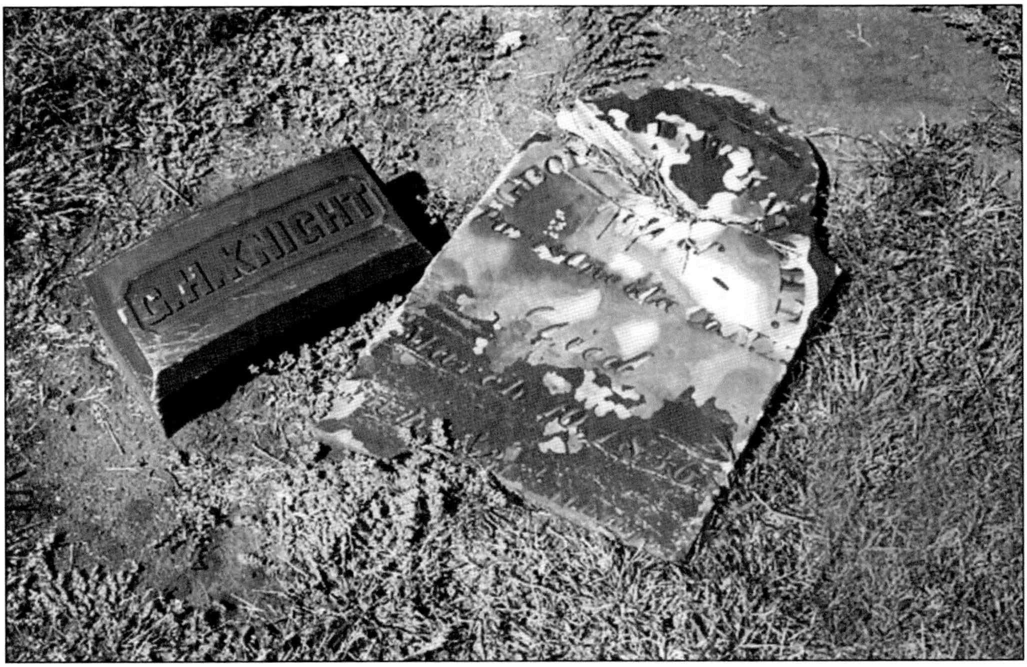

There are 17,935 burials in Erie Street Cemetery, though not all are marked. Walking through the cemetery one can find many interesting gravestones, some in good condition and some damaged by the elements or vandalism. It is the hope of the Early Settlers Association, in cooperation with Cuyahoga Community College, that restoration of the historic stones will be undertaken in the near future. (Cleveland Public Library.)

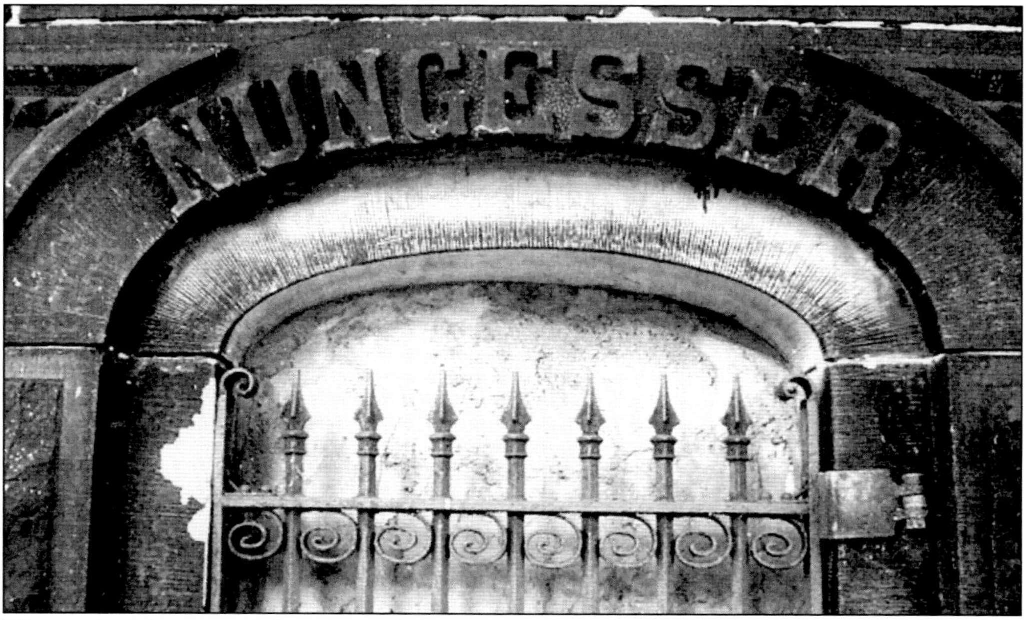

This is the Nungesser Mausoleum. John Nungesser came to America from Hesendamstrett, Germany, as a boy. His sons were George Franklin, John, and Edward. They followed their father in the cabinet-making trade. The daughter of George and Anna (née Fretta) Nungesser was named Irene. After graduating from Berkey & Dykes Business College, Irene went to work for attorneys Bernsteen & Bernsteen. While working for the firm, she became interested in the study of law and was admitted to the bar in 1921. In June 1923, she was appointed assistant US attorney for the northern district of Ohio.

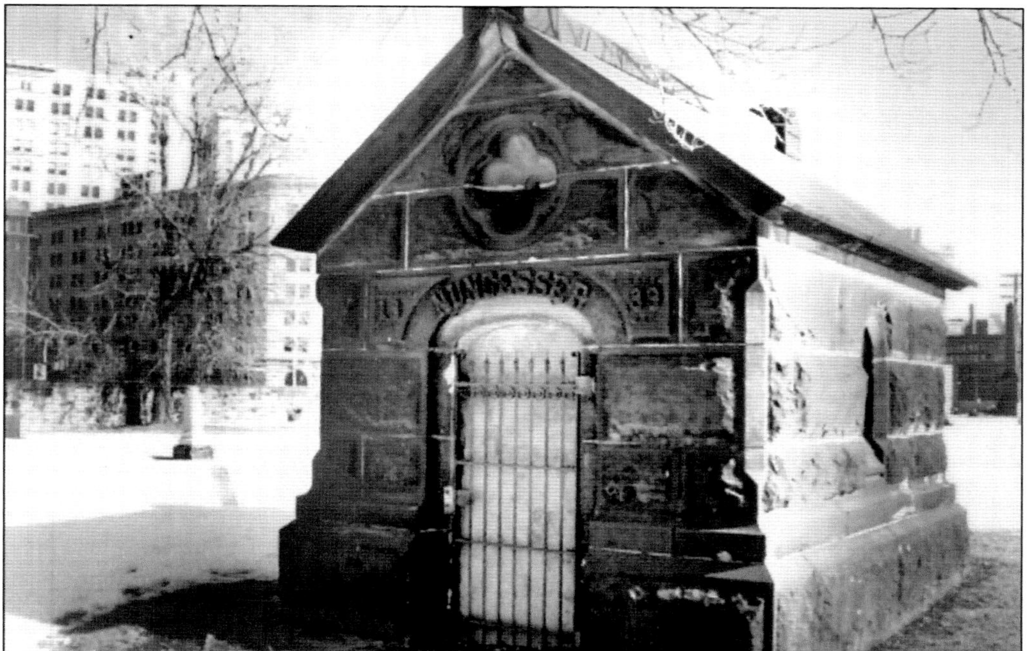

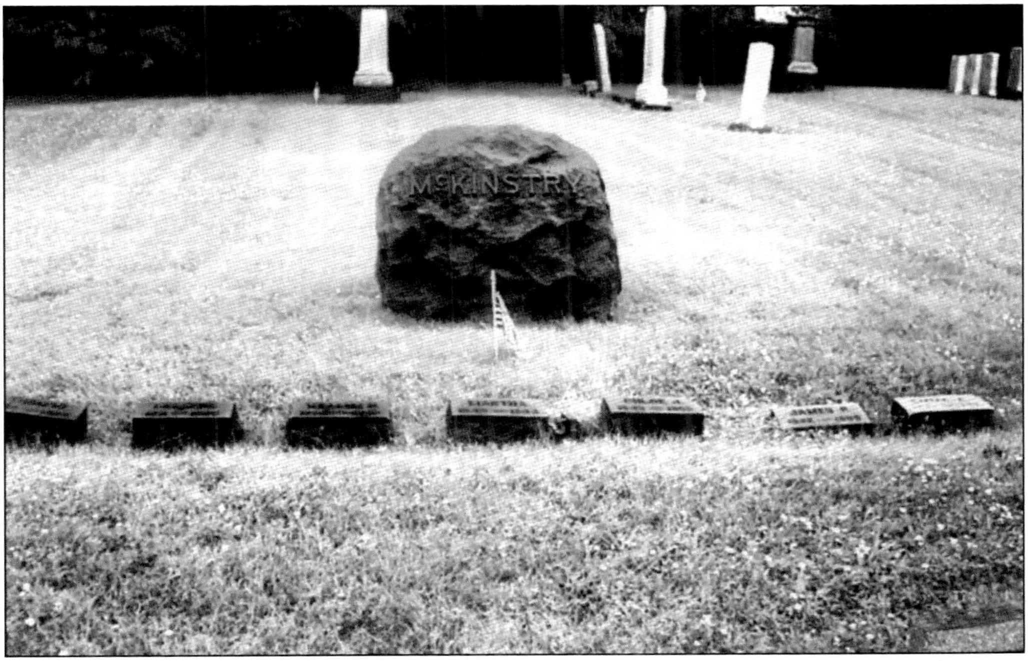

An impressive gravesite is that of the McKinstry family. The first McKinstry to come to America arrived in Massachusetts in 1718. Thomas McKinstry (1812–1882) served as superintendent of the Cleveland Police Department in 1869. James P. McKinstry (1842–1905) was a member of city council of the 13th ward in 1876 at the time that Nathan P. Payne was mayor of the city. Others buried in front of the McKinstry stone are Erexene (1811–1883), William H. (1839–1843), Martha (1843–1844), Chloe J. (1845–1855), and Emma A. (1841–1927).

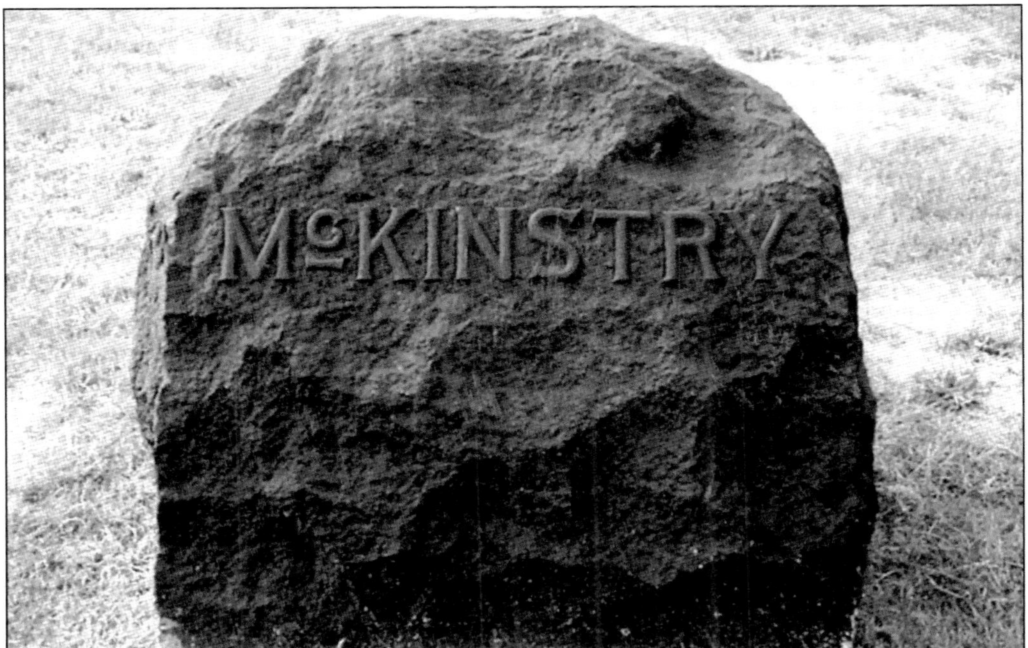

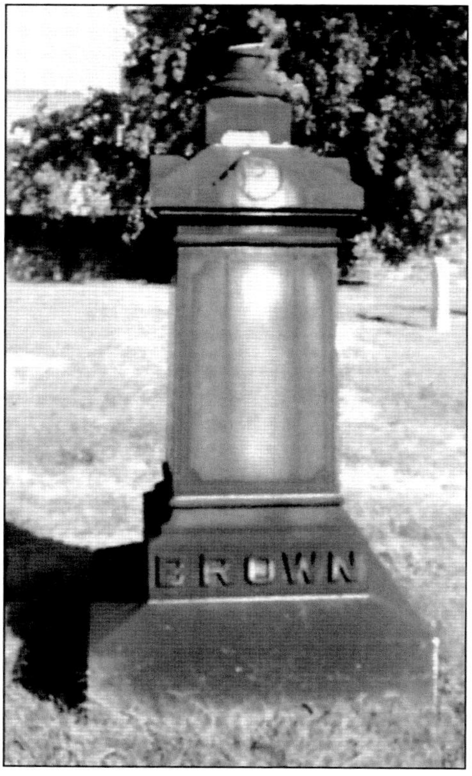

Dr. Asa B. Brown, physician and surgeon, began his work in Cleveland in the 1830s. His wife, Hannah Bliss, died a year after their marriage. She was only 20 years old. She had brothers who became prominent lawyers and a third brother who became the treasurer of the State of Ohio.

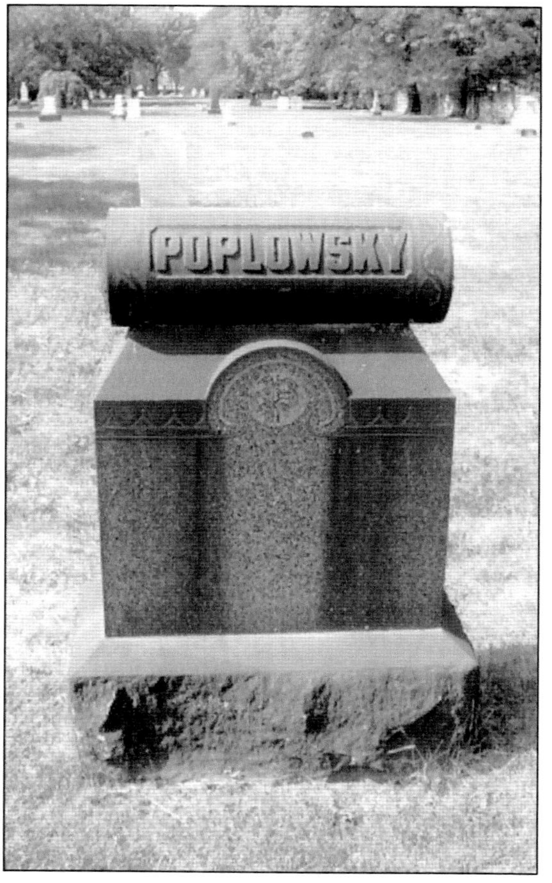

This is the Poplowsky family gravesite. William Poplowsky (1831–1891) died when he was 61 years old. His funeral was conducted at his residence at 62 Scovill Avenue. William's wife, Christina Poplowsky, died February 22, 1902, at the age of 70. Henry Poplowsky (1861–1913) died December 15, 1913. Charles Poplowsky died September 12, 1897. He was born in San Francisco on July 5, 1881, and died at the age of 16.

Jonathan Gillette was born in Windsor, Connecticut, in 1808 and came to Cleveland in the early 1830s. He was a successful Cleveland merchant. In 1839, he married Susan Sloan. He was identified with the growth of the city from the early 1830s until his death in 1862. His home on Euclid Avenue was said to be a place of beauty and a location of community hospitality.

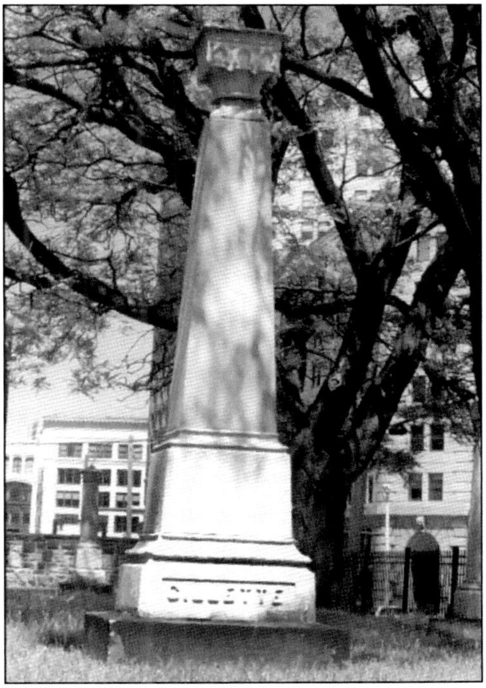

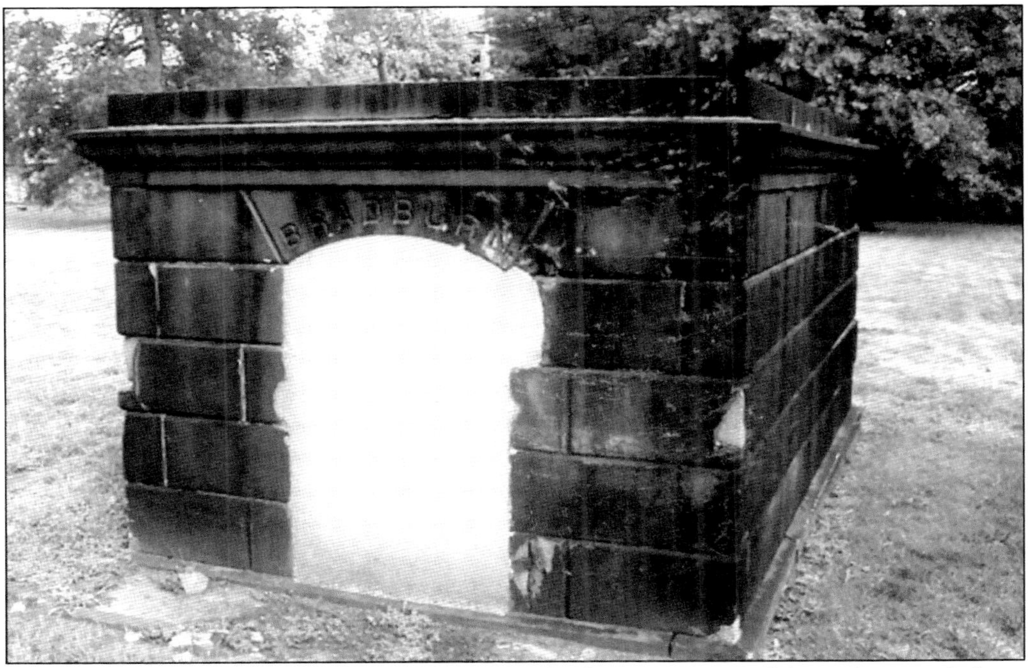

This is the crypt of Charles Bradburn (1808–1872) who was a successful merchant and also a leader in the organization and development of Cleveland's public schools. Central High School, opened in 1846, was Cleveland's first public school, and Bradburn helped establish it. He was called the "father of Cleveland schools." In 1853, he served on Cleveland's first school board and became its first president.

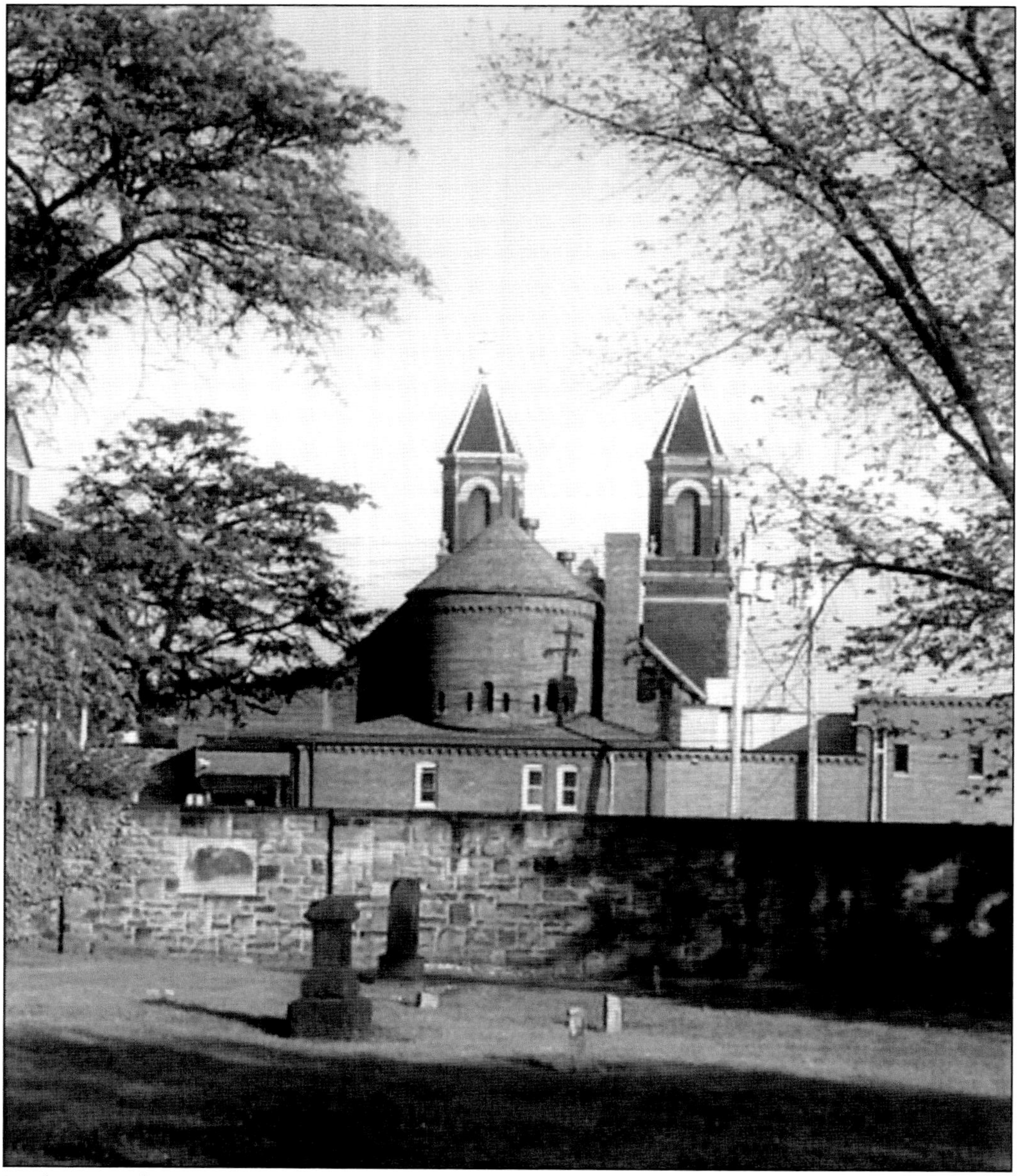

Looking south over Erie Street Cemetery's sandstone wall, St. Maron Catholic Church is visible. The church was originally built as St. Anthony of Padua Church in 1904. It was originally a landmark of Cleveland's Italian community, now it serves Cleveland's Lebanese Americans. St. Maron's Maronite Rite Catholic Church began in 1915 in a two-story apartment building that was remodeled into a church and rectory. In 1939, St. Maron's parishioners purchased St. Anthony of Padua Church. Maronites are followers of a saintly hermit, Maron, who lived in Antioch in the 5th century. The Maronite rite is one of the oldest orders in the Catholic Church. The liturgy is known as the Syriac liturgy of Antioch, ascribed to St. James the Less who was an apostle and the first bishop of Jerusalem. The liturgy is recited in Syriac-Aramaic, the language of Christ. The sect grew to become the largest Christian community in Lebanon. Today, the Maronites number about three million worldwide as reported by the Near East Welfare Association.

Three

Our Veterans, Lest We Forget

William C. Stark, volunteer archivist of the Cleveland Grays Armory, compiled the following survey of Erie Street Cemetery as completed in 2005 by Michelle Day, president of the Woodland Cemetery Association. The survey revealed a total of 168 veterans buried there. Findings included soldiers and sailors who had served in the American Revolutionary through the Spanish-American War and during periods of peace between those conflicts. Buried in the cemetery are four soldiers from the Revolutionary War; one from the pre–War of 1812; thirty-eight from the War of 1812; four from the post–War of 1812 militia; two from the pre–Mexican-American War; three from the Mexican-American War; one from pre–Civil War frontier duty; 98 from the Civil War; one from the post–Civil War Indian Wars; three from the Spanish-American War; one from the post–Spanish-American War; and three from a time period that is not known. The number of army veterans from all the wars totals 161. There are also seven navy Civil War veterans buried in the cemetery, for a total of 168 military men. A second field check that was conducted in 2009 showed that of the 98 Civil War army veterans, 37 had civilian gravestones or monuments, five had military headstones, and the remaining 56 had no gravestones at all.

It is important to remember that the information gathered is based on grave registration cards (GRCs) and often can be found incomplete or with errors. Research is presently being conducted to correct those errors if better information can be found. Over the years, Clevelanders did work to honor their dead.

At the Memorial Day rededication at Erie Street Cemetery on May 30, 1939, the following address was given by Thomas A. Knight:

> On this beautiful May morning we pause from our usual pursuits to pay honor to the dead in this oldest of Cleveland burial grounds, Erie Street Cemetery. Here today, are gathered Catholic, Protestant, Jew and Gentile, and American Indian. In this we recognize no race, no creed. We are universal in our reverence for those who are buried here whether their achievements in life were on the field of battle or in the less romantic field of civic endeavor.

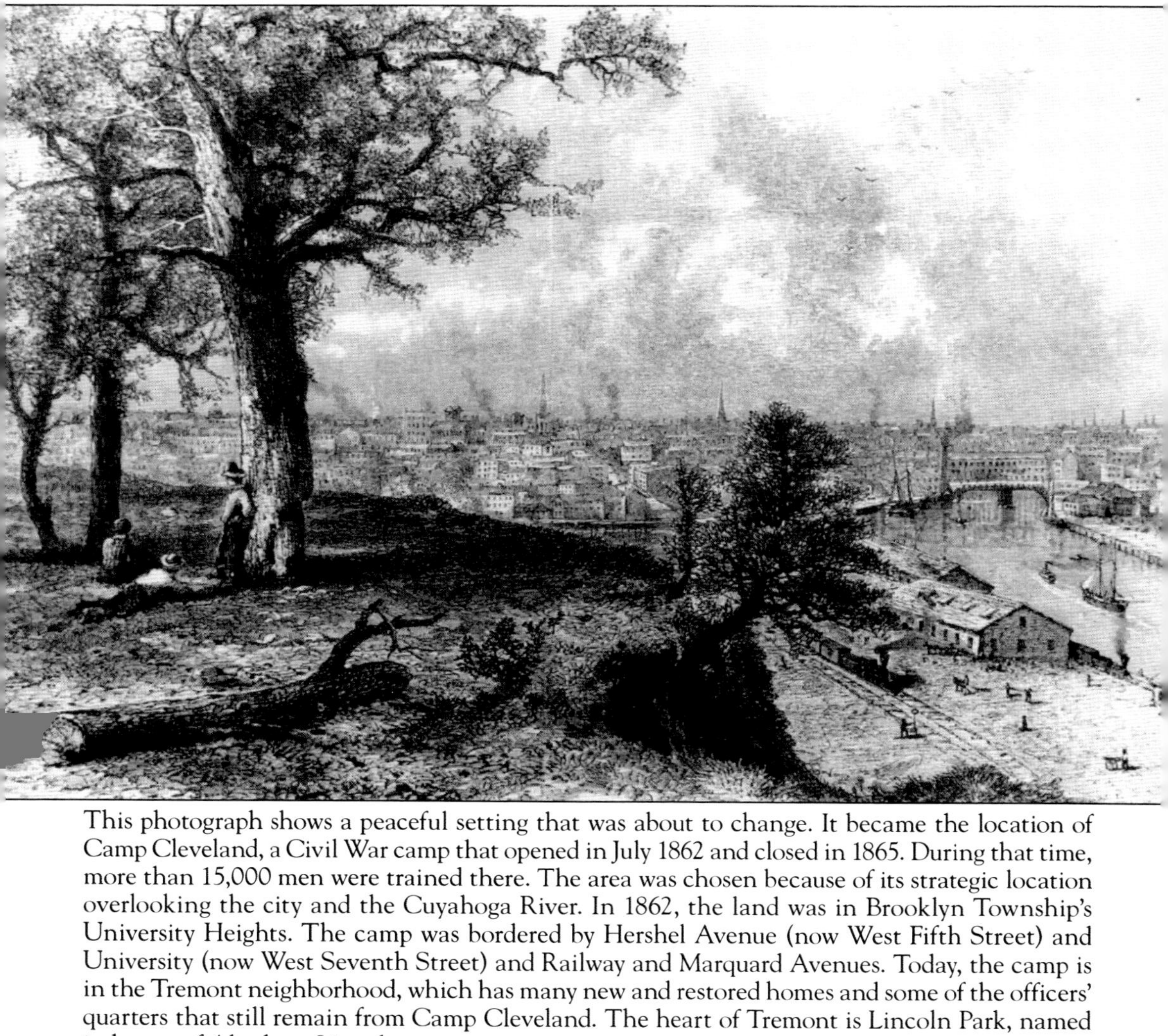

This photograph shows a peaceful setting that was about to change. It became the location of Camp Cleveland, a Civil War camp that opened in July 1862 and closed in 1865. During that time, more than 15,000 men were trained there. The area was chosen because of its strategic location overlooking the city and the Cuyahoga River. In 1862, the land was in Brooklyn Township's University Heights. The camp was bordered by Hershel Avenue (now West Fifth Street) and University (now West Seventh Street) and Railway and Marquard Avenues. Today, the camp is in the Tremont neighborhood, which has many new and restored homes and some of the officers' quarters that still remain from Camp Cleveland. The heart of Tremont is Lincoln Park, named in honor of Abraham Lincoln.

The historic marker was dedicated on October 11, 2003. It was erected by the Ohio Bicentennial Commission and the Scotts Company, a business founded by a Civil War veteran. The marker was funded by the Civil War Roundtable, the Early Settlers Association of the Western Reserve, and the Ohio Historical Society. There were seven Civil War camps located in the Cleveland area. Each was considered a camp of rendezvous and training where local regiments organized before entering the battlefield. Camp Cleveland was the largest and most developed of the camps. The historic marker overlooking the Flats tells the story of that camp. The 35-acre site was opened as Camp Cleveland in July 1862. In December 1862, there were 4,151 men in the camp. More than 15,000 men were trained there, and after the war's end in 1865, more than 11,000 soldiers were discharged from Camp Cleveland.

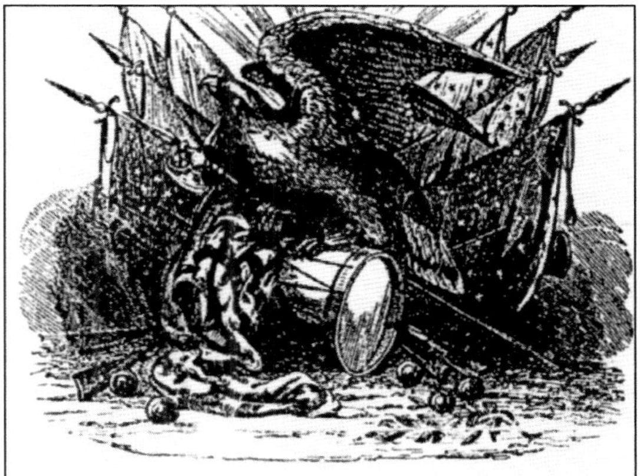

DEDICATION

Of an Ohio Bi-Centenial Marker
at the site of Camp Cleveland and
the United States General Hospital
Cleveland: 1862-1865

Saturday, October 11, 2003
at 1:15 P.M.

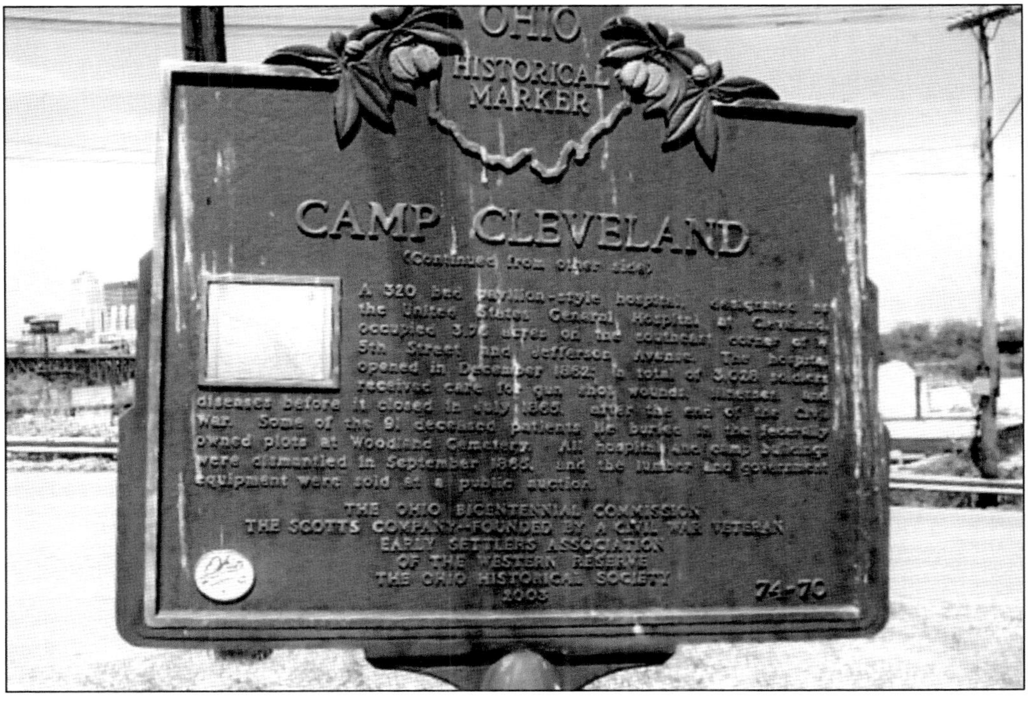

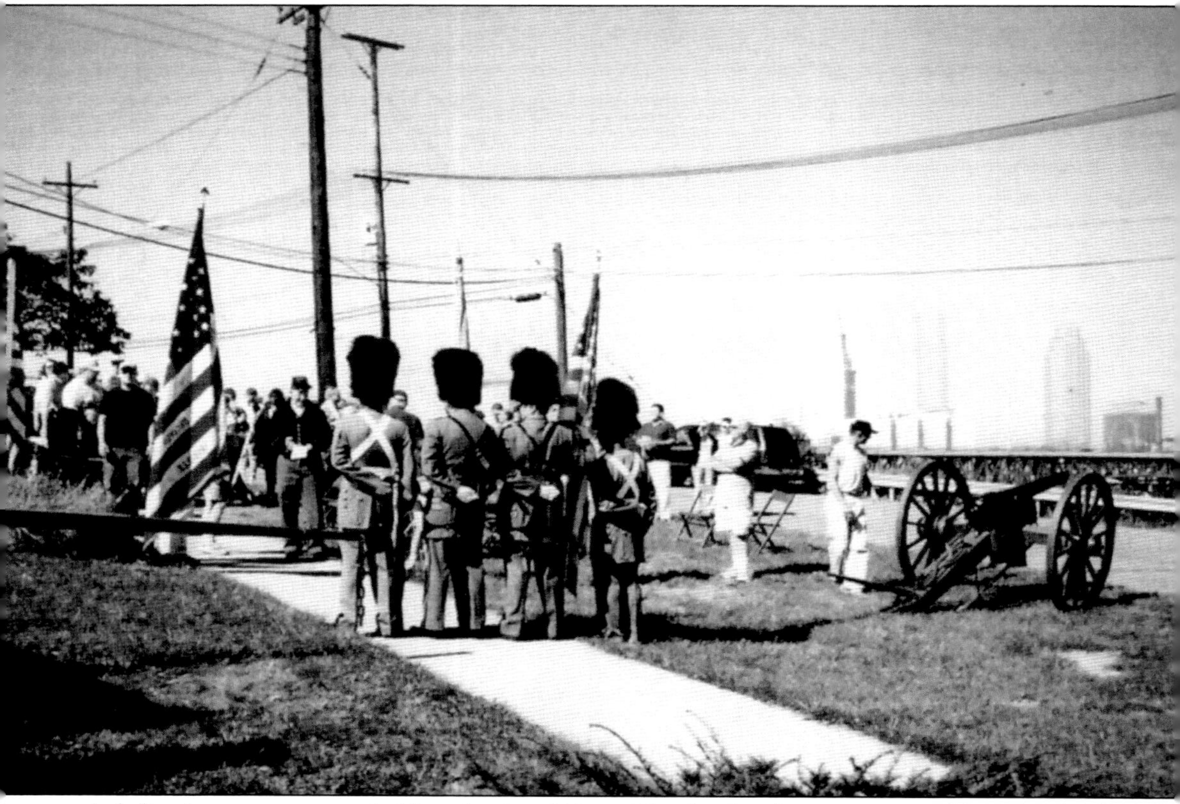

A dedication ceremony was held on the site of Camp Cleveland with participation of the Cleveland Grays and a Civil War reenactment group. Since their founding, the Grays have been active in programs to preserve Erie Street Cemetery. The Cleveland Grays joined the Union army as a unit and were mustered in as Company D of the Ohio Volunteer Infantry with their assignment being the defense of Washington, DC. It was reported that they were the first on the battlefield in the First Battle of Bull Run and the last to leave as they gave cover for retreating Union troops. The First Battle of Bull Run was a victory for Confederate forces. Approximately 5,000 men died in that battle and of those 3,000 were Union soldiers. There was a 320-bed hospital at Camp Cleveland that opened in December 1862. More than 3,000 soldiers were treated for gunshot wounds and other illnesses before it closed in July 1865. Some of those treated at the hospital were Confederate prisoners before they were transferred to Johnson Island in Sandusky, Ohio. (Dale Thomas.)

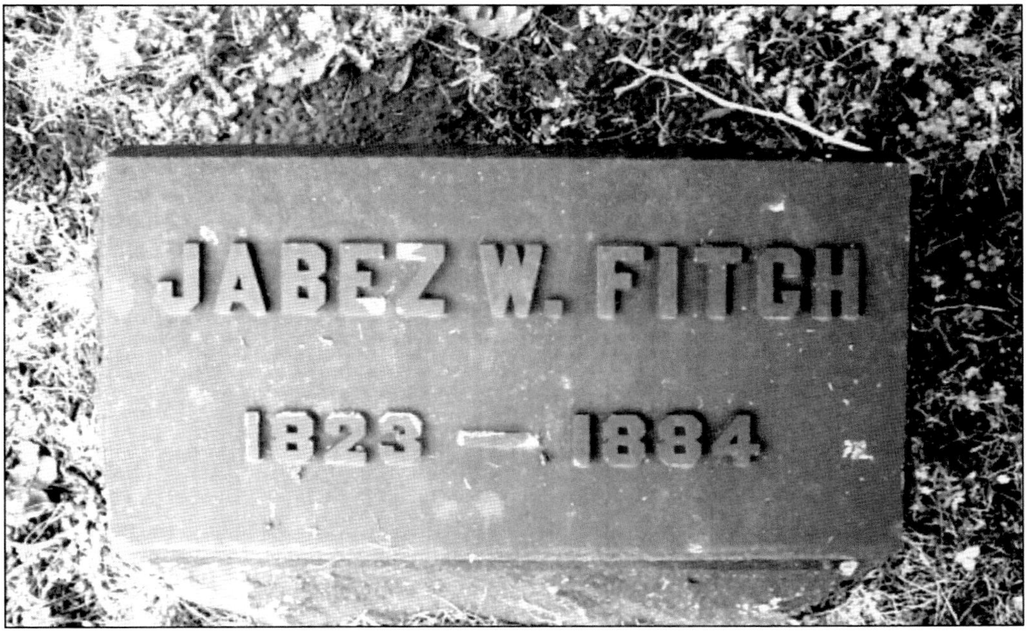

Jabez W. Fitch (1823–1884) was an attorney who served as a commandant of Camp Taylor during the Civil War. Camp Taylor was established on April 22, 1861. By April 27, several thousand soldiers were at the camp. Cuyahoga County furnished three companies of the 7th Infantry. In 1852, Fitch served as fire chief of the volunteer fire department, and in 1855, he was appointed US marshal when the seat of the northern district of the federal court was established in Cleveland. In 1875, Jabez was elected lieutenant governor of Ohio. At right is the family plot that includes the gravesite of Abby Fitch (1794–1893), who died at the age of 99. She was the sister of Gurdon Fitch and aunt of Jabez.

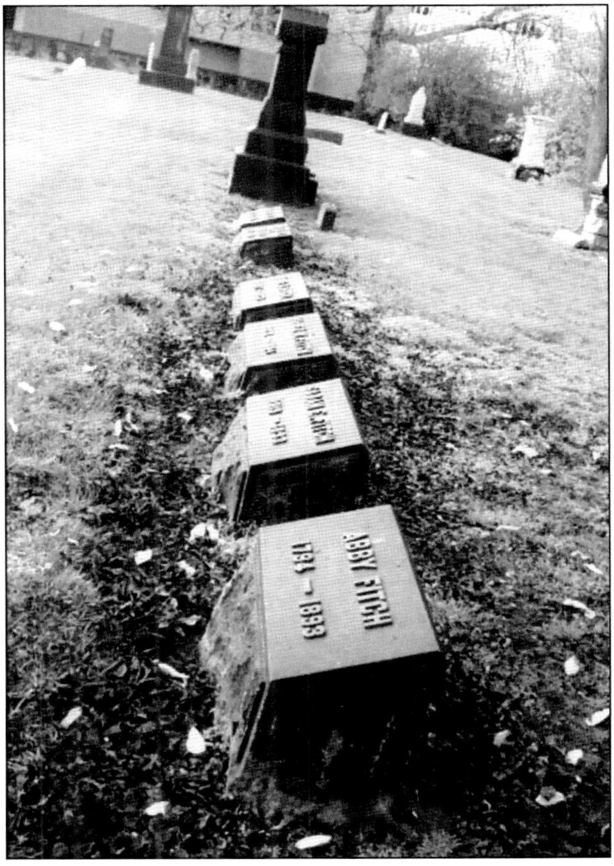

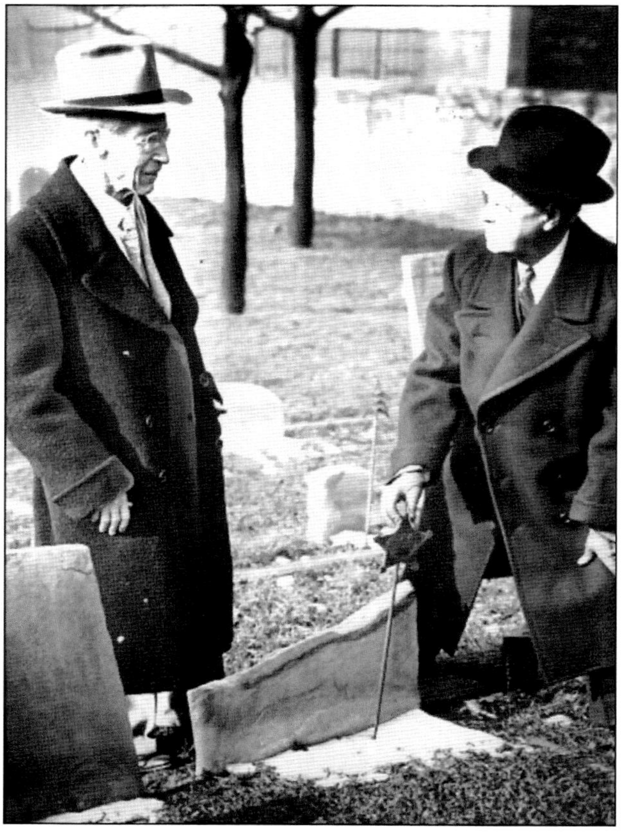

Pictured are John G. Eddy, superintendent of Erie Street Cemetery (left), and Thomas A. Knight, field secretary of what was then called the Western Reserve Historical Association and secretary of the Early Settlers Association of the Western Reserve. On February 19, 1941, Eddy and Knight visited the grave of Asabel Tuttle, a Revolutionary War hero. His gravestone had deteriorated and the committee ordered a new stone. (Cleveland State University, Cleveland Press Collection.)

Asabel Tuttle (1767–1837) served in the Revolutionary War as a private from April 24, 1781, to August 1, 1781. He served in Capt. Albert Van Deursen's company, which was authorized to seize the ships and property of the subjects of Great Britain. His gravestone has the logo of a Revolutionary War soldier.

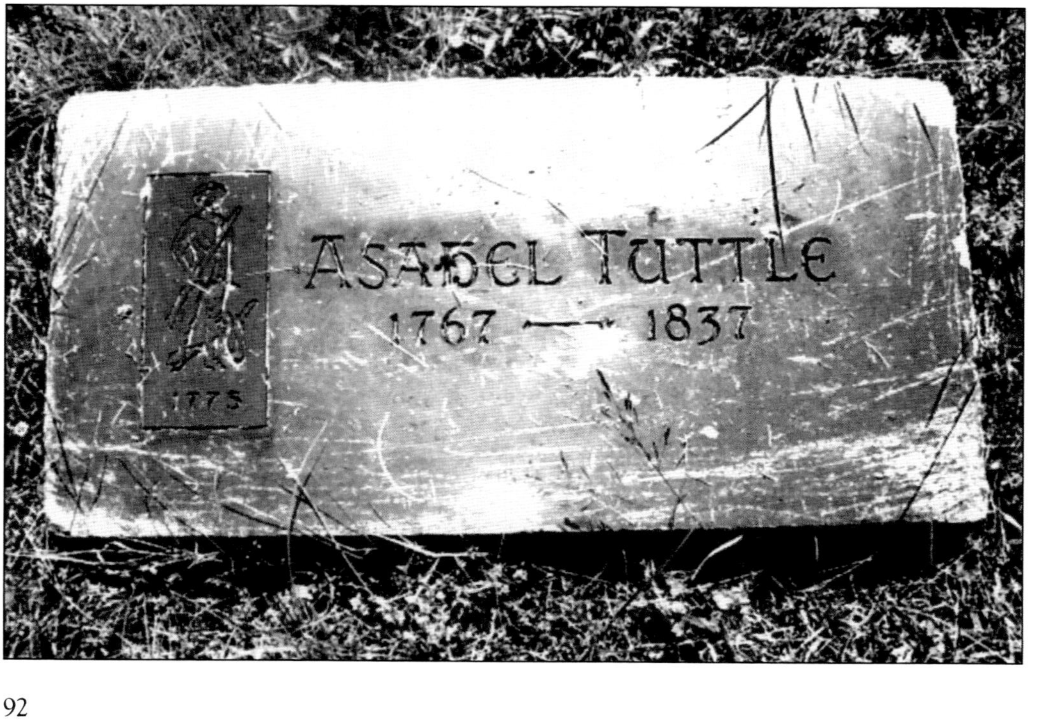

Charles A. Wolslangel (left) and Dan Chabek, a reporter from the *Cleveland Press,* examine the Fenton family gravestone. On it are the names of Gamaliel Fenton, a soldier of the Revolutionary War (January 31, 1763–August 19, 1849) and his wife, Elizabeth Webber (February 18, 1771–March 27, 1864). The Fenton Committee, the Pioneers Memorial Association, and the Early Settlers Association did not feel that a family stone was enough of a tribute to a soldier of the Revolutionary War. (Cleveland State University, Cleveland Press Collection.)

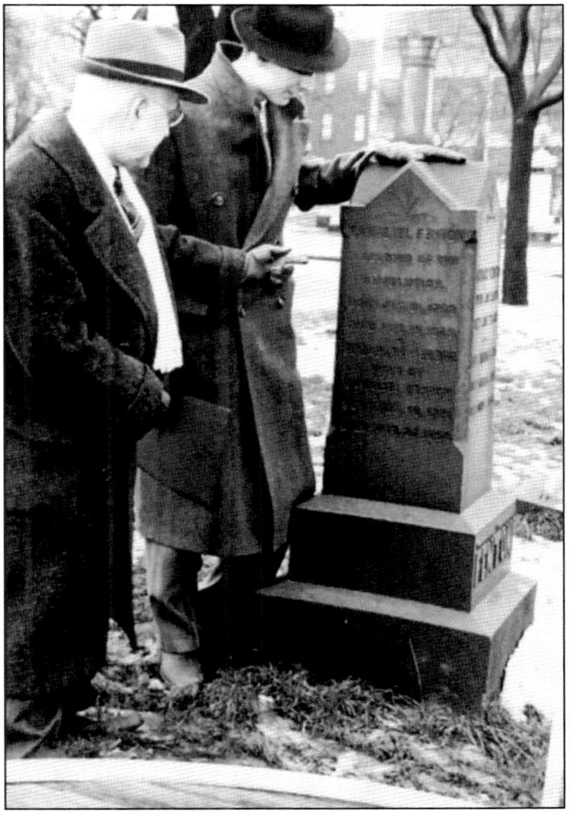

The effort of the Pioneer Memorial Association to improve Erie Street Cemetery and commission a monument to Gamaliel Fenton was successful. In this photograph, members of the Pioneers Memorial Association unveil the new Gamaliel Fenton monument. (Cleveland State University, Cleveland Press Collection.)

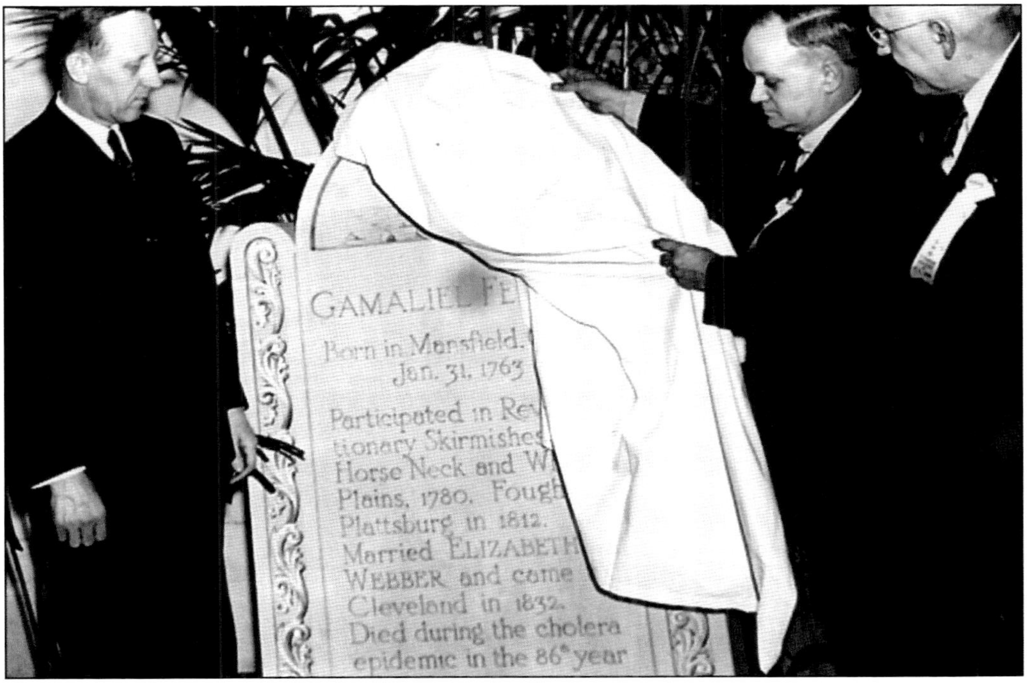

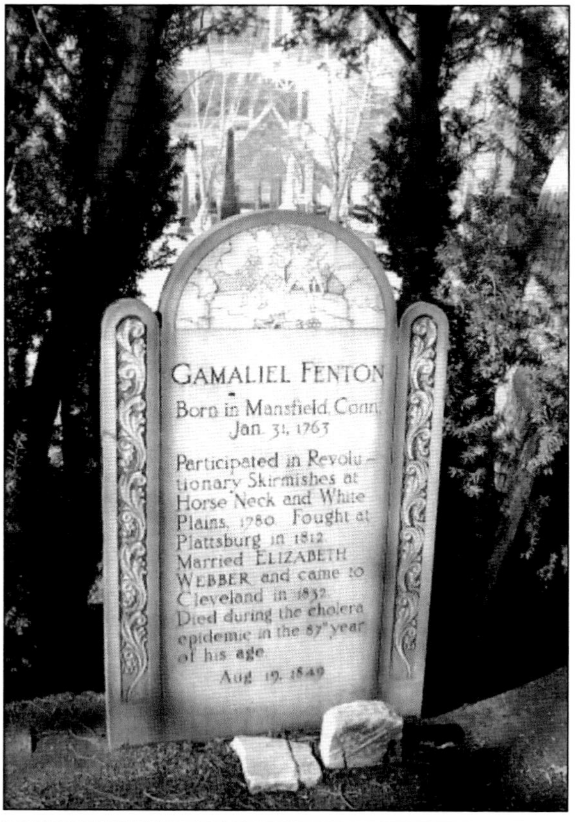

Walking through Erie Street Cemetery, one can often see people doing research. This is the Gamaliel Fenton gravesite. Fenton was born in Mansfield, Connecticut, on January 31, 1763. He enlisted in the Connecticut militia at age 17. His first assignment was the protection of the coast near New London, Connecticut. When his enlistment concluded, he returned home. He then reenlisted and fought in the Battle of Horse Neck in Connecticut on February 26, 1779, the Battle of White Plains in New York, and in New Jersey during the Revolutionary War. Fenton also fought in Plattsburgh, New York, during the War of 1812. In 1832, he and his wife, Elizabeth, and their two sons came to Cleveland. Fenton died on August 19, 1849, at the age of 86 during the cholera epidemic.

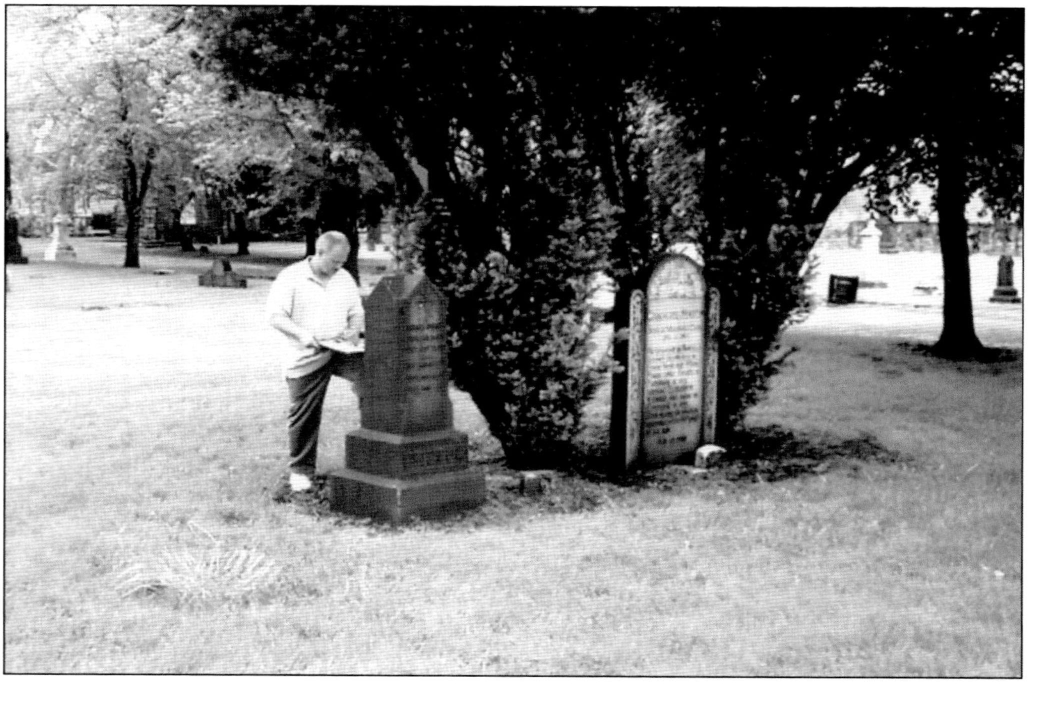

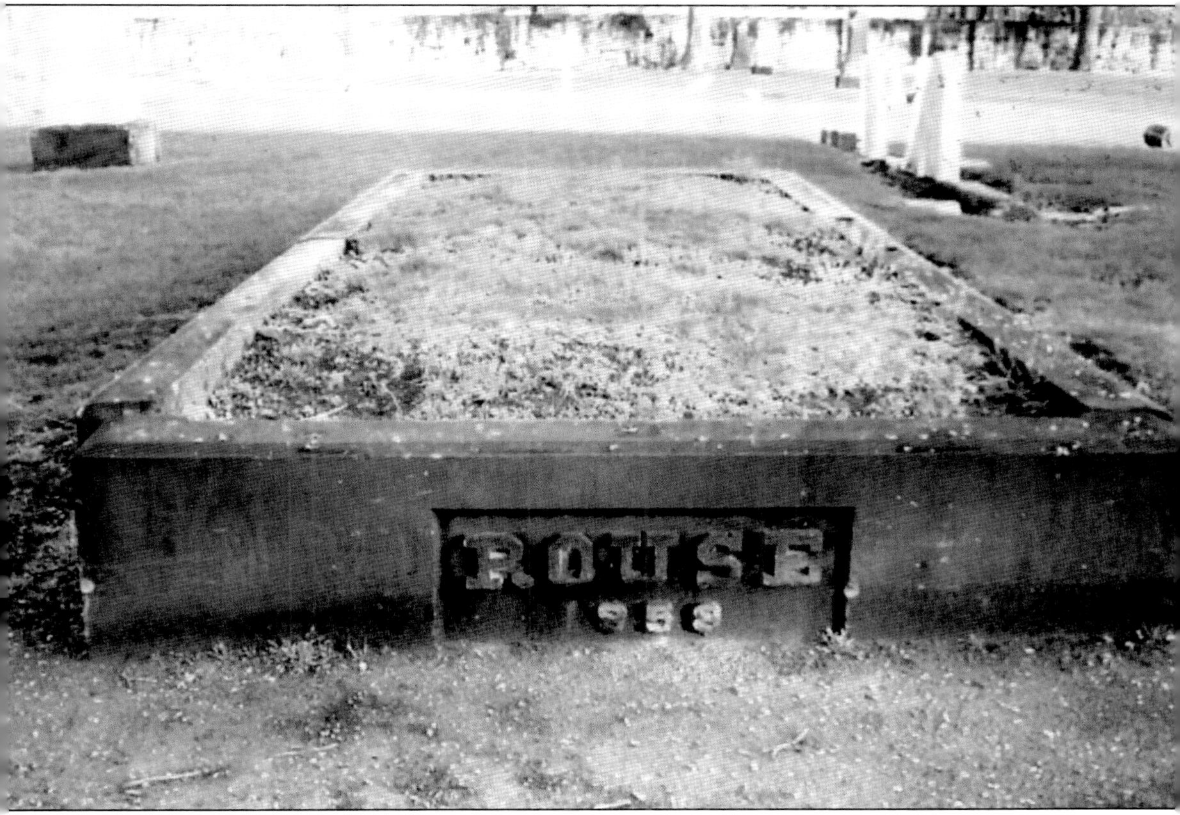

The unfinished mausoleum shown here was the Rouse gravesite. It was reported that construction of the mausoleum was so slow that the Rouse family became impatient. When the underground portion was finished, construction was brought to a halt. Benjamin Rouse (1795–1871) and his wife, Rebecca Elliott Rouse (1799–1887), are now buried in Lake View Cemetery. Benjamin served in the War of 1812 when he was only 17 years old. He married Rebecca in 1825, and he and his family came to Cleveland in 1830. Benjamin moved to Cleveland to spread the gospel, not as a minister but as a religious book distributor. He opened a small store for the sale of such books. He became the western agent of the American Sunday School Union and established the village's first Sunday school. He and Rebecca were founders of the First Baptist Church. Benjamin traveled around the country, presiding at religious services in churches that did not have regular pastors. He was also a builder and contractor.

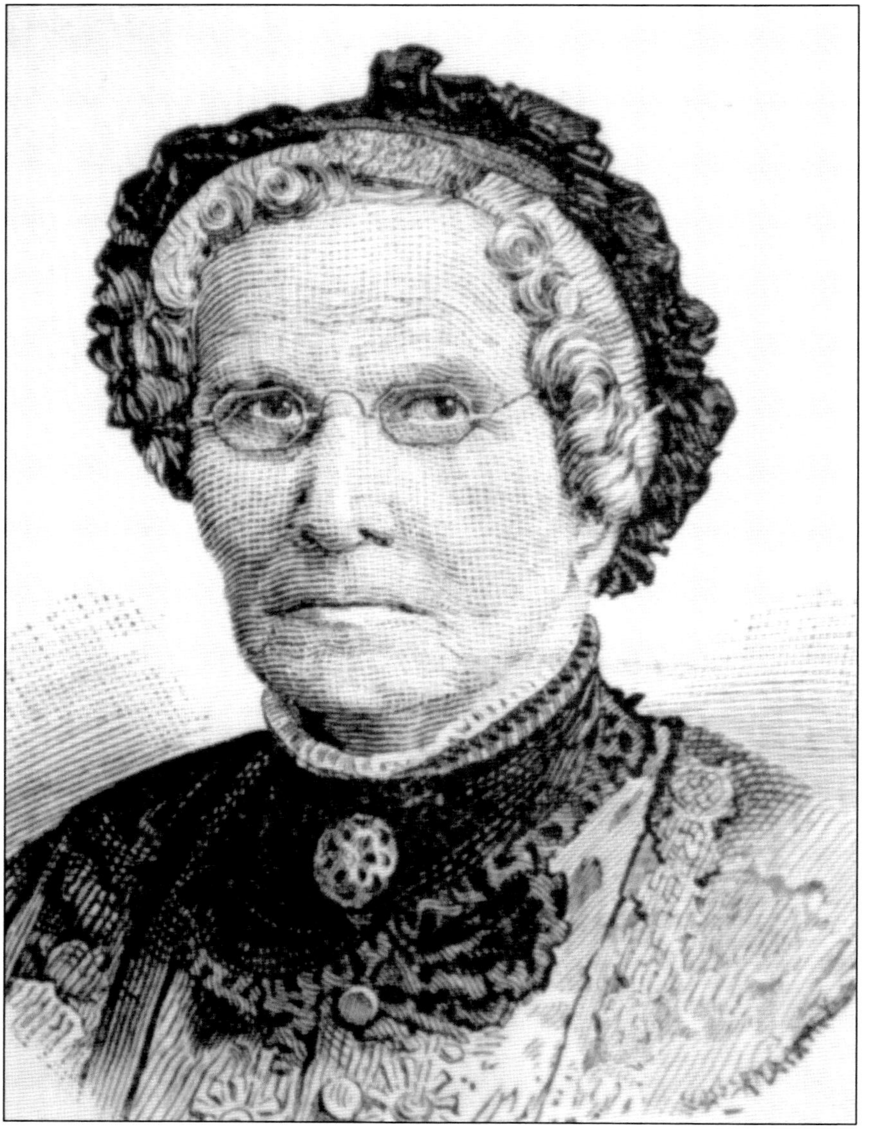

Rebecca Elliott Rouse, born in Salem, Massachusetts, came to Cleveland with her husband and three children in 1830. Upon their arrival in Cleveland, Rebecca and her husband, Benjamin Rouse, opened a religious bookstore. The Rouses were charter members of First Baptist Church, established in 1833. They were ardent temperance workers who tried to wipe out the heavy drinking they felt was infecting the town. Rebecca helped organize the Cleveland Ladies Temperance Society, and in 1842, she organized the Society of Martha Washington and the Dorcas Society to care for needy children and elderly or sick people. That work helped to establish the Cleveland Protestant Orphan Asylum. The Civil War brought national attention to Rebecca, who organized the Soldiers Aid Society that was headquartered in Cleveland but gave aid to soldiers throughout the nation. In 1861, she led an effort to establish the Ohio State Soldiers Home in Columbus. There is a bronze panel located in the Soldiers' and Sailors' Monument on Public Square commemorating Rebecca's efforts for soldiers during the Civil War. (Early Settlers Association.)

James Willis's (1838–1880) gravestone is a totally weathered, white marble, upright, military headstone. He was born in England in 1838. He served in the 1st Regiment of the Ohio Volunteer Light Artillery in the Civil War. The first Ohio Volunteer Light Artillery consisted of six companies. Of the six companies, four were from Cleveland: A, B, D, and E. Its commanding officer was Gen. James Barnett. Each company had but one gun (canon), making it only a six-gun battery. Barnett, with four guns, was stationed in Grafton, West Virginia, and fought at Laurel Hill. The military grave registration card also includes James Willis's service record. The Veterans Administration recently replaced the weathered gravestone with a new gray granite military headstone. Over time, it is hoped many more deteriorating gravestones will be replaced. (William Stark.)

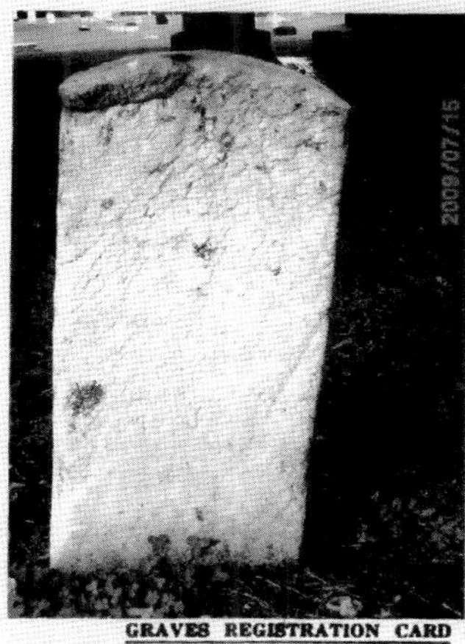

Totally weathered white marble, upright, military government headstone of Bugler James Willis (1838–Jan. 8, 1880) who served in the 1st Regiment, Ohio Volunteer Light Artillery in the Civil War.

A new gray granite upright military head stone from the Veterans Administration will replace it in 2010.

Below is a copy of his Graves Registration Card

GRAVES REGISTRATION CARD Cuyahoga Co.

Name: WILLIS JAMES
Address: 126 Broadway, Cleveland, Ohio
Date of Death: Jan. 8, 1880 — Place:
Cause: Debility — Date of Burial: Jan. 10, 1880
Date of Birth: 1838 — Place: England
Name of Cemetery: Erie — Location: Cleveland, Cuya.Co., O.
Lot No. 57 — Section No. 1 — Block No. — Grave No. 1 from N.
Marker: Flat — Upright X — None
Next of Kin: F.A.Willis (Name)

SERVICE RECORD Ohio Official Roster Vol. 10, Pages 371 & 373

War Served In: Civil War
Date Enlisted: 8-10-61 — Date Discharged: 4-1-62 — Serial No.
Branch of Service: Light Arty. — Rank: Bugler
1st.Bat.Ohio Volunteer Light Arty.

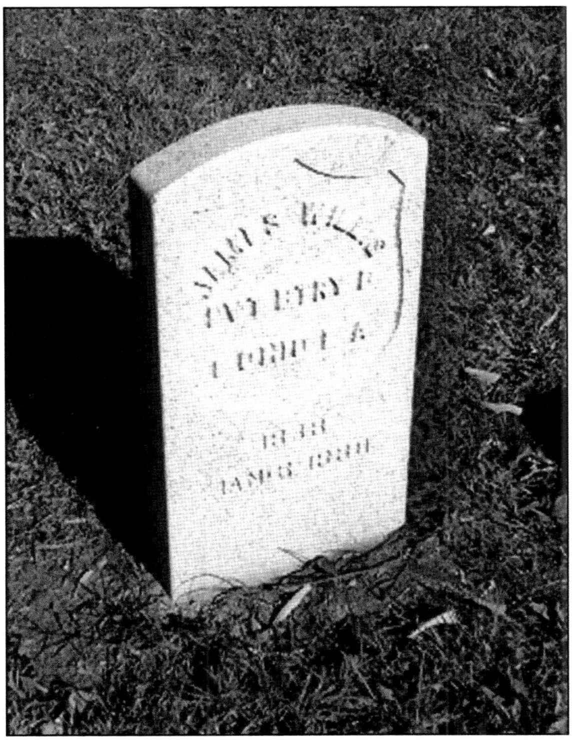

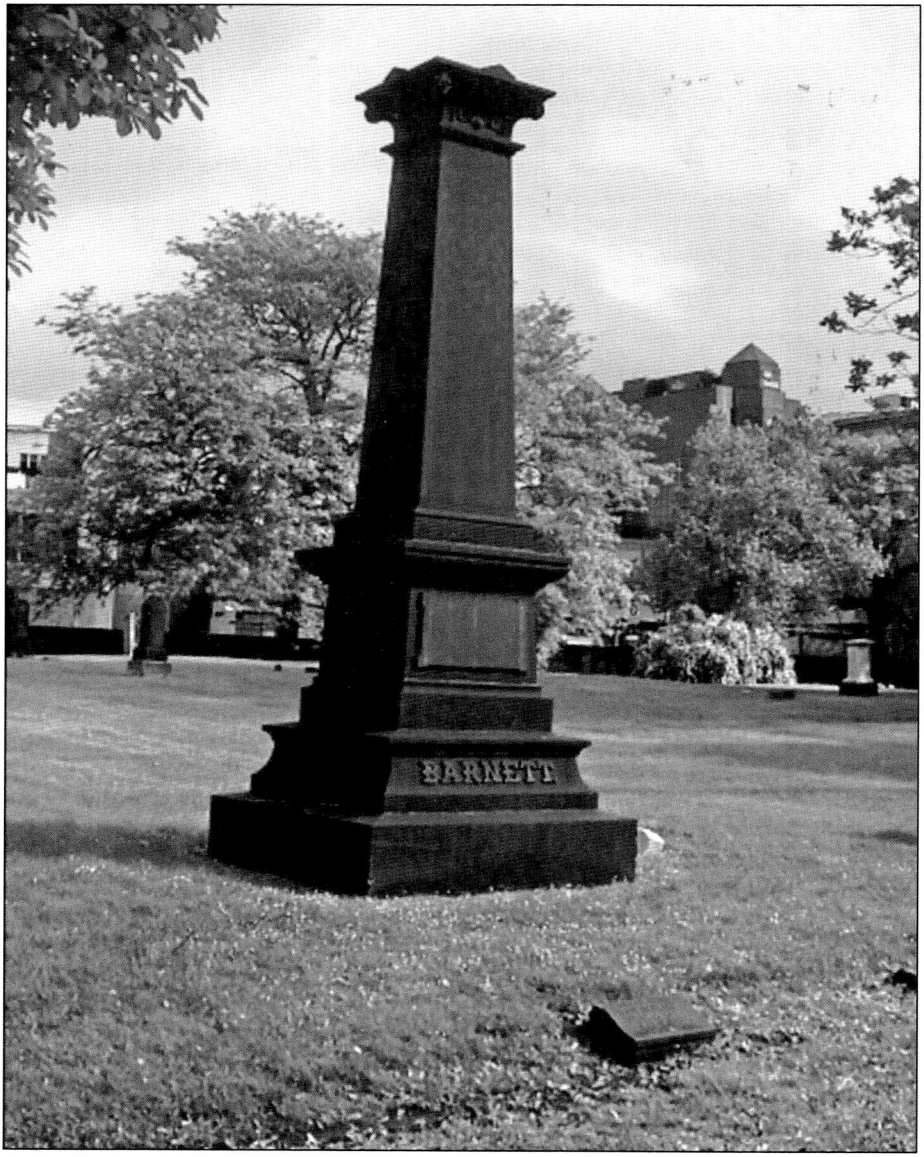

This is the Barnett monument and family gravesite. Melancton Barnett was born in May 1789 and left New England as a young man to go to western New York where many other New Englanders were relocating. He was encouraged to come to Cleveland by a friend who wanted Barnett to join him in a dry goods store business. He did so in 1826 and became very successful. His wife, Mary Clark (1792–1840), was born in New Lebanon, Connecticut. She was the daughter of Capt. Jerome Clark, a Revolutionary War hero who fought at the Battle of Bunker Hill. Their son James went on to distinguish himself as an officer in the Civil War and a business leader in Cleveland. Gen. James Barnett led a welcome by the Cleveland Grays for President Lincoln during his Cleveland visit. He lived to serve on the commission appointed in 1888 to plan and construct the Soldiers' and Sailors' Monument on Cleveland Public Square as a tribute to Union defenders during the Civil War. He joined the volunteer fire department as a very young man and continued as a member until his death.

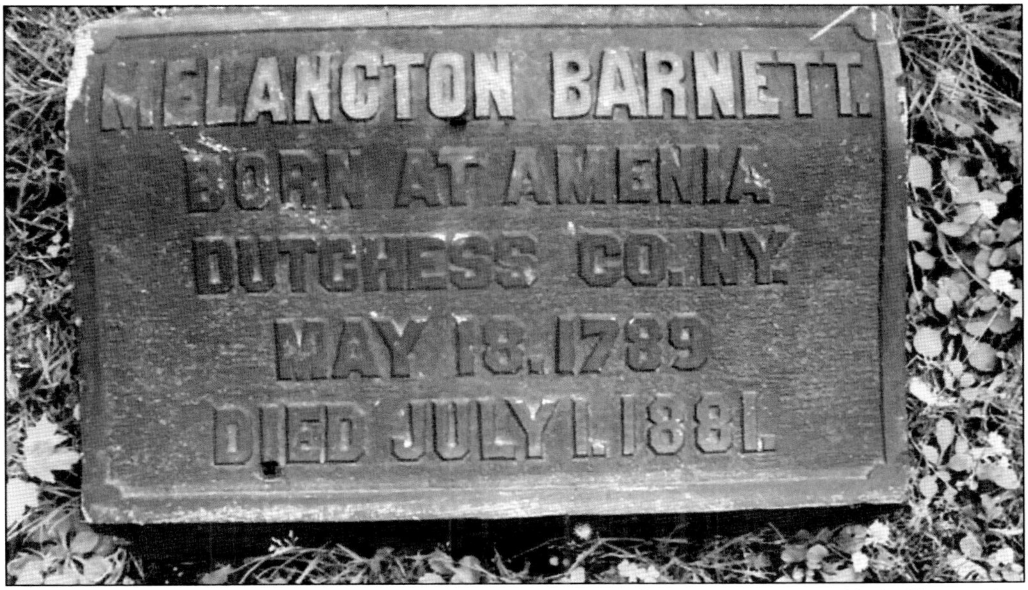

Melancton Barnett (1789–1881) was born in Amenia, Dutchess County, New York. He met his wife, Mary Clark, in Cherry Valley, New York. Both were children of the American Revolution. His civic life included service as a member of city council, justice of the peace, and Cuyahoga County treasurer. Their son Gen. James Barnett was a hero of the Civil War. After the war, James had a distinguished career in Cleveland civic and business affairs as a banker and president of the George Worthington Company, succeeding the founder of the company. More information about James Barnett and other Clevelanders can be found on the Internet under Cuyahoga County, Ohio, biographies.

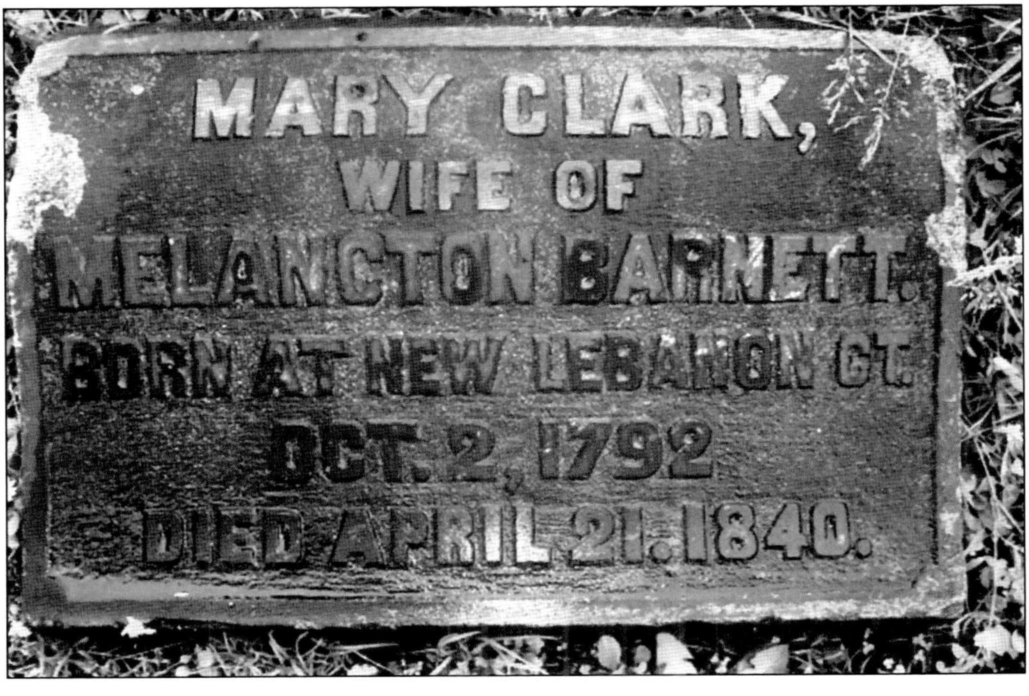

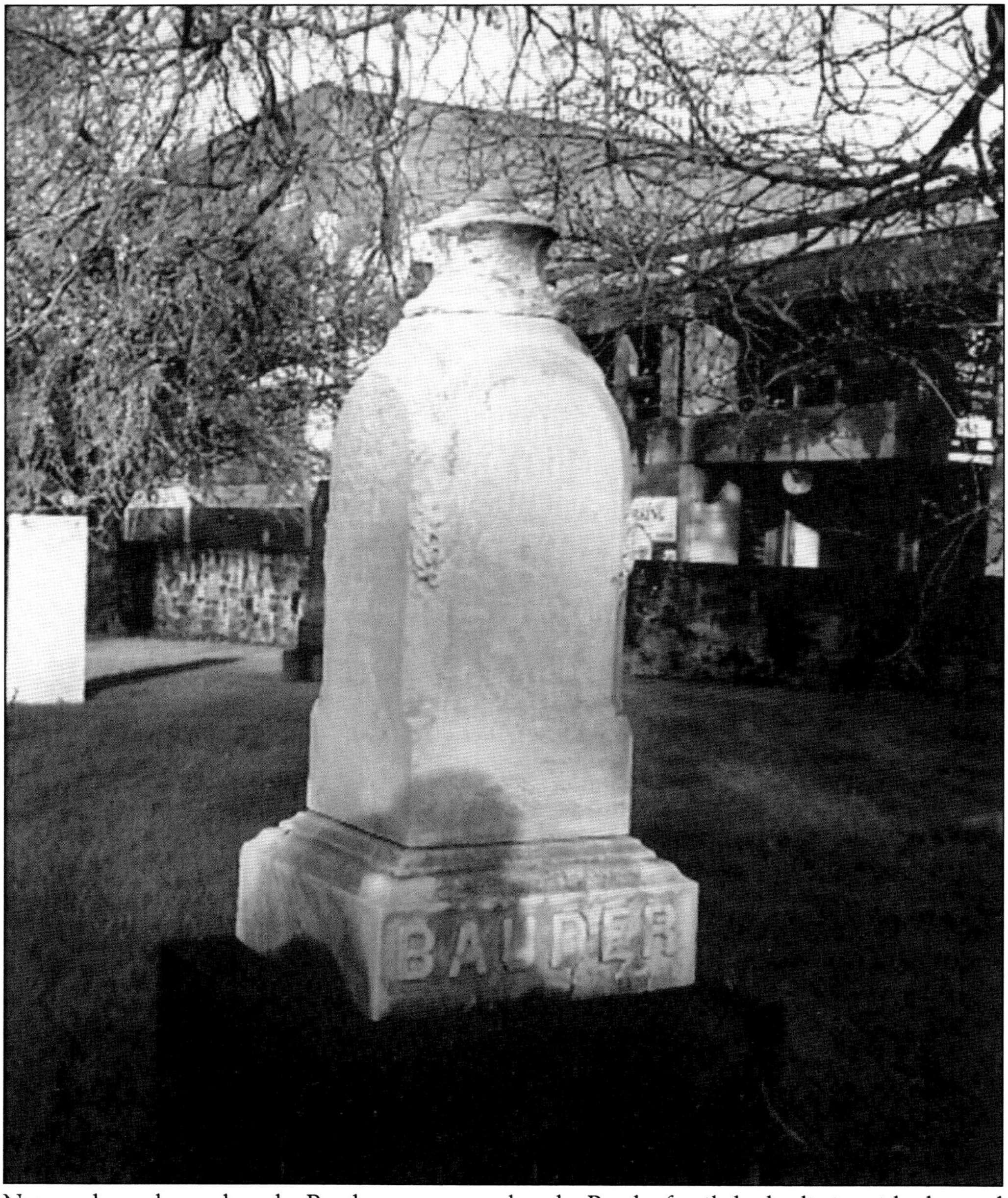

Not much can be read on the Bauder monument, but the Bauder family had a distinguished record for military service to the country that dates back to the Revolutionary War. Melgert and Peter Bauder served in Col. Jacob Klock's battalion in the Revolutionary War. Both men were captured by Indians and taken to Canada. They escaped, but their sister did not and she was never heard of again. Catherine Klock Bauder (1773–1853) was a real "daughter of the revolution," who actually came under fire during the war. Her father, Joseph Klock, was a soldier in the Revolutionary War, and her husband, Lodwick, and brother-in-law were soldiers in the War of 1812. Capt. Walter S. Bauder died in Cleveland from an illness contracted during the Spanish-American War. Catherine was the mother of three sons, Charles, Michael, and Levi, who were Cleveland pioneers. They were cabinetmakers until the Panic of 1857 destroyed their business.

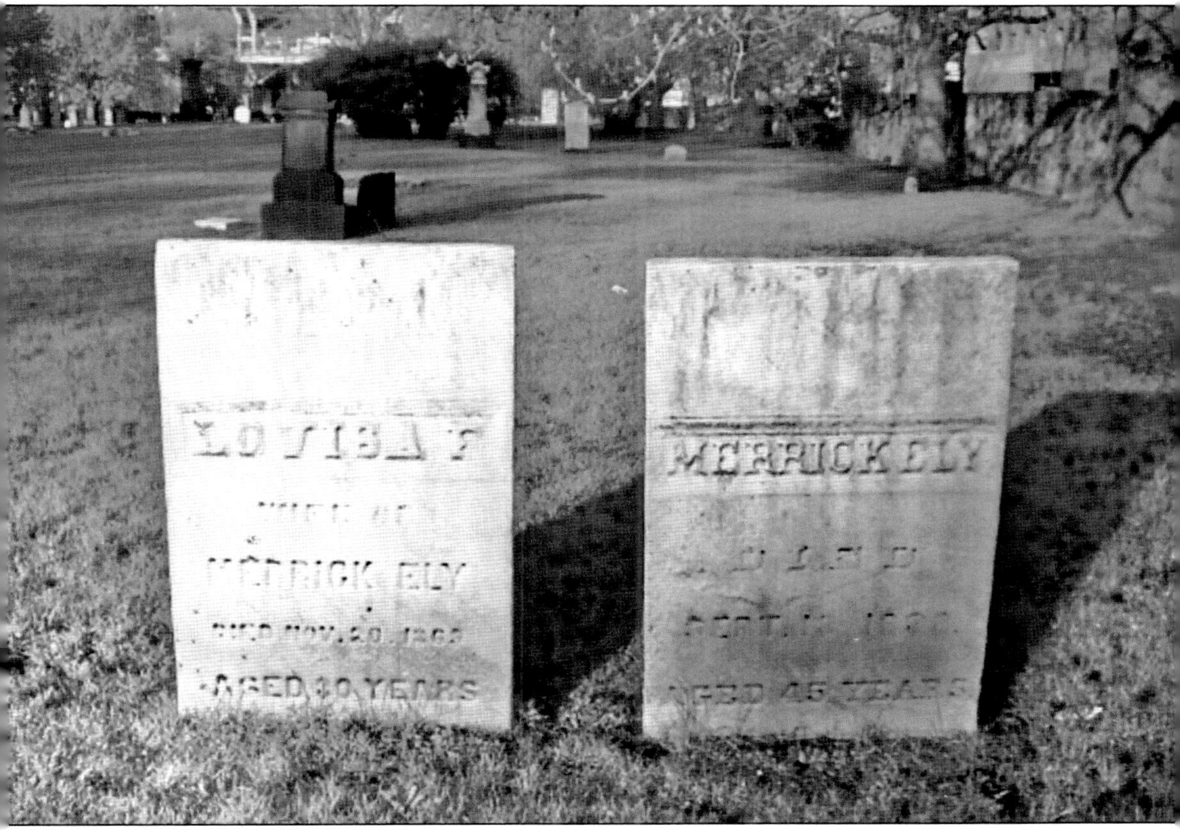

Two well-preserved gravestones mark the graves of Merrick and Louisa Ely. Merrick Ely's father, Lewis Ely, was a soldier in the Revolutionary War and came to Deerfield, Ohio, from Granville, Massachusetts. Louisa, Merrick's wife, was born in Blanford, Massachusetts, but moved to Deerfield, Ohio, when she was a young girl. Her father, Elisha Farnum, was also a Revolutionary War soldier. Before Merrick married, he and his brother had a general store in Deerfield. Merrick was a major in the state militia, and both he and William H. Otis carried mail from Pittsburgh to Cleveland. This was a passion that called him to Washington, DC, two or three times a year. In Deerfield, Ohio, Merrick and his wife raised a son and four daughters. In 1834, they purchased a farm on what is today Kinsman Road, about five miles from Public Square. They also had business interests in Cleveland. Merrick died in 1838, only four years after reaching Cleveland at the age of 45. All of the Ely children became schoolteachers; their son served in the Civil War.

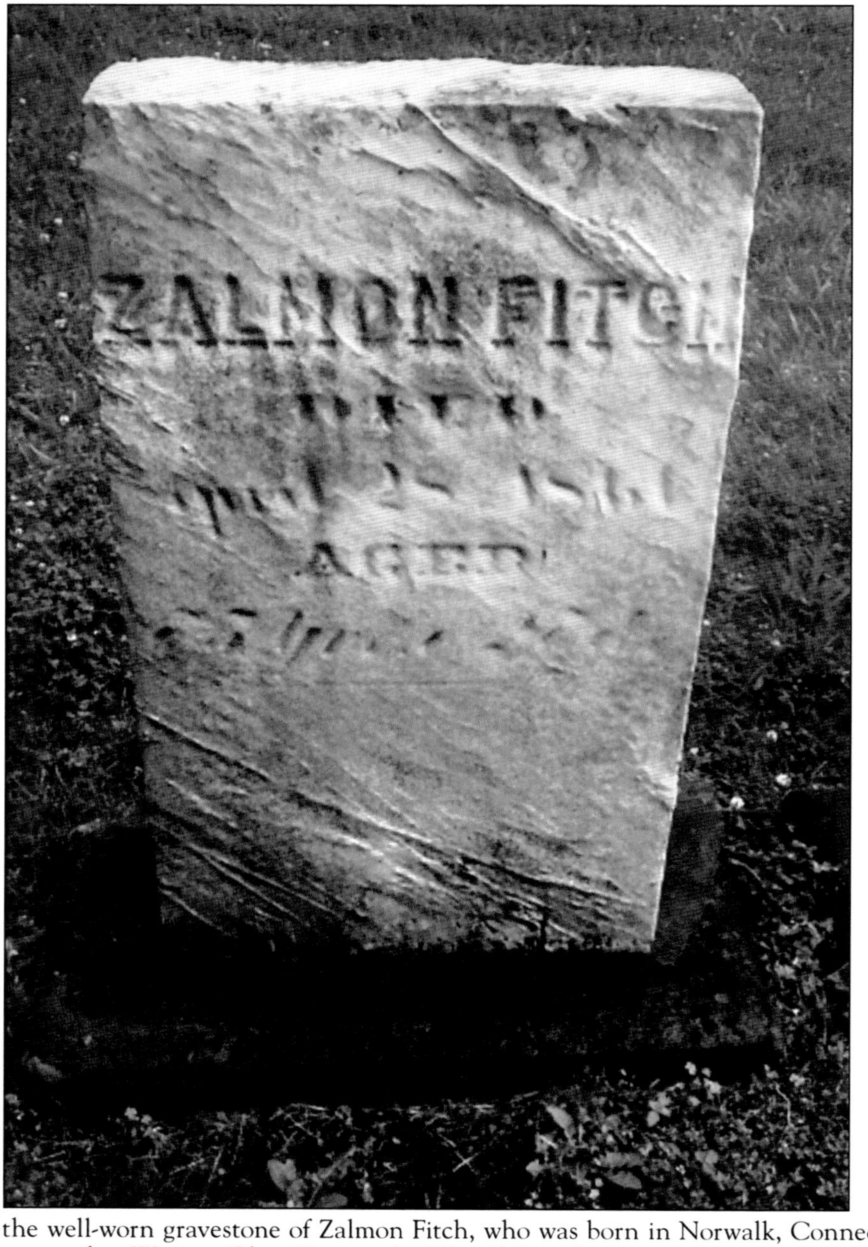

This is the well-worn gravestone of Zalmon Fitch, who was born in Norwalk, Connecticut, and later moved to Warren, Ohio. During the War of 1812, he served under Maj. Gen. Elijah Wadsworth while defending the Ohio frontier. Wadsworth was a captain in the Revolutionary War and became a major general in the War of 1812. He was also from Warren. After the war, Fitch became a cashier in the first bank in the Western Reserve, the Western Reserve Bank, which was established in 1813 and located in Warren. Fitch eventually became the bank's president. He was a leading figure in financial circles. When he came to Cleveland in 1838 at the age of 51, it was said that he straightened out the Bank of Cleveland, which ran into difficulties during the panic of 1837 that was caused by the collapse of the Cleveland real estate boom. In his later years, Fitch became a partner in George Williams and Company, a private banking and brokerage firm.

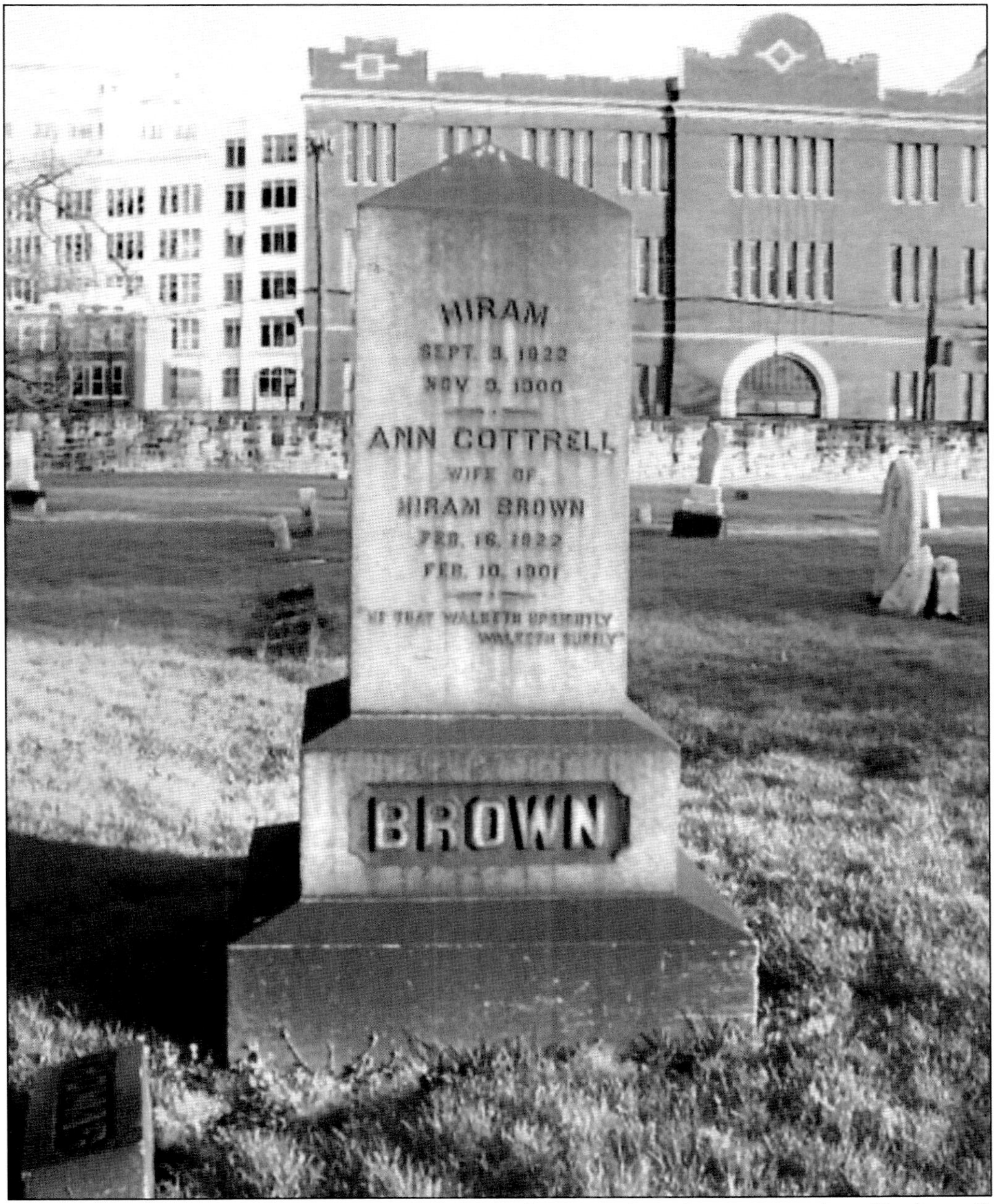

Hiram Brown enlisted in the Union army on November 28, 1861, and was mustered out (discharged) on June 27, 1863, due to a disability. He was a member of Company K of the 2nd and 6th Cavalry. He was born September 3, 1822, and died November 8, 1900. His wife, Ann Cottrell, came from a family of early settlers who lived on Hill Street, which was called Newburgh Bluff Road, a location near what is today East Seventy-first Street and Broadway Avenue. Newburgh Bluff Road became the principal road of early settlers on their way to Cleveland. Many of those pioneers moved back from Cleveland to the highlands of Newburgh and built homes near the road to escape the mosquitoes that infested the flat land along the Cuyahoga River and brought disease to their family. However, by the 1930s Newburgh Bluff Road was almost completely deserted.

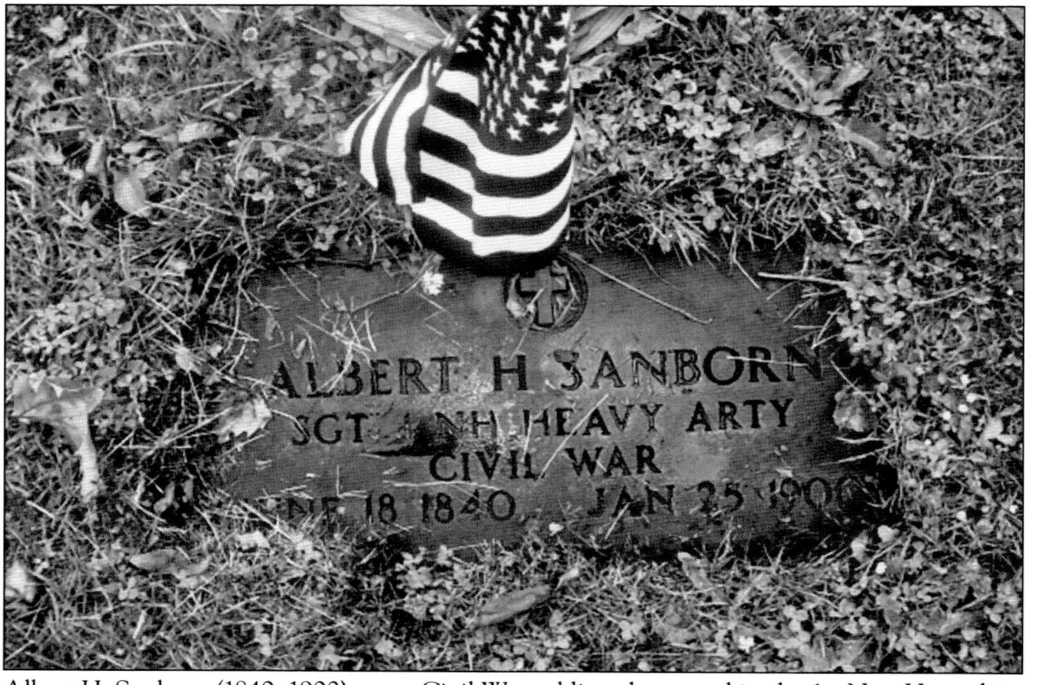

Albert H. Sanborn (1840–1900) was a Civil War soldier who served in the 1st New Hampshire Heavy Artillery Volunteer Regiment. The regiment filled its ranks within two weeks of President Lincoln's call for 70,000 men on April 15, 1861. Albert Sanborn came to Cleveland from New Hampshire and returned to his home state to serve in the war. After the war, he returned to Cleveland. For more information, visit the 1st New Hampshire Heavy Artillery Regiment Roster online. The Sanborn family retained its residence in Cleveland. Next to Albert Sanborn's grave is that of Mayry E. Spooner (1892–1914), wife of Calvin B. Sanborn. She was the daughter of Bryon Spooner, who lived in Toledo before coming to Cleveland.

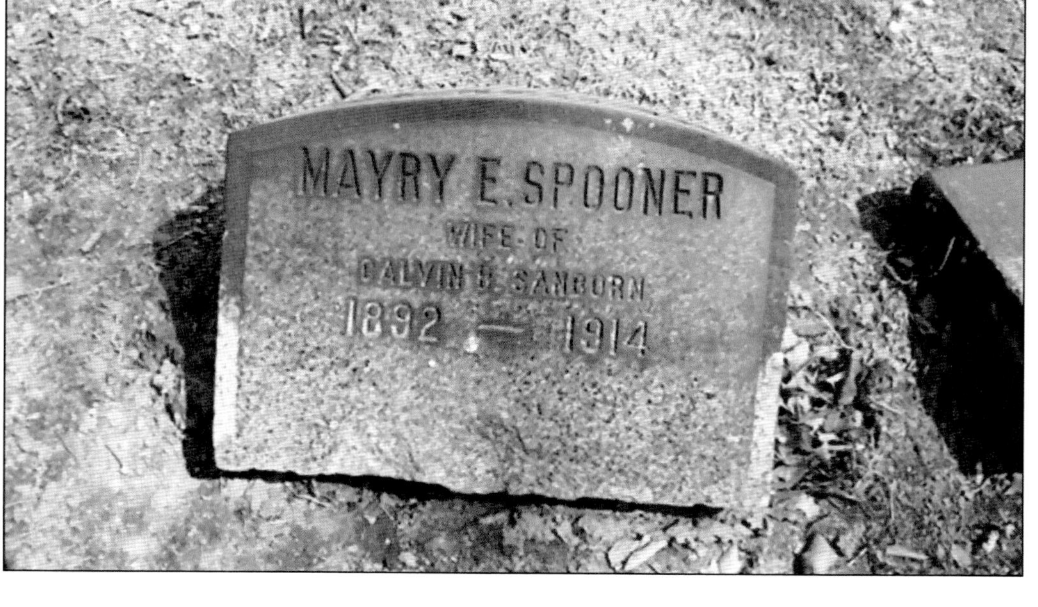

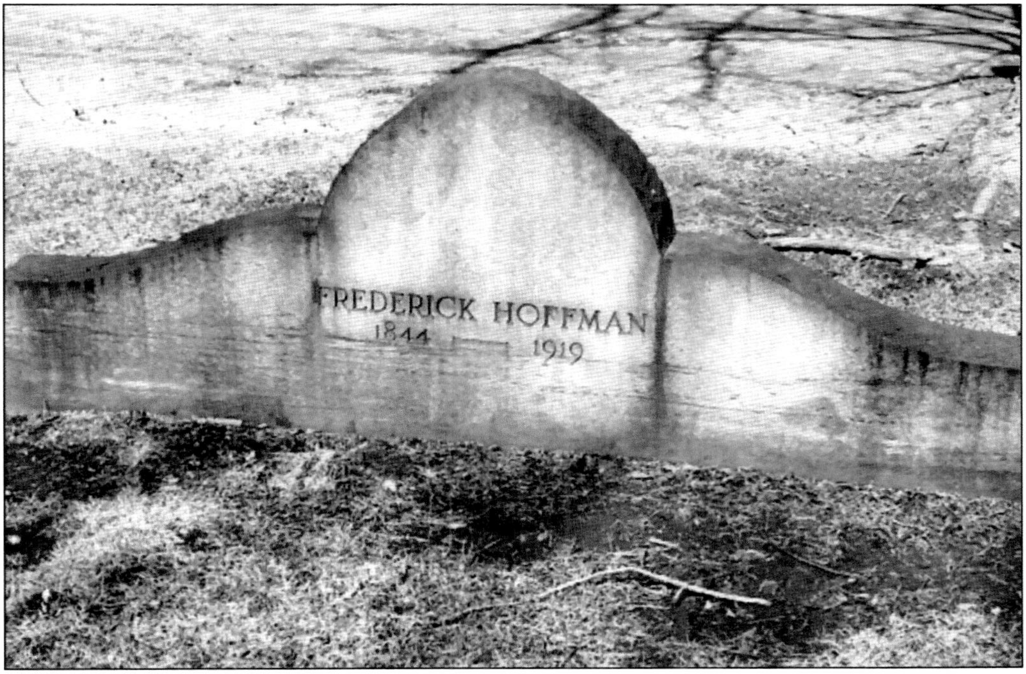

Frederick Hoffman died on November 28, 1991, at the age of 75. His residence was at 3802 Central Avenue. He was the son of the late Henry Hoffman, and he passed away at Charity Hospital. Funeral services were held at Koebler's Parlors located at 2340 East Fifty-fifth Street. Hoffman is listed as a soldier in Company B of the 150th Ohio Infantry during the Civil War. That infantry was mustered out on August 23, 1864.

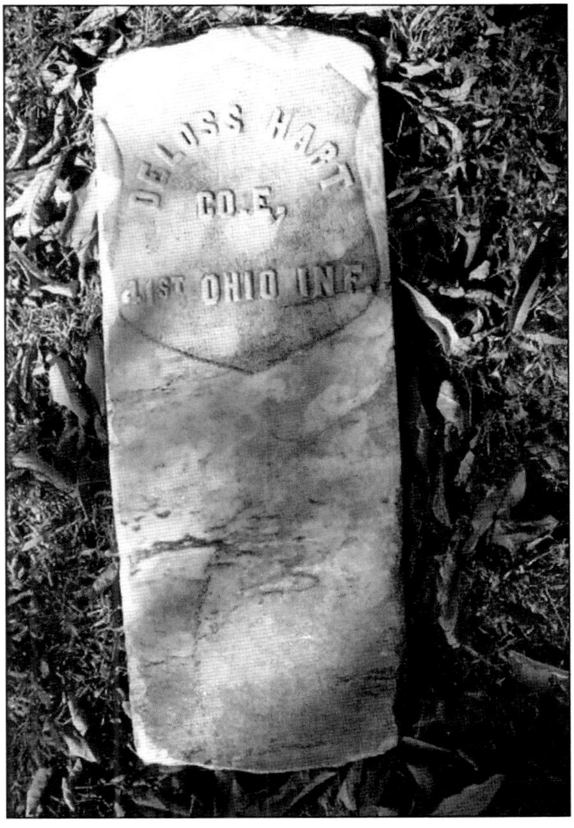

The Deloss Hart marble military stone was upright and properly set, but today it lies flat on the ground. The stone reads, "Company E, 41st Ohio Volunteer Infantry." There is no grave registration card maintained at the Cleveland Public Library for Hart, and he is not listed in Chrisfield Johnson's book *History of Cuyahoga County*, published in 1879. Hart is a mystery that will require further study.

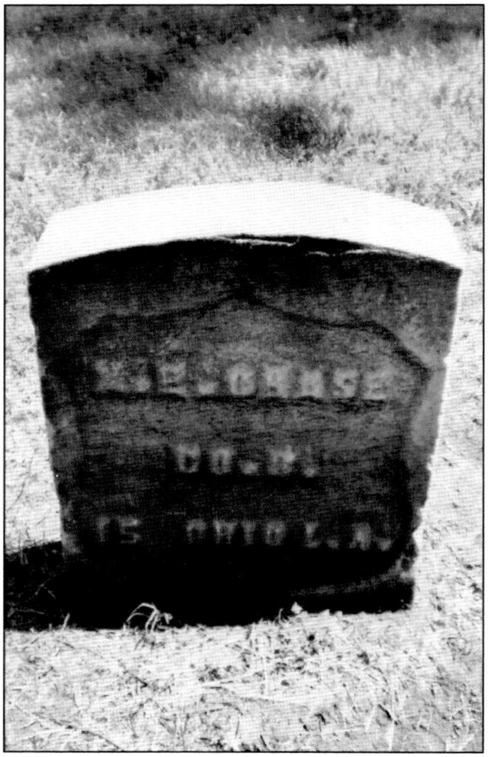

This is the government, upright, white marble military headstone of Nathaniel E. Chase (1846–1891), who served in Battery B, 15th Independent Battery, Ohio Volunteer Light Artillery. The stone reads, "N. E. Chase, Co. B., 15 Ohio L.A."

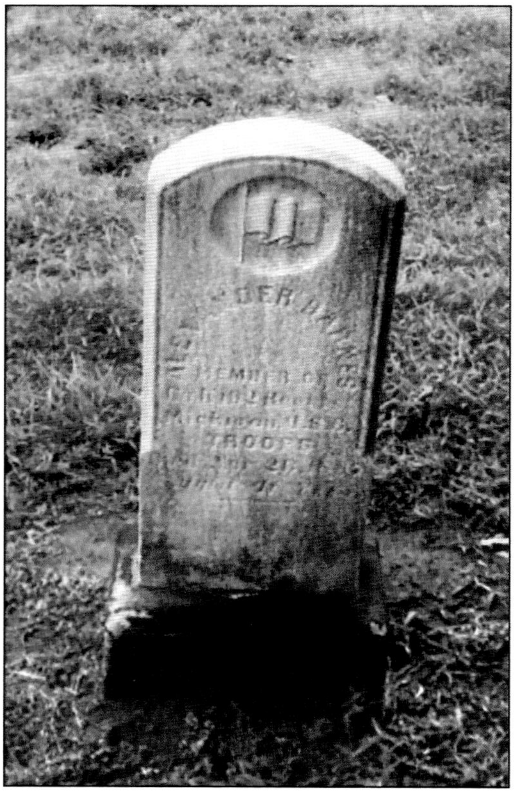

Pictured here is a civilian gravestone with a military motif. Alexander Barnes (1846–1887) served in Company B, 102nd Infantry Regiment, US Colored Troops with the rank of corporal in the Civil War. Over time, more information about the lives of the people buried in Erie Street Cemetery will be gathered so the full story of their contributions to the city can become a part of Cleveland's rich history.

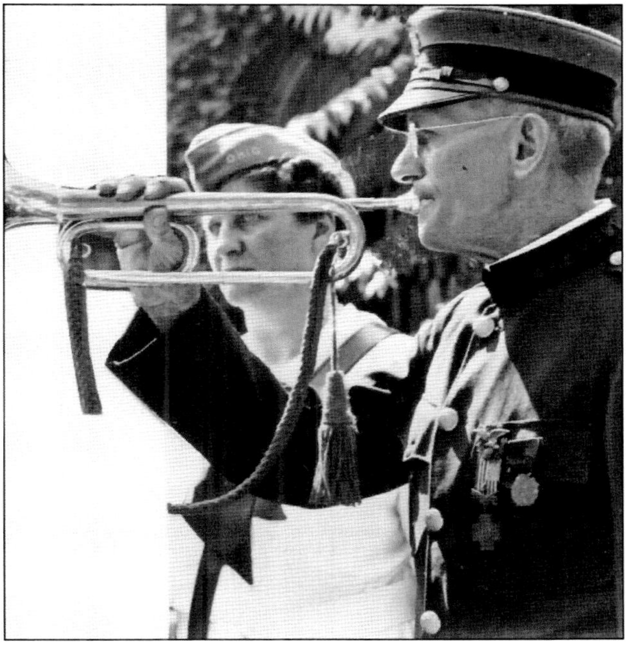

A tribute to veterans and a flagpole now fill the space where the Erie Street Cemetery chapel once stood. A flagpole was erected and the area was beautified by the Disabled American Veterans, American Legion, and AMVETS. A program was held on Memorial Day 1955 to commemorate the site, during which a plaque was presented that reads, "Dedicated to the veterans who served, lived, and died for their Country." (Cleveland State University, Cleveland Press Collection.)

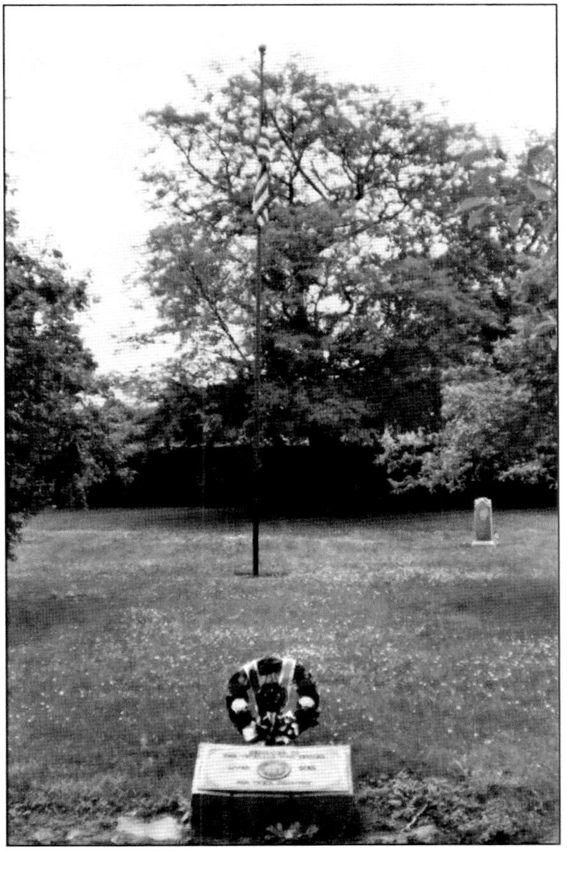

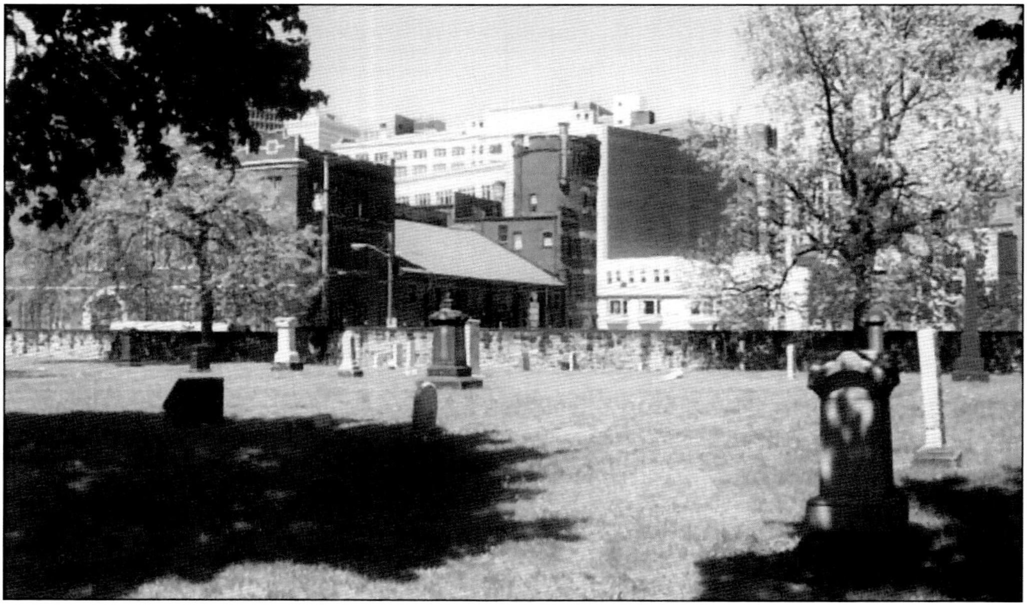

Overlooking Erie Street Cemetery behind its sandstone wall, one can see the Cleveland Grays Armory. It was February 22, 1837—George Washington's birthday—that a group of young men got together to form a private military company they called the Cleveland City Guard. The adoption of a gray colonial-style uniform prompted the name change to the Cleveland Grays. By the mid-19th century, most American cities of the east had their own volunteer militias. Cleveland became the first city west of the Allegheny Mountains to have its own city guard. Its members have served in every American conflict since the Grays were founded. The armory and museum has served as the headquarters of the Grays since it was built in 1893. Today it is the location of many social and community programs. The Grays have served with distinction in many civic events at Erie Street Cemetery.

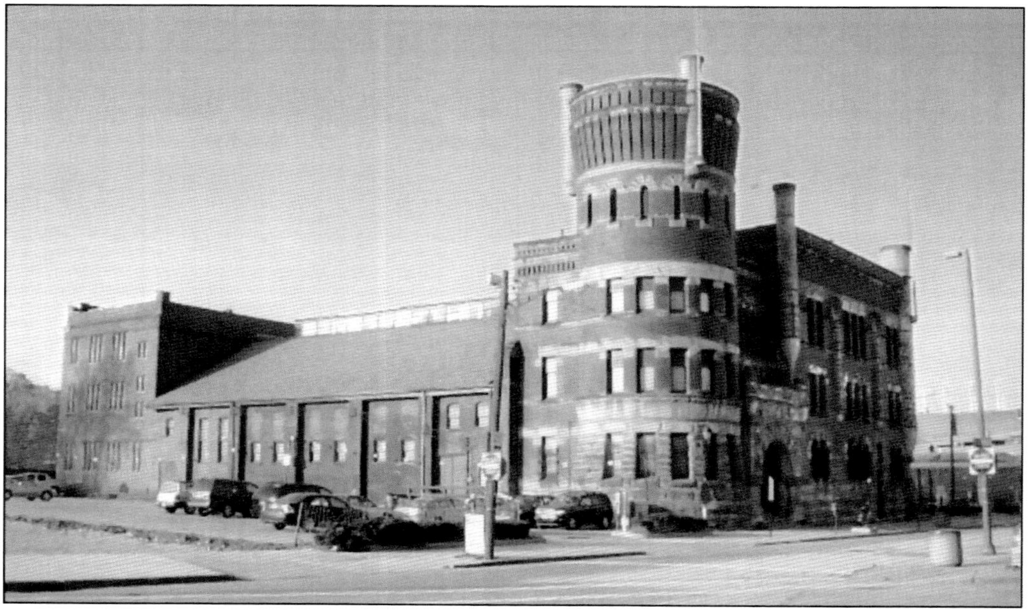

Four

Now and in the Future

If Erie Street Cemetery is to remain a place of history, restoration is essential to the gatehouse and other structures, as well as the gravestones that continue to deteriorate as time goes on. The last major improvement effort was in 1939 and 1940. In 2009, the Ohio Cemetery Alliance, with the support of the Early Settlers Association of the Western Reserve, placed an Ohio Historical Marker just to the north of the Gothic entrance to the cemetery on East Ninth Street. The Cuyahoga Community College Honors Program students undertook a cleanup of the grounds in preparation for the historic marker ceremony. An ongoing, long-term partnership between the Cuyahoga Community College Honors Program, the Early Settlers Association, and the City of Cleveland seeks to facilitate assistance in the maintenance of the cemetery, provide educational service regarding its historic significance, and create a learning site in downtown Cleveland.

The study of Erie Street Cemetery will continue through the improvement of records that often are found to be incomplete or incorrect since, as earlier stated, no records were kept before 1840. Ohio did not enact a statute to require birth, death, and marriage registration until 1856 and 1857. A third law went into effect in December 1908 that set up the current record-keeping system in Ohio.

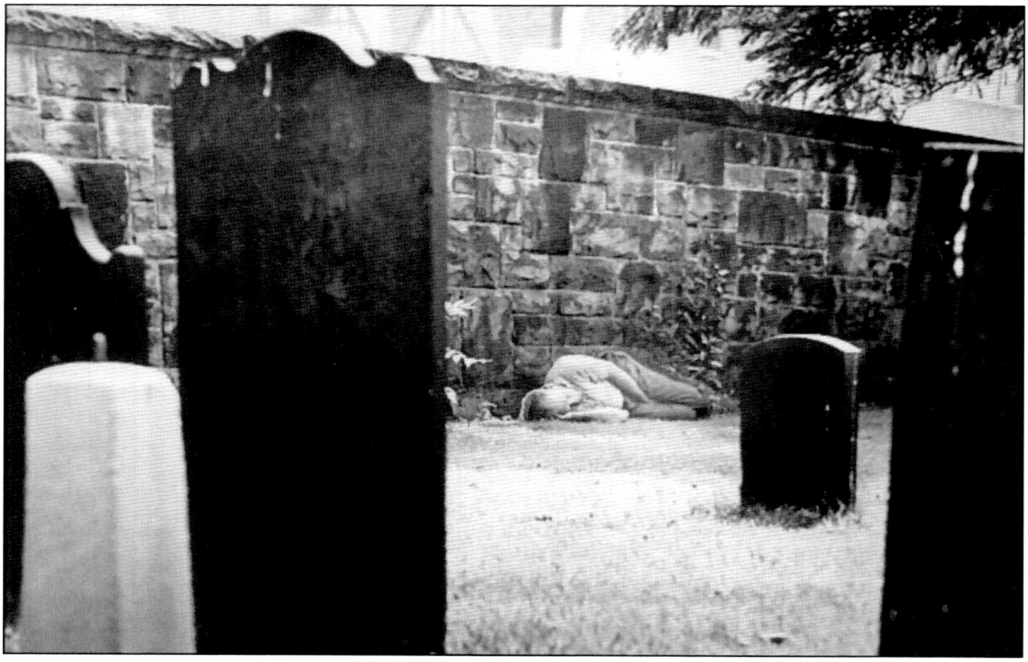

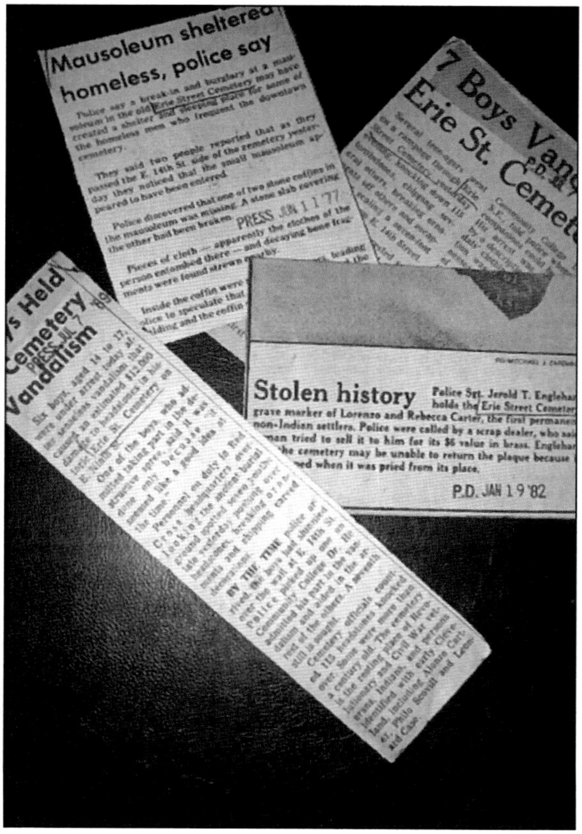

It looks like some people just cannot wait for their headstone. Over the years, the homeless or those who had too much to drink have used Erie Street Cemetery as their bedroom. As seen in the newspaper reports below, Erie Street Cemetery has been plagued by vandalism. Today, the city has established a security patrol that rides bicycles and keeps people from using the grounds inappropriately. (Cleveland State University, Cleveland Press Collection.)

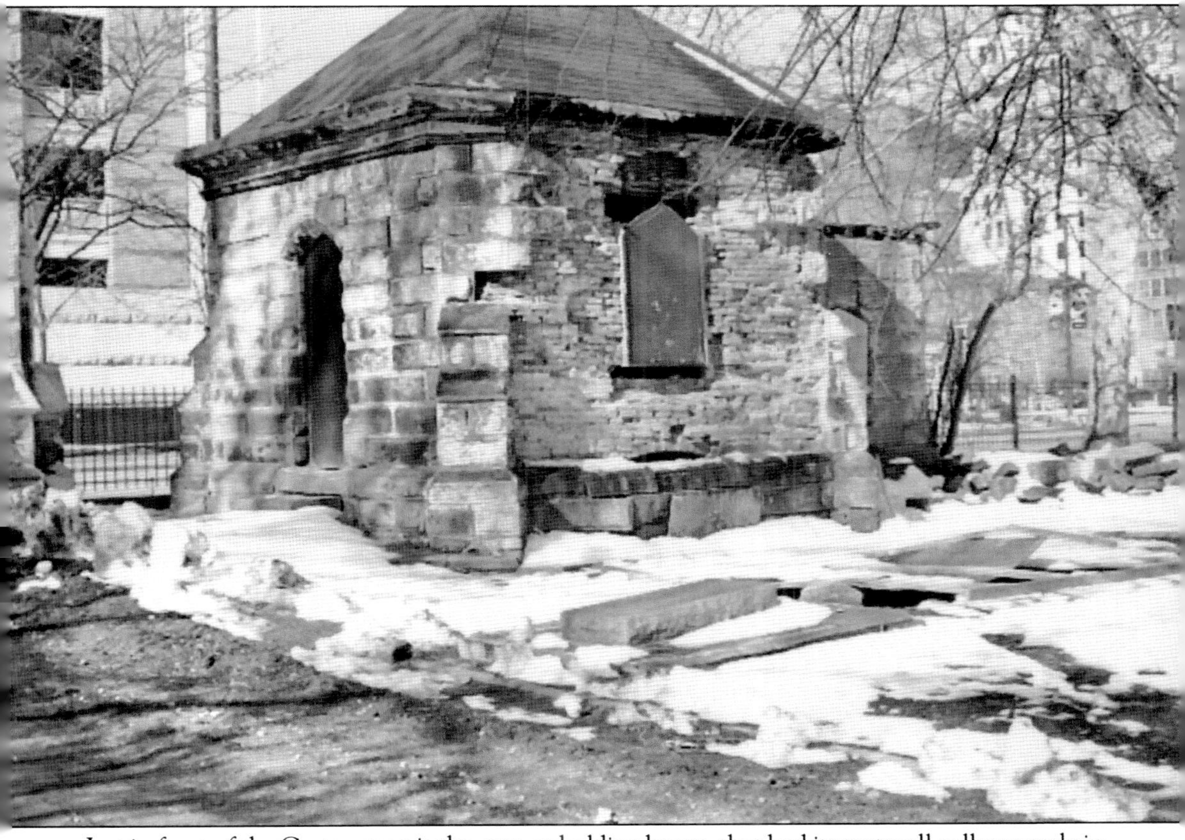

Just in front of the Carter grave is the gate, or holding house, that had its east wall collapse early in 2009. Hopefully it will be rebuilt in the near future. In August 2010, legislation was introduced in Cleveland City Council for capital improvement funding for assessment and repair of the archway and gatehouse of the Erie Street and Monroe Cemeteries. A number of construction groups have also pledged their assistance to the restoration efforts. The goal of the Early Settlers Association and the Honors Program of Cuyahoga Community College is to restore the gravestones of people like John Willey, Cleveland's first mayor; Peter Weddell; Henry Everett, also a mayor of Cleveland; and many others who can help tell the story of the city's history.

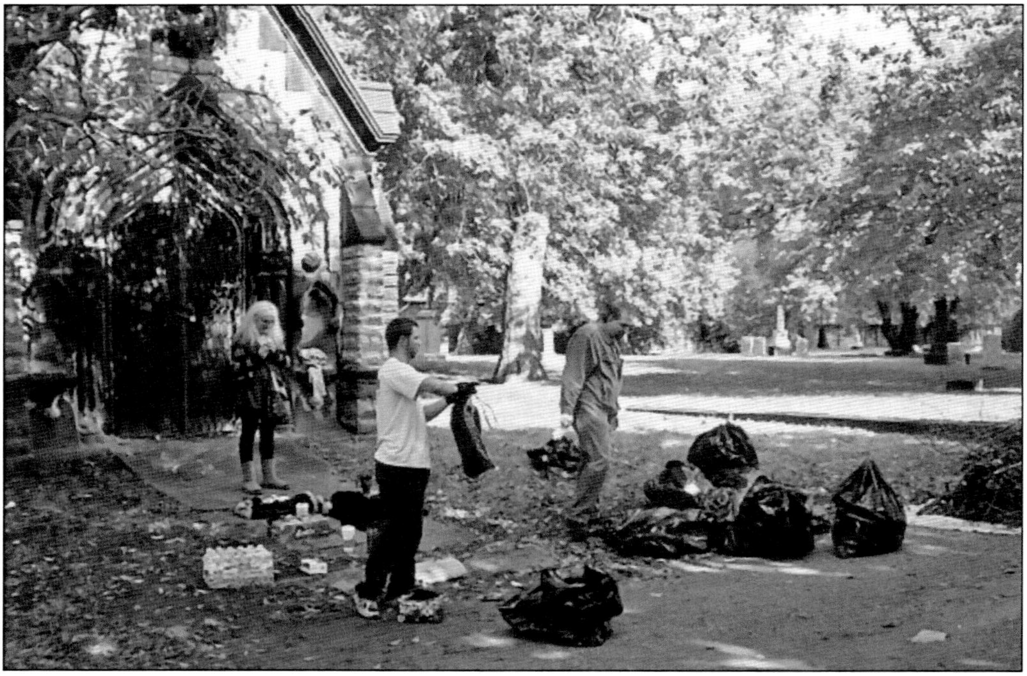

There is a need for volunteers to assist in the cleanliness and preservation of all of Cleveland's cemeteries. The photograph above is of the cleanup of Erie Street Cemetery prior to the dedication of a historic marker.

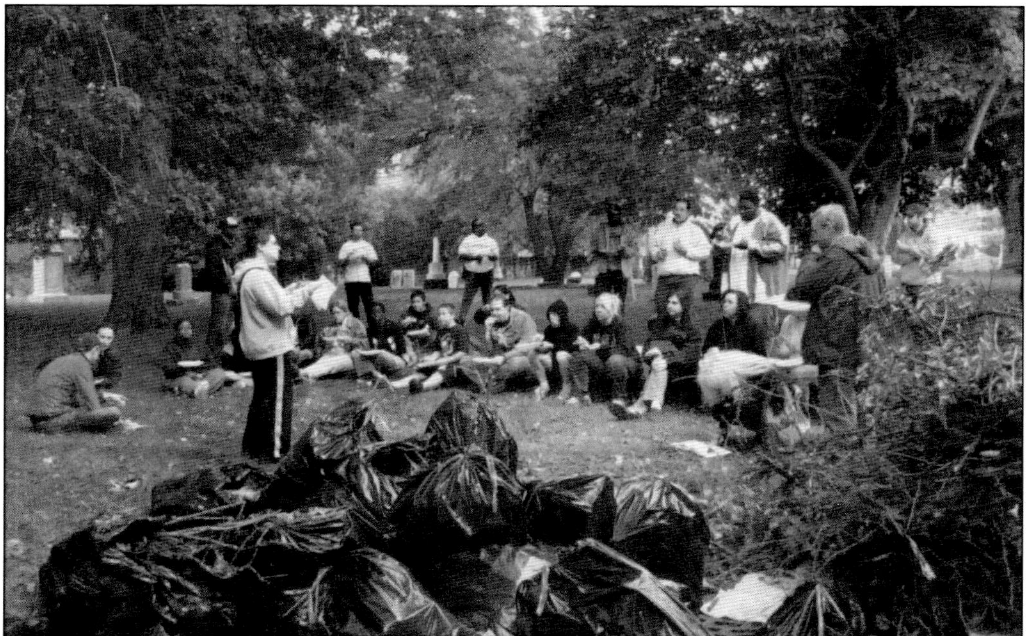

Students and faculty from Cuyahoga Community College Honors Program take a break to hear a lecture on the history of Erie Street Cemetery.

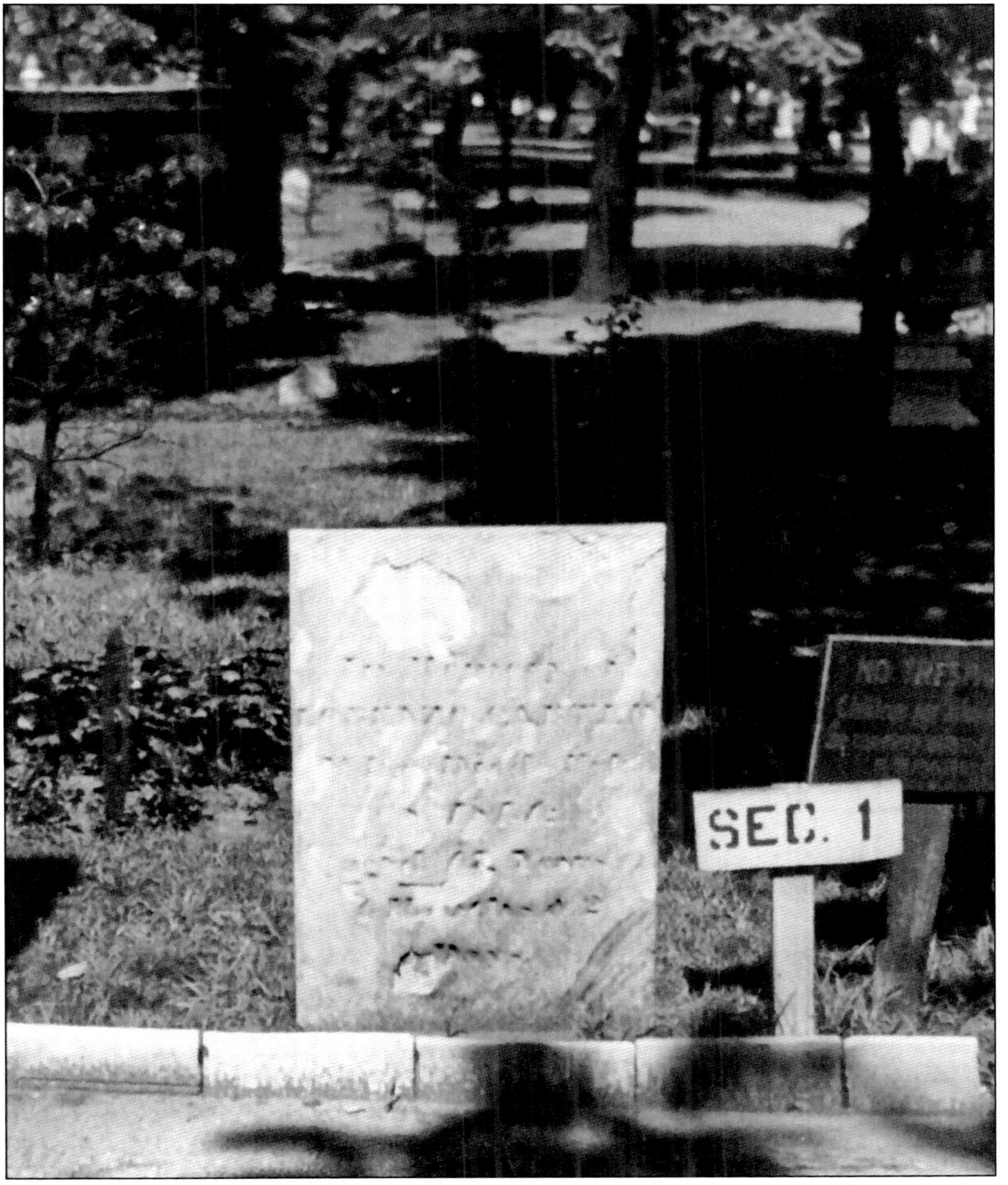

When Lorenzo and Rebecca Carter's graves were moved from the Ontario Street Cemetery, they were appropriately reburied in section I of the Erie Street Cemetery, near the entrance. This was a proper location for the graves because the Carters are honored as Cleveland's first permanent settlers. Seen here is the gravesite of the Carters as it appeared in June 1954. Due to threats of closing the Erie Street Cemetery, lots for the Carters were purchased in section l, lot 76 of the Lake View Cemetery. The lots are vacant today; their bodies were never moved. Records of the Erie Street Cemetery are kept at the Western Reserve Historical Society and Highland Park Cemetery, but those records are incomplete. No records were kept for the cemetery before 1840. The first improvement to the Carter gravesite came in 1938 when a bronze marker was dedicated at an event held on July 22, the anniversary of the founding of Cleveland. (Michelle Day.)

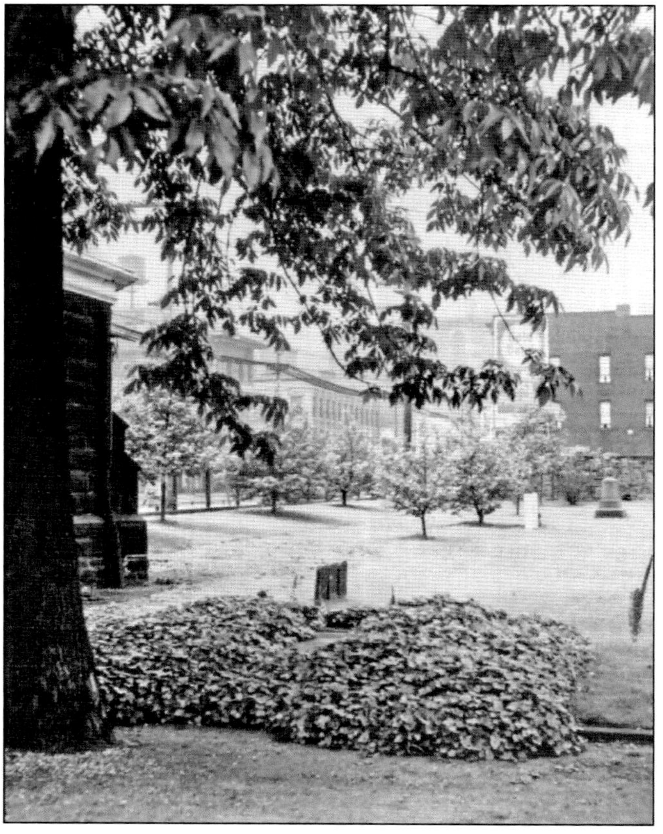

At left is a photograph of the Carter gravesite as it appeared in the 1960s, overgrown with ivy; the bronze plaque that placed there in 1938 was gone. It was damaged in an attempt to steal it. Below shows preparation for the unveiling of the new Carter gravestone on Saturday, June 3, 2006. Lorenzo Carter and his brother-in-law traveled to what became Cleveland a year before Moses Cleaveland to look over the land to decide if this was a place to bring his family. When Moses Cleaveland arrived, his task was to conduct a survey of the land. It is also interesting to note how many gravestones had been removed. (Cleveland State University, Cleveland Press Collection.)

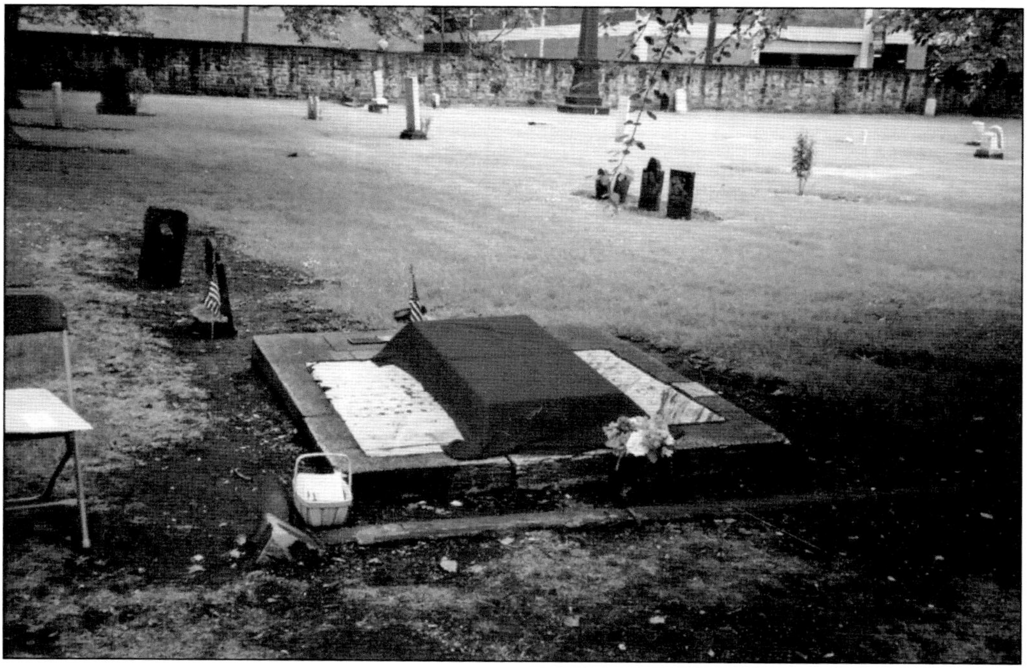

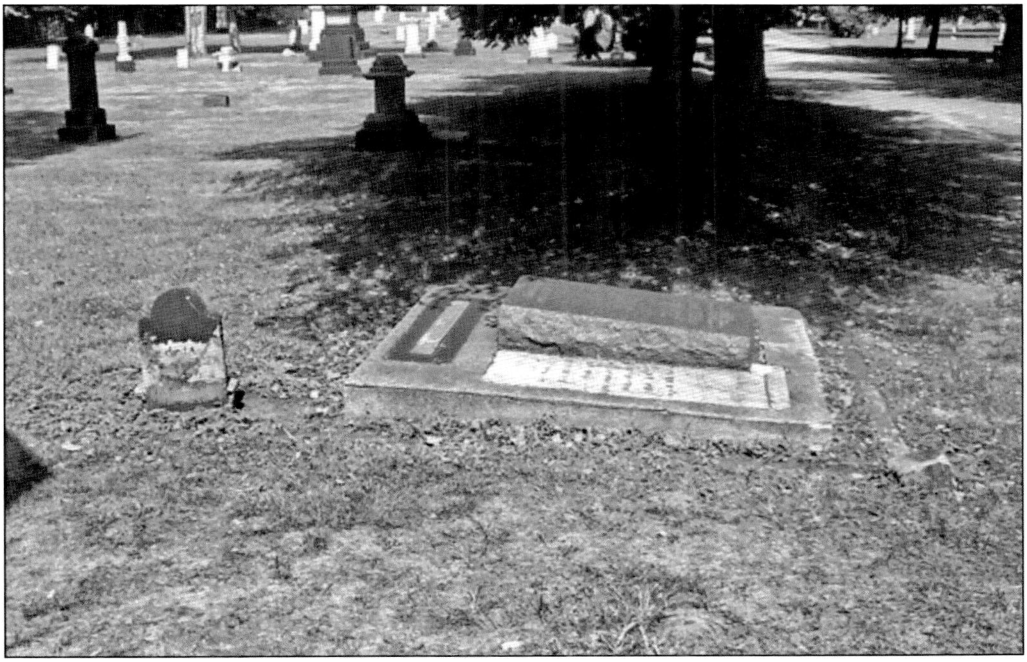

Lorenzo Carter and his wife, Rebecca Fuller Carter, had three children when they began their journey to the Western Reserve. Their children were ages six, four, and two. Rebecca had five more children after arriving in Cleveland. The only Carter child who has her own gravestone is Rebecca, who died at three years old in August 1803. It is just to the north of her parents' gravesite, seen in this photograph at left center. The first daughter named Rebecca was born in 1794 and died in 1797. Even with all of their hardships, "They Remained—Others Fled" is inscribed on the Carters' gravestone.

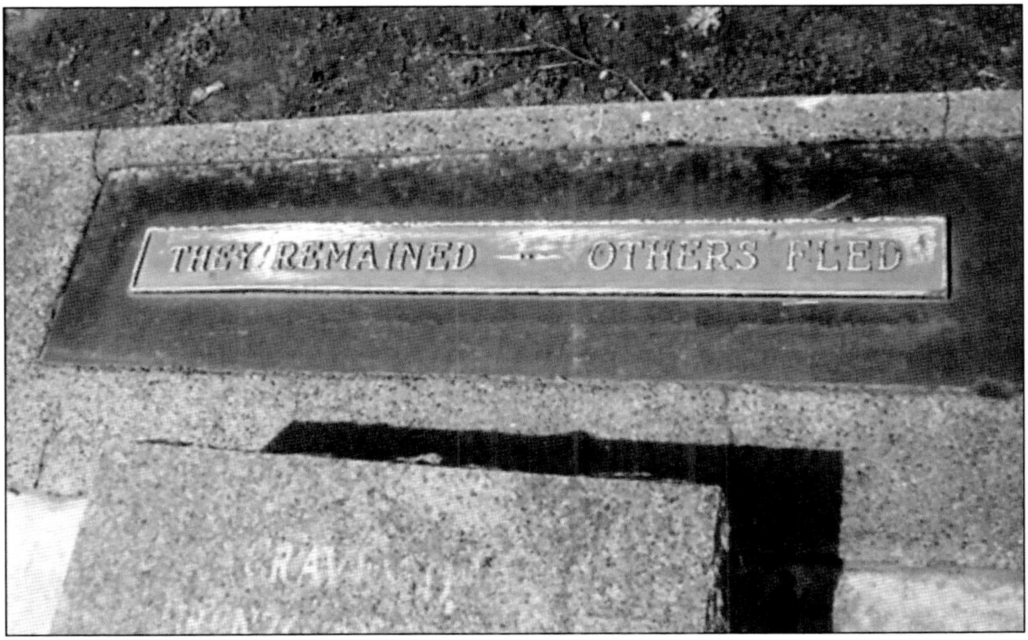

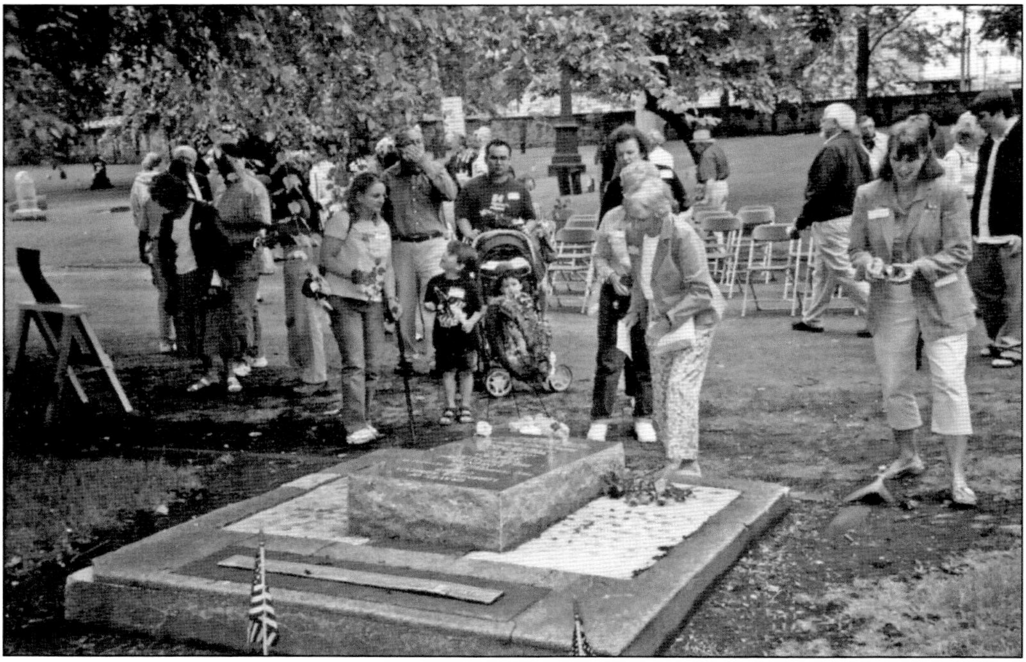

Erie Street Cemetery is appropriately the final resting place of Lorenzo Carter, who is credited as being Cleveland's first permanent settler. The first gravestone for Lorenzo Carter was dedicated in Erie Street Cemetery on July 22, 1938, by the Early Settlers Association. The original bronze historic marker had to be replaced because of vandalism. A granite stone was provided by the Early Settlers Association during a ceremony attended by many of the Carters' descendants, as well as members of the Early Settlers Association who gathered to pay tribute in June 2006. A military salute was part of the program.

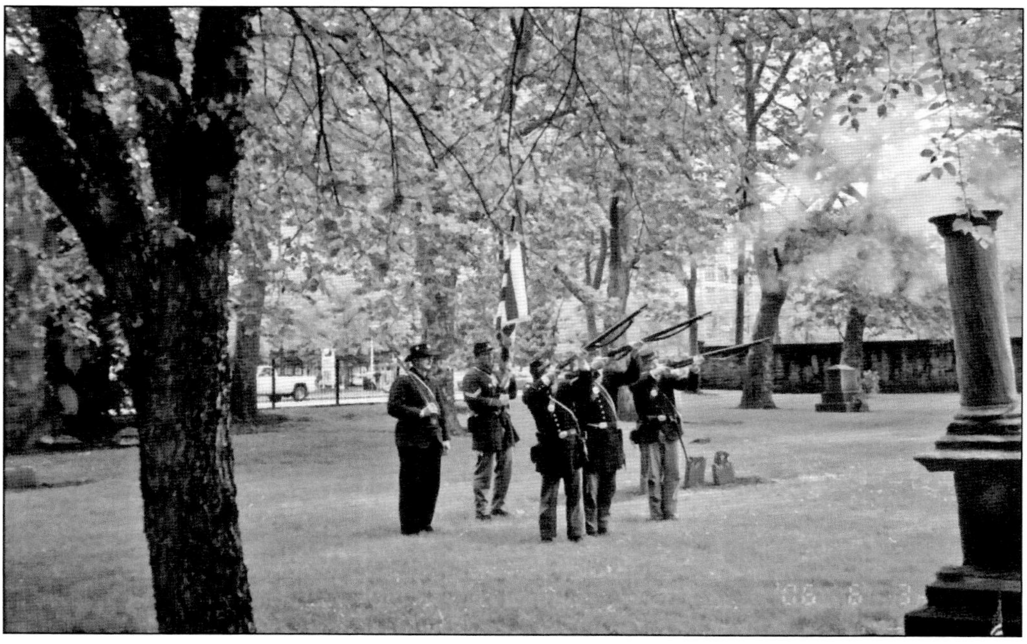

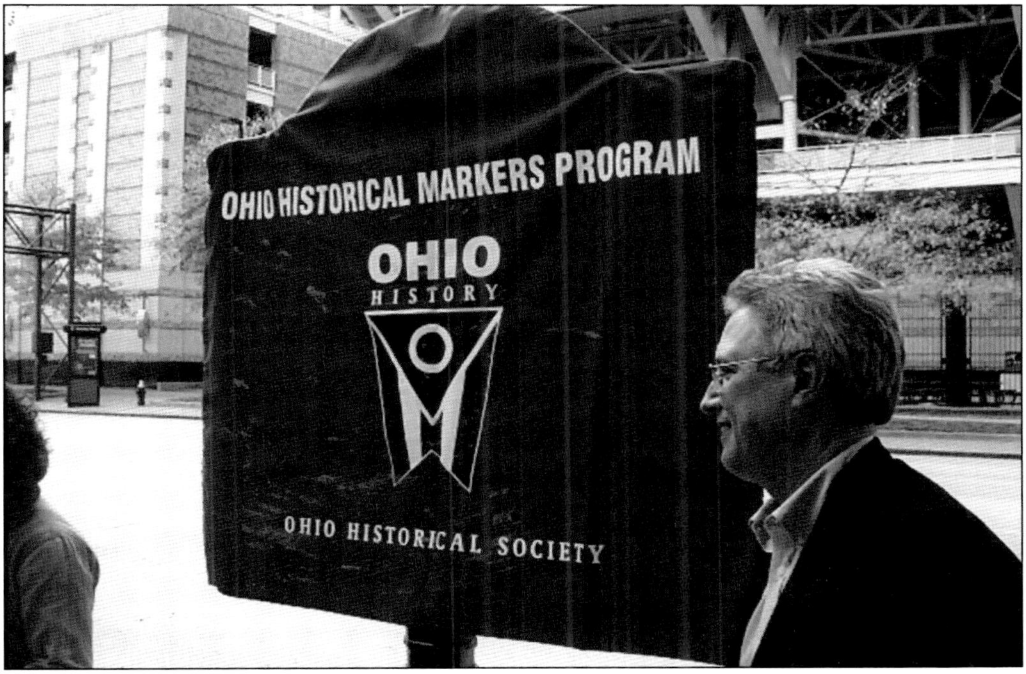

On October 3, 2009, Ted Prasse, president of the Board of Trustees of the Ohio Historical Society, unveiled a historic marker just to the north of the Erie Street Cemetery gate. The marker was erected due to the efforts of the Ohio Cemetery Alliance and the Early Settlers Association. The historic marker reminds visitors that in 1826, when Cleveland's first cemetery was closed, the village trustees purchased the land from Leonard Case Sr. for $1 and the land was dedicated as a cemetery. The marker reads, "Built on what became prime property, the cemetery touched off a century long struggle between residents and local government." (Early Settlers Association.)

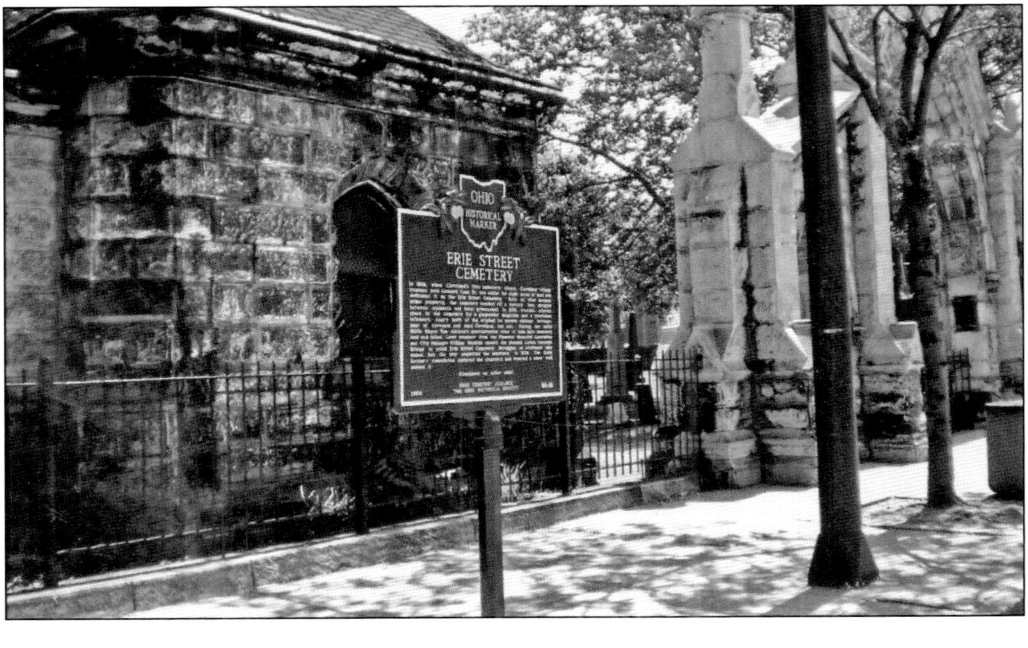

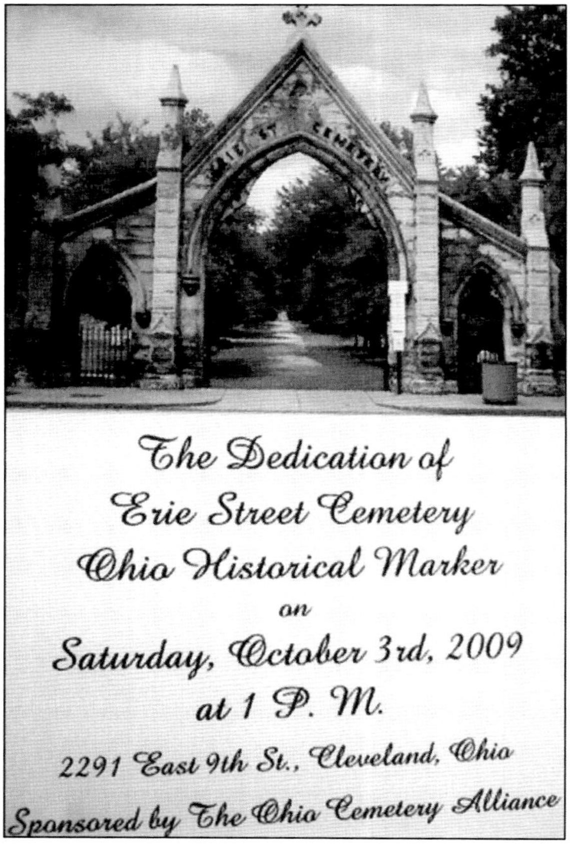

At left is an invitation to the October 3, 2009, dedication program held at Erie Street Cemetery. Photographed below are, from left to right, John D. Cimperman, president of the Early Settlers Association of the Western Reserve and author of this book; Vicki Blum Vigil, of the Ohio Preservation Alliance; and Robert K. Searson, district director of the Honors and Experimental Learning Program of Cuyahoga Community College. The trio stands in front of the Stickland monument in Erie Street Cemetery on Saturday, October 3, 2009.

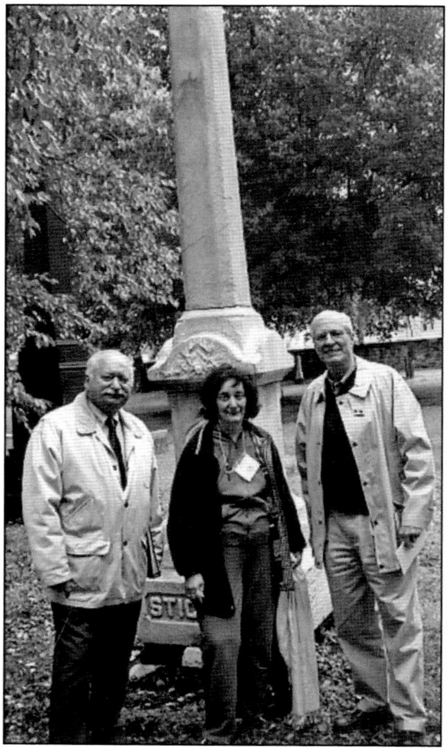

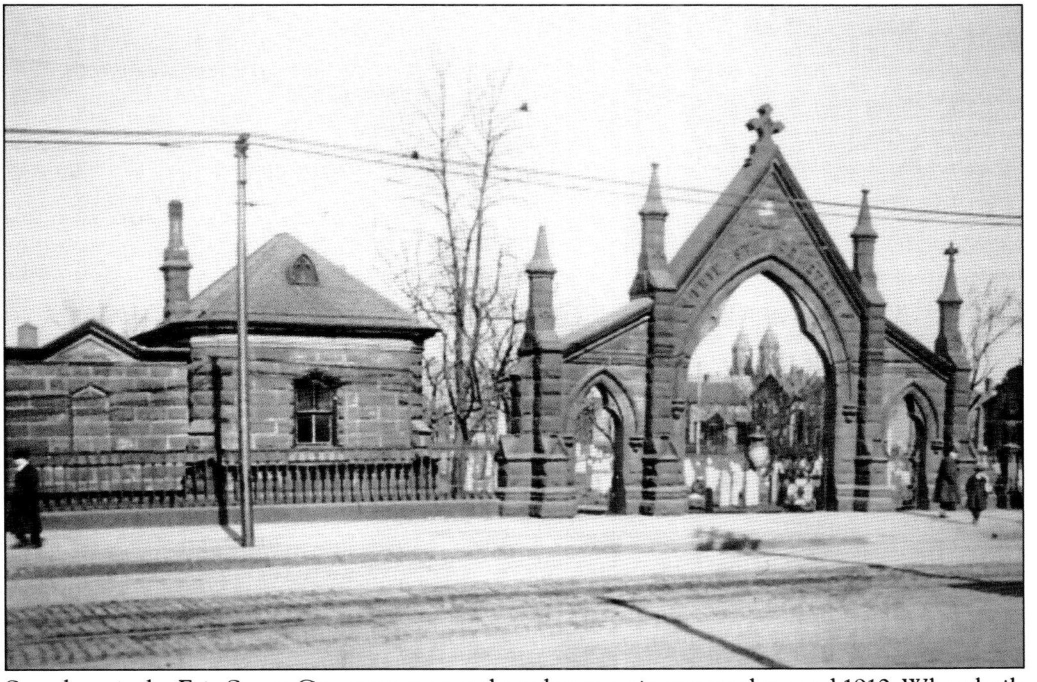

Seen here is the Erie Street Cemetery gate and gatehouse as it appeared around 1910. When built in 1870, the Gothic gateway cost $8,196. By as early as 1860, almost all of the lots in the cemetery were sold. (Cleveland State University, Cleveland Press Collection.)

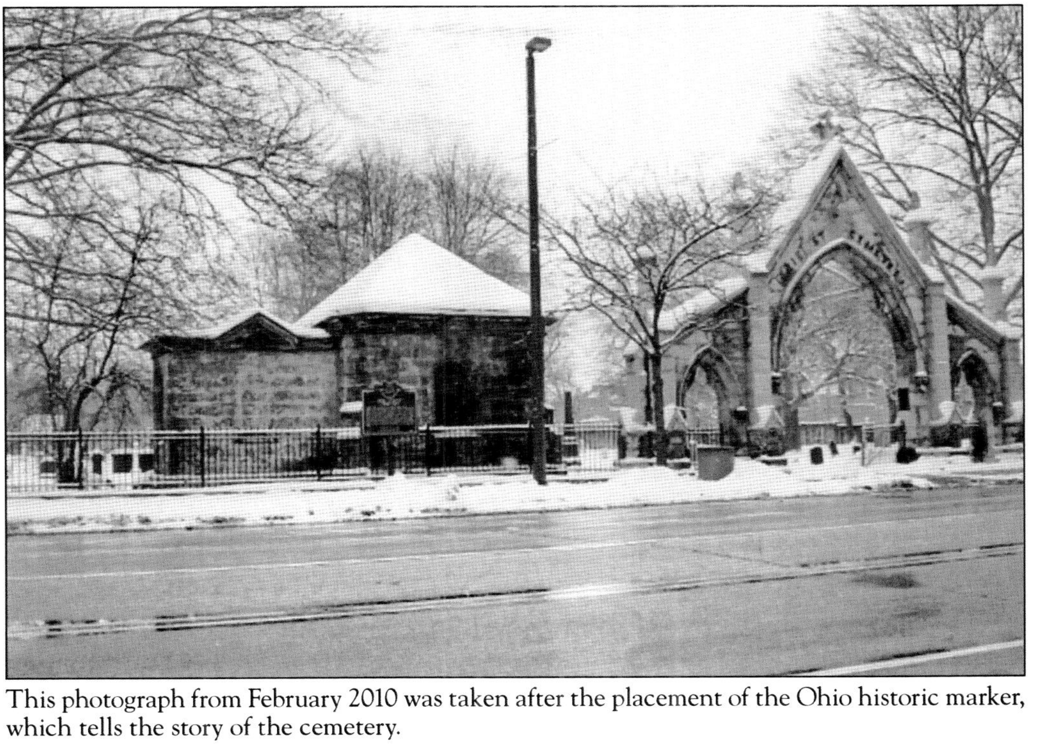

This photograph from February 2010 was taken after the placement of the Ohio historic marker, which tells the story of the cemetery.

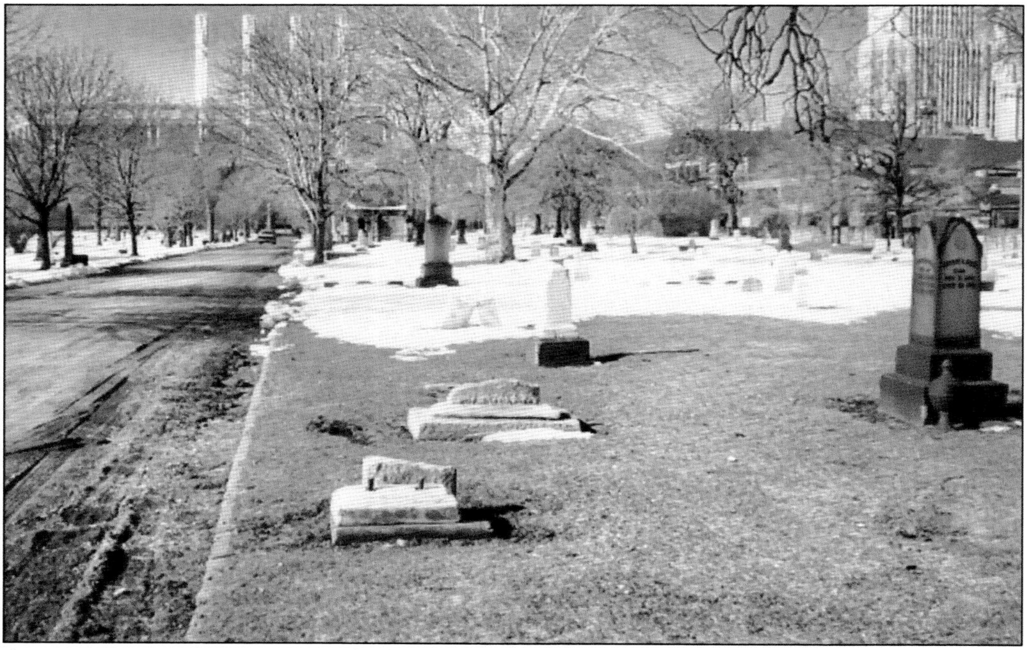

As winter passes, one can notice the loss of headstones and, in many cases, the further desecration of gravesites. There is a need for continual attention or for a nonprofit corporation to be established that would tend to the needs of the historic cemetery.

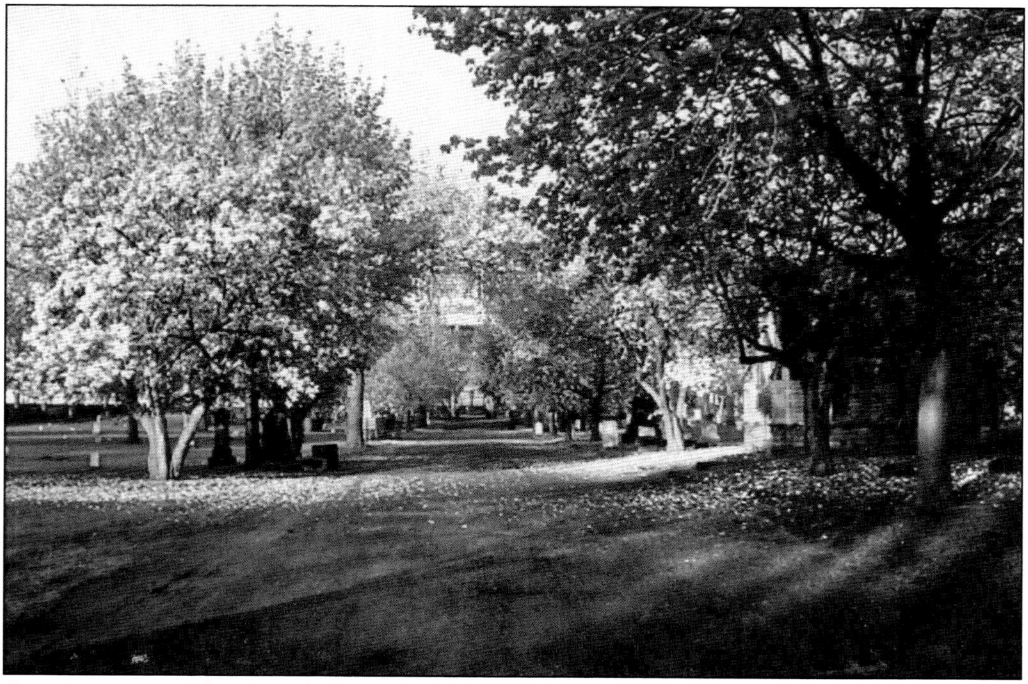

As spring arrives, the trees that were planted in 1939 and 1940 are in full bloom.

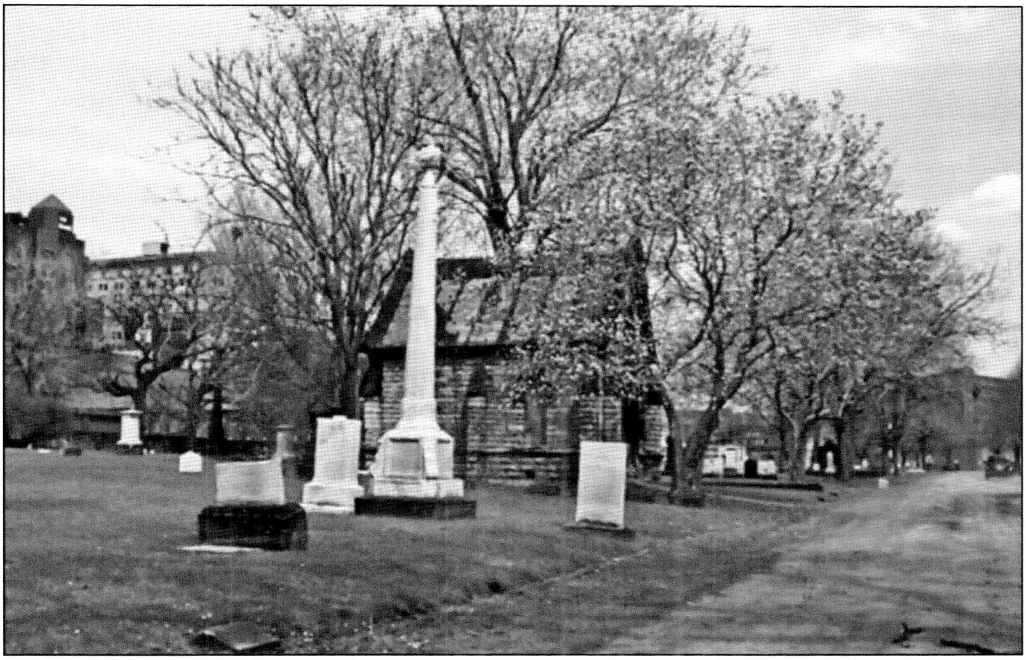

This photograph looks east at the Hilliard monument and the Harris mausoleum in the spring. As summer brings more leaves to the trees, the view from the upper deck of Progressive Field becomes less impressive. The photograph below was taken from the upper deck of Progressive Field in August 2010. In the spring, this spot provides a great view of the cemetery.

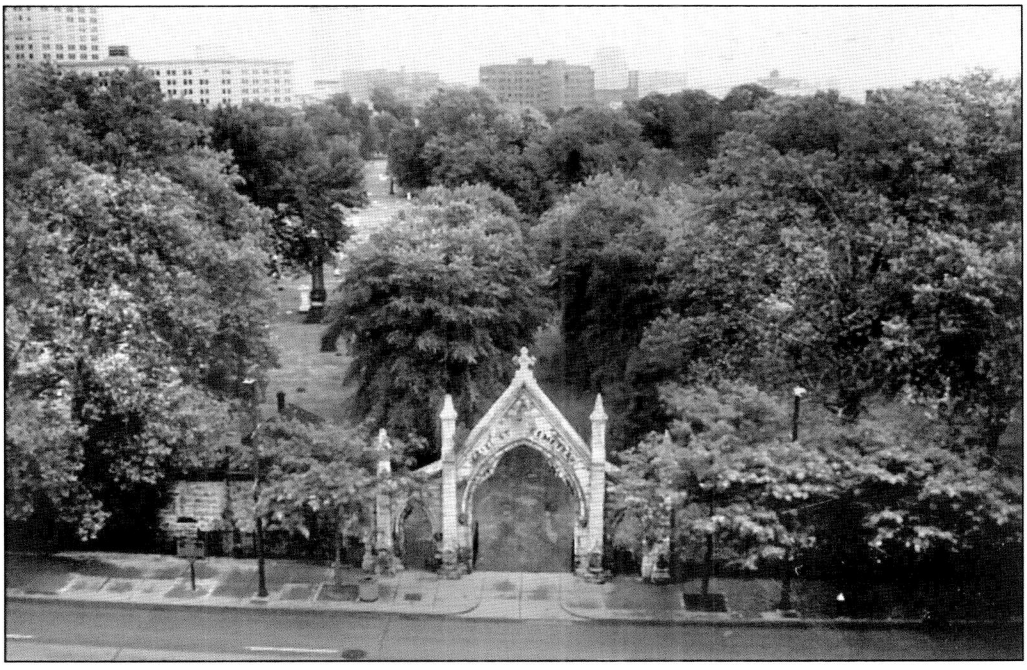

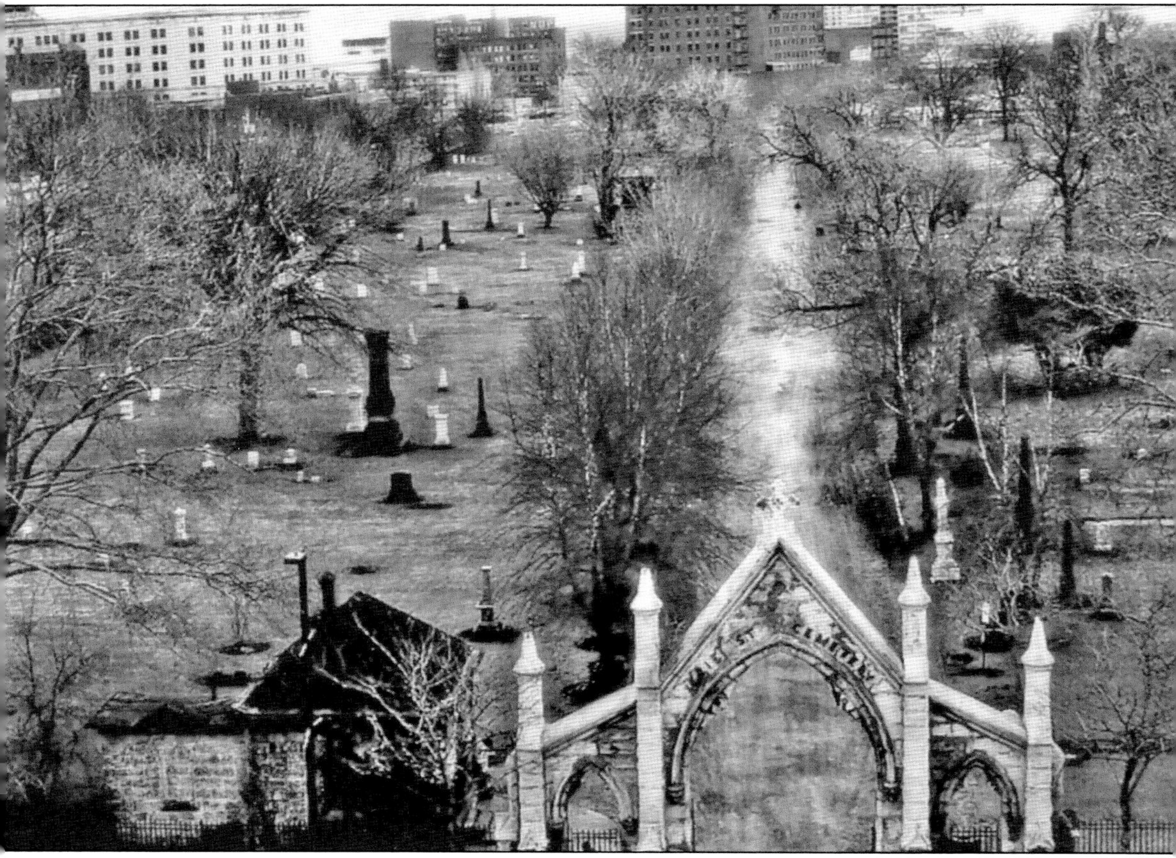

This photograph was taken from the upper deck of Progressive Field in the spring before the trees began to bloom. This land has remained as it was originally planned, as the final resting place for many of Cleveland's early settlers. By the 1860s, all of the lots had been sold, but because of the many threats to sell the cemetery for other purposes, many bodies were removed to other cemeteries. (Barbara Hale.)

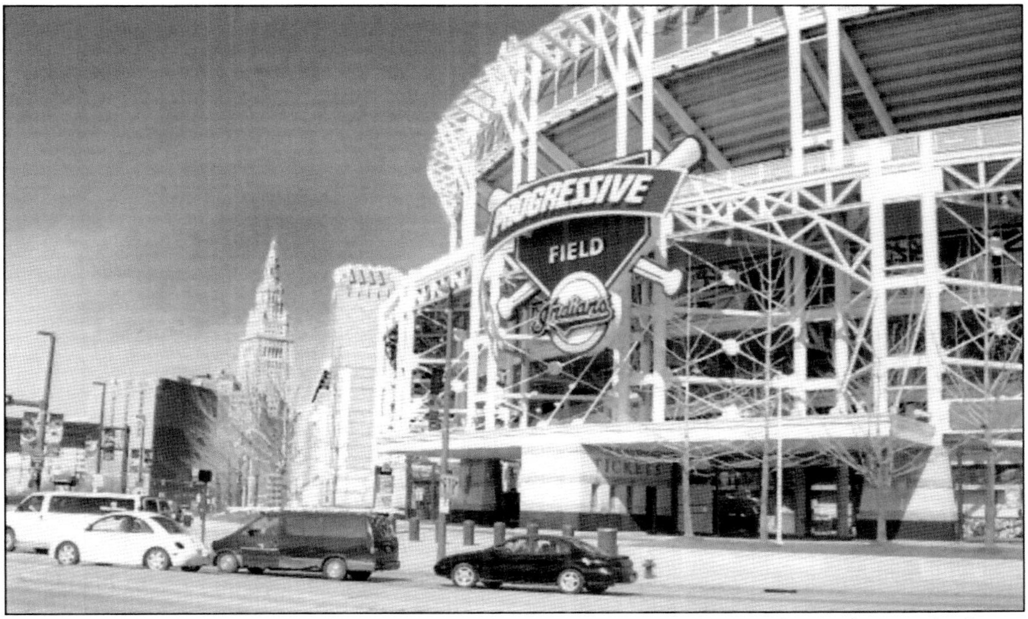

Progressive Field dwarfs the 1870 entrance gate of Erie Street Cemetery. The stadium is the home of the Cleveland Indians baseball team. The ballpark was built in 1994 as Jacobs Field, named for the owners Richard and David Jacobs. It was renamed Progressive Field before opening day in 2008 after Progressive Insurance purchased the naming rights. On April 4, 1994, the Indians played their first game at the new stadium. Pres. Bill Clinton threw out the first pitch, and the Indians defeated the Seattle Mariners 4-3 in 11 innings. On game days, large crowds travel through the pleasant surroundings of Erie Street Cemetery to Progressive Field.

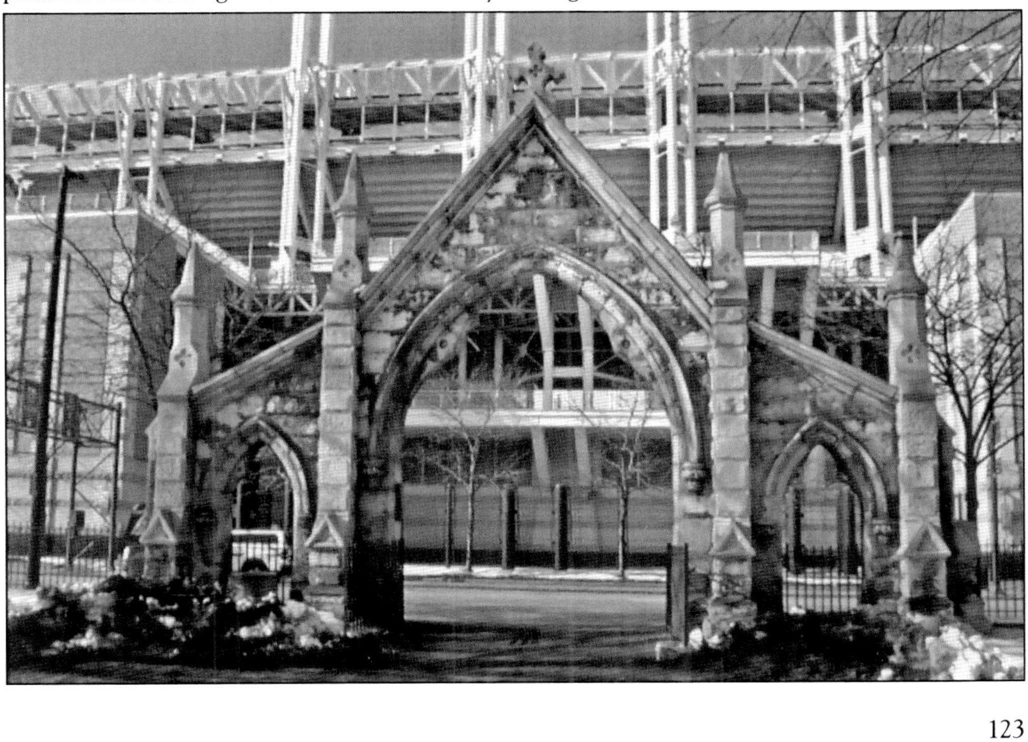

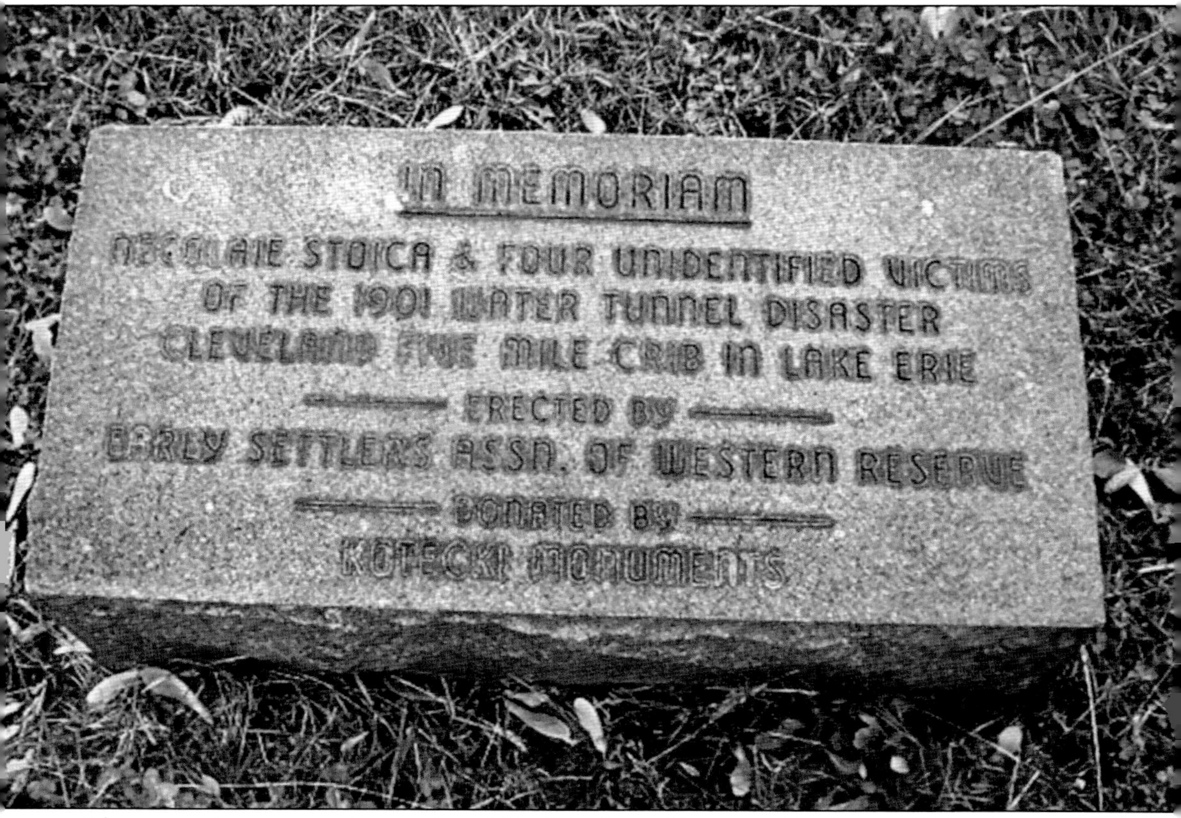

The story of many tragedies can be told in Erie Street Cemetery. On August 15, 1901, nineteen lives were lost in the construction of the Five Mile Crib, a project to bring clean water to the city. One of the men who died that day was Nicolae Stoica, an immigrant from Romania who came to the United States before the turn of the century. He left his wife and nine children in Romania hoping to send for them when he could afford to bring them to America. Unfortunately, that did not happen, as he died on that tragic day. Stoica and four other victims were not identified and were interred in a common grave. Years later, Stoica's daughter came to America, married, and raised a family. Eventually, they discovered that Stoica was buried at Erie Street Cemetery in an unmarked grave. The family appealed to the Cleveland Landmarks Commission for help since the cemetery is city property. Through the help of the commission, the Early Settlers Association, and Kotecki Monument Company, a gray granite stone finally told the story of Nicolae Stoica.

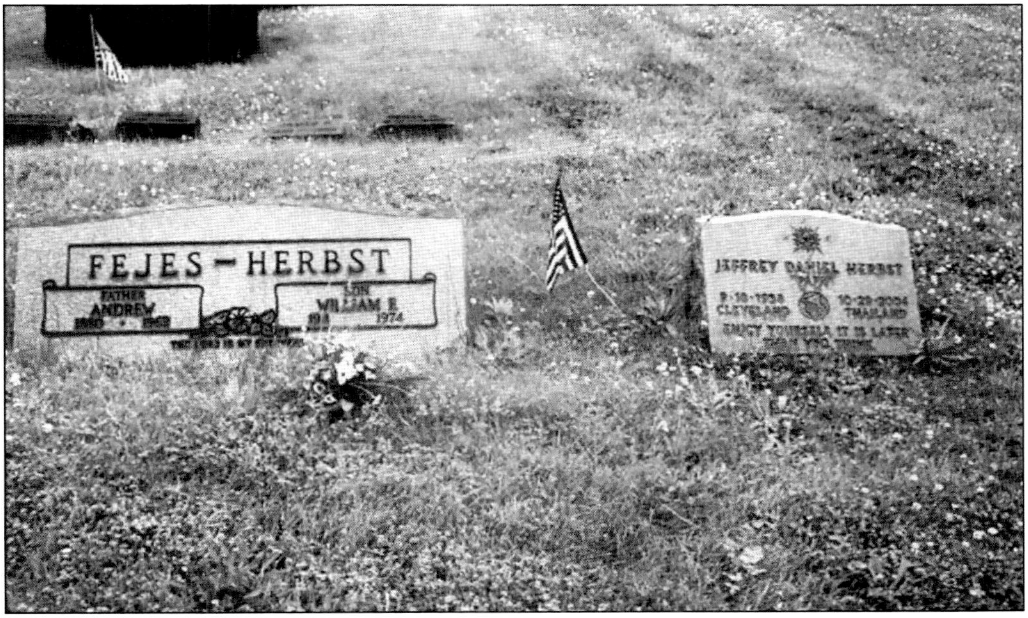

Walking through Erie Street Cemetery, one's attention may be drawn to the recent gravestone of Jeffrey Daniel Herbst, who died in Thailand on October 29, 2004. His obituary states that he died suddenly in Pattaya, Thailand, and that he was an avid adventurer who traveled and lived in numerous countries throughout the world. In the last few years of his life, he was teaching English. He was a dedicated member of Alcoholics Anonymous for 26 years, helping others attain sobriety. He served in the US Air Force from 1959 to 1963. His gravestone reads, "Enjoy yourself, it is later than you think."

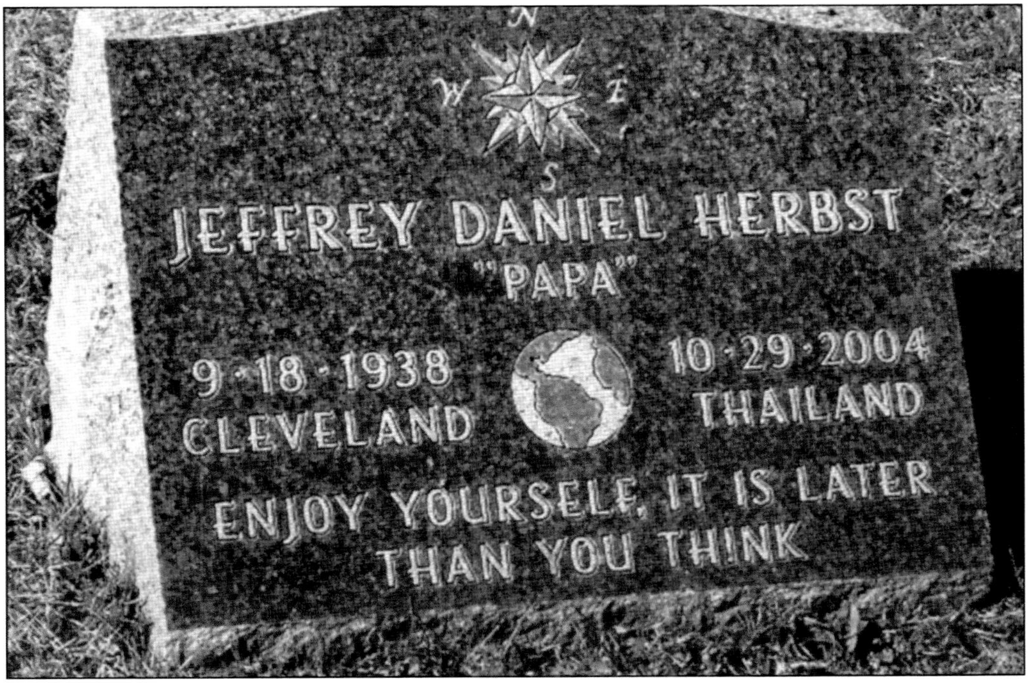

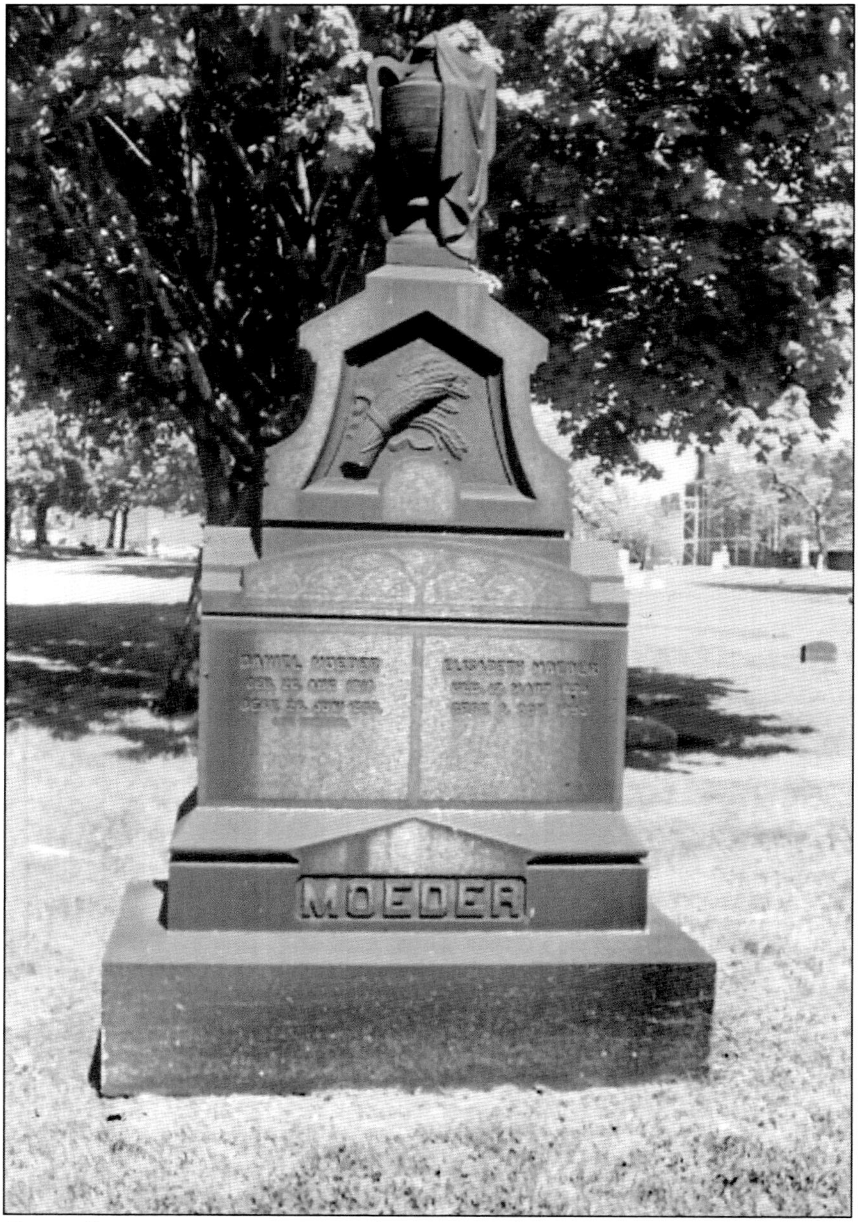

In the Erie Street Cemetery are monuments that may not be included in this publication. One that can not be missed because it is near the road is the Moeder monument. The names on the front panel are those of Daniel, who died in 1888, and Elizabeth, who died in 1895. On the side panels are the names of Andrew, who died in 1887; Dan Meders, 1878; George Eberts, 1866; Henrietta, age 5, 1863; Catherine, 1847; and J.A.W. Moeder, 1850. In gravestone symbolism, the monument tells a story. The draped urn may symbolize immortality, the last partition between life and death, or mourning. The sheaf of wheat can represent the divine harvest. The interpretations may differ, and there are many different studies available today for those interested in gravestone symbolism. The history of Erie Street Cemetery and Cleveland are one story; it is a legacy that should not be lost.

Bibliography

Annals of the Early Settlers Association of the Western Reserve. Proceedings of the years 1888 to 1959. Published under the direction of the Executive Committee.

Avery, Elroy McKendree. *A History of Cleveland and Its Environs*. Chicago and New York: The Lewis Publishing Company, 1918.

Butler, Margaret Manor. *A Pictorial History of the Western Reserve 1796 to 1860*. Cleveland, OH: A joint publication by the Early Settlers Association of the Western Reserve, the Western Reserve Historical Society, and the Lakewood Historical Society, 1963.

Chapman, Edmund H. *Cleveland: Village to Metropolis*. The Western Reserve Historical Society and the Press of Western Reserve University, 1964.

Ellis, William Donahue. *Early Settlers of Cleveland*. Cleveland, OH: Cleveland Ethnic Heritage Studies, Cleveland State University, 1976.

Gresser, John A. *Burials and Removals Erie Street Cemetery 1840–1918*. Cleveland, OH, 1919.

Hatcher, Harlan. *The Western Reserve: The Story of New Connecticut in Ohio*. Cleveland and New York: The World Publishing Company, 1966.

Johnson, Crisfield. *History of Cuyahoga County, Ohio*. D.W. Ensign & Co., 1879.

Peskin, Allan. *North into Freedom—The Autobiography of John Malvin, Free Negro, 1795–1880*. Cleveland, OH: The Western Reserve Historical Society, 1996.

Reference Guide to Cuyahoga County, Ohio Cemeteries. Western Reserve Historical Society.

Rose, William Ganson. *Cleveland: Making of a City*. Cleveland, OH: The World Publishing Company, 1950.

Van Tassel, David, and John Grabowski. *The Encyclopedia of Cleveland History*. Second edition. Bloomington, IN: University Press, 1987.

Wickham, Gertrude Van Rensselaer. *The Pioneer Families of Cleveland 1796–1840*. Vol. I and Vol. 2 (Under the auspices of the Executive Committee of the Women's Department of the Cleveland Centennial Commission–1896), Evangelical Publishing House, 1914.

Wilson, Ella Grant. *Famous Old Euclid Avenue of Cleveland*. Vol. II. 1937.